*Track and field
fundamentals
for girls and women*

Track and field fundamentals for girls and women

FRANCES WAKEFIELD, M.S.

AAU Women's Track and Field Official,
College of the Canyons,
Valencia, California

DOROTHY HARKINS, Ed.D.

Professor of Physical Education and formerly Women's Track
and Field Coach, Eastern Kentucky University,
Richmond, Kentucky

with

JOHN M. COOPER, Ed.D.

Associate Dean and Professor of Physical Education and
Track and Field Researcher, Indiana University,
Bloomington, Indiana

FOURTH EDITION

with 189 illustrations

The C. V. Mosby Company

Saint Louis   1977

FOURTH EDITION

Copyright © 1977 by The C. V. Mosby Company

All rights reserved. No part of this book may be reproduced
in any manner without written permission of the publisher.

Previous editions copyrighted 1966, 1970, 1973

Printed in the United States of America

Distributed in Great Britain by Henry Kimpton, London

The C. V. Mosby Company
11830 Westline Industrial Drive, St. Louis, Missouri 63141

Library of Congress Cataloging in Publication Data

Wakefield, Frances.
    Track and field fundamentals for girls and women.

    Includes index.
    1. Track-athletics for women. I. Harkins,
Dorothy, joint author. II. Cooper, John Miller,
1912-   joint author. III. Title.
GV1060.8.W3 1977   796.4'2   77-170
ISBN 0-8016-5328-2

GW/M/M 9 8 7 6 5 4 3 2 1

This book is dedicated
to the many women teachers and coaches
who wish to know as much as they possibly can
about track and field;
to the many girls and women
who want to develop an appreciation for,
an interest in, and an understanding of these activities;
to the many girls and women
who wish to participate satisfyingly in track
and field activities at a competitive level;
and finally to those women participants
who aspire to be the very best in their events.

Preface

The interest shown by so many female athletic performers and women teachers and coaches originally promoted the idea of a book written on the subject of track and field fundamentals for girls and women. The idea has proved to be a worthwhile undertaking, since this book is now in its fourth edition.

The fact that the two women collaborators were aided and abetted by the ideas of a man has obviously been well received. The knowledge of women in this area increased greatly in the last few years; yet it was considered beneficial to blend the man's and the women's concepts into one publication so that all aspects of this area would be presented.

The advice and opinions of many teachers and performers were again sought to ascertain what was needed in a book of this nature. It was found that both general and specific information was needed in all areas, some of which should be updated. Several women coaches voluntarily furnished new ideas and concepts. Everyone interviewed expressed the desire to have the contemplated changes placed in her possession immediately.

In this fourth edition we have attempted to meet their requests. This volume is divided into seven parts—an introductory section (which includes a discussion of girls and women in track and field as well as principles of conditioning and training) and sections on running, hurdling, jumping, throwing, pentathlon, beginning a track and field program, and managing and planning aspects. In each section, where appropriate, a discussion is conducted concerning the novice, the competitor, teaching progression, a training program, and techniques of performance.

Furthermore, wherever possible, suggestions are made concerning the use of improvised equipment when standard equipment is not available. In fact, an entire chapter is devoted to this subject.

An attempt has been made to provide information for the teacher, the beginner, and the more advanced performer. We believe we have achieved this goal.

We take responsibility for the mention of any new ideas, the positive statements made regarding controversial points, and the interpretation of research findings. It is believed that track and field has become an integral part of most school programs for girls, and support of this concept is found throughout the book. The very latest and best ideas we could find are contained herein. However, it is recognized that ideas and concepts will change as a result of future research findings and experiences. We are dedicated above all else to the improvement of track programs at all levels.

We wish to thank all the typists who helped in the preparation of the manuscript, especially Charlianna Cooper. We are also grateful to Joan Schutz, Joanna Adang, and Diane Wollery for their illustrative drawings and photographs from the third edition that have been retained in the fourth edition. We thank Kay Flatten for revision suggestions and for presenting us with some fine photographs taken by Gary Dahle. We acknowledge the use of photographs from the Eastern Kentucky University sports information office. Other photographs have been obtained from various sources too numerous to mention specifically. We believe all the contributions add greatly to the understanding of the written ideas.

In this revision we have updated records, revised the discussion on skill performances in the various events, deleted some and combined other sections, redrawn some of the diagrams, added new photographs and drawings, and replaced some of the other illustrations. Wherever possible, the metric system is used. We believe the value of the contents has been increased.

Frances Wakefield

Dorothy Harkins

John M. Cooper

Contents

PART ONE

Introduction

CHAPTER 1

Participation of girls and women in track and field

Track and field activities are exciting and challenging, and they are becoming increasingly popular in the United States in school and college programs and in organized track clubs. Girls given the opportunity to run, jump, and throw may find that the experience fulfills certain physical and psychologic needs. Many girls find the experiences and challenge of track and field so strongly satisfying that they are spurred on to participate in higher levels of competition in national and international championships.

SPECIAL CONSIDERATIONS

Opportunities for participation. Track and field programs offer an opportunity for many types of performers to participate and excel, provided they are willing to work diligently. No other sport can be enjoyed by so many, and no other sports activity offers the average or even the poorly coordinated girl such possibilities for enjoyable participation. It is the average and below average in skill who need the most attention and encouragement in this sport; the naturally gifted or highly skilled girl will usually participate in such strenuous activity without much encouragement. The skilled girl may also find pleasure in a highly organized competitive track and field program. The girl who loves to run or jump just for the thrill of running or jumping will be an eager participant and will need little motivation (Fig. 1-1).

Physiologic values. The physiologic values derived from track and field activities are evidenced by the attainment of health, vigor, and a high degree of physical fitness. Rigorous training programs and competitive situations develop good neuromuscular coordination and cardiorespiratory endurance. There should also be an accompanying increase in strength, speed, power, balance, flexibility, and agility.

The emphasis on development and maintenance of a high level of physical fitness should increase the participant's awareness of the conditioning value of participation in the vigorous track and field activities. To be able to run and jump with ease is useful in almost any gross body movement. Girls may be able to avoid accidents and injuries because of this ability, and they may use it in the successful performance of some activities other than that found in track and field programs.

People will naturally pursue those activities in which they find pleasure and success. Thus track and field actions that involve refinement of the basic skills of running, jump-

Fig. 1-1. Note the intensity of the runners. Just to have the opportunity to participate appears to be worthwhile.

ing, and throwing have carry-over value for persons who wish to increase their ability in these or related activities and who find participation in such activities satisfying and challenging.

Often the developmental powers of the body are enhanced, and a feeling of fitness and well-being is enjoyed by those participating in track and field events. Competitive sports have a great appeal for girls as well as for boys, and participation in track and field events affords the most all-around basic competition for the greatest number of persons. The physiologic effects of track and field activities have been carefully evaluated, and it is believed that such participation can be recommended for women.

Other significant aspects. Social and psychologic values derived from track and field activities are enhanced as girls develop qualities of cooperation, leadership, self-discipline, and self-sufficiency in learning to compete with other girls. In addition, many educators believe it is important for girls to learn to be gracious winners as well as cheerful losers (Fig. 1-2).

Certain cultural and intellectual values develop as a girl gains self-knowledge and realizes her potentialities; she learns of her limitations and of her special aptitudes. Certainly, movement experiences in track and field can help a girl acquire a practical self-image and become more aware of her movement potential. As she works with others in group situations, she will learn to lead as well as follow while she is forming relationships that may prove valuable to her in adult life. Also, a girl at the competitive level can become aware of the athletes of other countries and learn to appreciate them for what and who they are. At the same time she may increase her geographic, lingual, and cultural knowledge of the world.

With the advent of the hormone tests for female athletes in Olympic competition, there has been a noticeable ''feminizing'' of international women competitors in track and field.

Fig. 1-2. Sprinters in the set position. These girls are competing in a regularly scheduled meet in southern California. Notice the starter is in correct attire and stationed in a good position. The girls in the second and third heats are lined up behind the first row, quietly waiting for their turns. These girls are seasoned competitors and well indoctrinated in meet protocol. The clerk of the course is seen checking in another group. These girls are in the 10- to 11-year age group.

The women athletes must not have an overbalance of male hormones in relation to the female hormones, as determined by the results of these tests, to be eligible to compete. There has been evidence that the so-called superwoman syndrome had allowed some women to take unfair advantage of the women who did not have this overabundance of male hormones. At the present time, if a woman athlete fails to submit to the hormone test, she is automatically disqualified. Some well-known foreign competitors, who are world record holders in their events, have withdrawn from further competition because of the requirements of the hormone test.

Challenges. Track and field sports offer a definite challenge to the skilled performer because her success depends on her own ability to execute the desired action, not on the efforts of others. The victory or the blame is hers; on the other hand, she may receive satisfaction from just comparing her present with her past performances.

Participants in track and field suffer few limitations that are not self-imposed. They should learn to turn themselves loose and participate without self-consciousness. Most girls, when they can do this, will have a wonderful time performing activities that involve the natural movement patterns of running, jumping, and throwing. These are the same movement patterns used in dancing and in daily living. A girl may utilize her natural abilities to realize some measure of success in this area; however, she may increase her natural ability by the use of tested learning methods and thus, through systematic training, excel in performance. Girls seem to find greater success in some areas than in others by virtue of their body types, but there are many notable exceptions. Examples of those exceptions are the short heavy girl who is successful at sprinting and the tall slender girl who is able to put the shot or throw the discus well.

Menstrual periods do not keep a healthy girl from training or competing; in fact, many women turn in their best performances following these times. Girls and women who become athletes tend to perform in a superior manner when they are relaxed and at ease. It is possible that the release of tension evident with the onset and continuance of the menstrual flow accounts for the superior performance of women athletes following the menstruation period.

Learning. Even though people learn many different things, all learning occurs the same way—through the nervous system via the senses. Many learning theorists would proclaim these four significant elements necessary for learning to occur:

1. *Drive*—a stimulus that triggers action, causing a person to want to learn something.
2. *Cue*—the stimulus that guides the action, causing a person to notice something and to relate past knowledge or experience to the action.
3. *Response*—the action itself, in which a person is involved in doing something.
4. *Reward*—the result of the action, in which a person receives something for her efforts.

Because of these elements, the following principles of learning are important.

Readiness to learn. The ability that the beginner brings to the learning situation will largely determine the degree of skill development that will occur.

The physical attributes necessary for success in track and field skills are strength, endurance, coordination, speed, agility, balance, power, and flexibility. The maturation level of the girl will determine the kinds of track and field activities with which she can find success. Emotional maturity is important in the performance of track and field because of the stringent demands of self-discipline and control that result from competing against oneself. Intelligence is also an important prerequisite for learning track and field because of the complex motor movements found in some of the events.

Suitable motivation will largely determine the amount of interest, effort, and perseverance that the beginner displays. For good track and field experiences to be realized, a girl needs high levels of these qualities. Positive motivation is largely the key condition for involvement of the beginner. Unless she is completely involved, she will not focus her attention on well-defined goals.

Goal-centered learning. Cues readily picked up by the beginner and related to past knowledge and experience will lead her to reasonable goals. Track and field knowledge is based on the natural abilities of pupils to run, jump, and throw. The teacher or coach should present a clear picture of what is to be attained through challenge, problems to solve, and good demonstrations; she should then provide opportunities for ample and progressive practice. In this way the goals of track and field activities can be realized. It is important that verbal cues be kept brief and that demonstrations be made correctly because what the girl perceives affects her ability to learn.

Methods of practice. Once the girl gets the idea of the action needed, it is important that she become actively involved in the learning process. She learns by doing, by correcting errors, and by refining movements and retaining skill through overlearning. Pupils usually learn faster when they are presented skills using a whole-part method. For beginners, practice sessions should be short and frequent.

Three practice sessions a week are considered minimum for optimum learning to occur. The length of the practice session should be no less than 60 minutes and can easily be extended to 90 minutes if attention is given to varying the activities during the session. The competitive athlete will be able to train for longer periods of time 5 or 6 days a week.

It is extremely important that practice schedules be individualized to conform to the needs of the athlete. What is best for one person may not be best for another. Girls and women need to experiment to find a schedule that best helps them to improve their performances.

Immediate feedback and a suitable learning environment. The beginner needs to be rewarded or reinforced by having a sense of "this is it" or "I've got the idea." This awareness may occur as a result of a teacher's verbal comments and her noting of improved performances based on records or by other evaluative techniques. In track and field, knowledge of results is immediate; beginners note how they rank in relation to other competitors and also how they have improved their own achievements.

There is little doubt that a friendly environment is most conducive to learning and that the social climate of the class influences both the quality and quantity of learning. Democratic leadership is preferred to a laissez-faire or autocratic leadership. An insecure or tense learning environment that is uncontrolled or semicontrolled is not the best learning situation.

It is also true that the coach has to be strict. She will need to impose demands on the athlete and to be firm so that the athlete will push herself toward excellence. The coach must be aware of the pain that an athlete sometimes endures, but she must not always allow the athlete to realize this. In this manner the coach becomes a source of added strength for the athlete. The coach must combine empathy for the athlete with firmness to really serve the athlete in important ways in the learning situation.

Thus the elements necessary for the learning of track and field skills are the same as those required for the learning of any motor skill, or for any kind of learning. It is hoped that this information will be of special value to the beginning coach.

HISTORICAL BACKGROUND

Historically most sports and games were designed for men. Only later were adaptations made for girls and women. Track and field activities for girls and women have evolved in much the same manner as other sports, and they are now being accepted as excellent activities for girls and women. Perhaps their growth has been slow because, in the past, women physical educators were not trained to direct these activities for girls, and indoor and outdoor track and field facilities did not exist for women to the degree that they did for men. These and other handicaps are gradually being overcome as up-to-date physical educators recognize the value of track and field activities for girls. Newspaper publicity is also helping to influence public opinion in favor of offering such activities for girls in the schools. Furthermore, men coaches are helping to increase the participation of girls and women by assisting women coaches and by helping them promote women's track and field programs. Physical educators are realizing that track programs can be carried on effectively in a school environment with a minimum of equipment and limited facilities. Finally, with the advent of federally mandated Title IX in the mid 1970s, public schools and colleges were obliged to offer equal athletic opportunities to girls and women. Creation of coaching positions, teams, and development of league structures further advanced track and field knowledge, participation, and competition.

Ancient Olympic Games. Women were not allowed to compete in the early Olympic Games, which originally consisted of only track and field events. Not only were they barred from participation, they were punished by death for even watching the games. There was quite a disturbance when the mother of Pisidorus, one of the better runners in the early games, became excited by her son's winning and stood up at the games, thereby revealing her disguise. However, the death penalty was not inflicted on her—perhaps because she had taken charge of Pisidorus' training after the death of his father and had come to the stadium in disguise to watch him perform.

Women were not to be kept from competing, however; under the influence of Hippodameia the Heraea Games were organized to provide competition for women. These games, for women only, were held secretly every 4 years midway between the Olympiads. The Roman Conquest ended this effort in behalf of the ''Women's Olympics.'' Although the status of women was improved somewhat after the birth and ministry of Jesus Christ, the woman's role in sports was still minimized, and not until the end of the nineteenth century did women compete seriously in any sport.

Advent of the modern Olympics. In 1896 in the rebuilt stadium of Athens, the first Olympic Games of the modern era were held. An intelligent Frenchman, Baron Pierre de Coubertin, a hard worker who understood the dreams and needs of youth, was chiefly responsible for this revival. The new Olympic Games still did not include any events for women. Equestrian and tennis events for women were introduced at the Paris games in 1900, but no women's events were included in the St. Louis games of 1904. In 1908 in England, women competed in archery during the summer games and in skating during the winter games; they participated in swimming events in Stockholm in 1912. At the Antwerp games in 1920 there was competition for women in tennis, archery, swimming, and fencing.

Two women who indirectly helped to set the stage for the entrance of women into competition in track and field events were the tennis champions Suzanne Lenglen of France and Helen Wills of the United States. They demonstrated that women could be great performers and still act and be feminine.

At the Amsterdam games in 1928 there were 121 women competitors from all over the world taking part in five track and field events. Nineteen of the 101 athletes from the United States were women. The events for women included the 100-meter dash, the 400-meter relay, the running high jump, the 800-meter run, and the discus throw. This Olympiad and those of 1932 and 1936 provided outstanding performances by Mildred ''Babe'' Didrikson (Zaharias), Stella Walsh, and Helen Stephens.

Since the entry of women into track and field competition in 1928, women competitors had been more or less simply tolerated. The picture changed in 1948 when Fanny Blankers-Koen, a Dutch housewife and mother of two who was coached by her husband, went to London and won four gold medals. She finished first in the 100-meter dash (11.9 seconds), the 200-meter dash (24.4 seconds), and the 80-meter hurdles (11.2 seconds), and ran as a member of the winning team in the 400-meter relay (47.5 seconds). The 200-meter dash, the broad (later changed to long) jump, and the 4-kilogram (8 pounds 13 ounces) shot were added as new women's events in the 1948 games.

Women performers who had received little attention from news reporters were pushed into the headlines because of the contest between the United States and Russia that made the 1952 games at Helsinki something of a dual meet. Unfortunately the only track and field points scored by the United States women's team was a victory in the 400-meter relay.

In 1956 at Melbourne only one record for women was set: Betty Cuthbert of Australia ran 200 meters in 23.4 seconds.

In 1960 the United States sent its strongest women's team ever to the seventeenth Olympiad, held in Rome. Wilma Rudolph, a long-limbed lass from Tennessee Agricultural and Industrial State University, earned three gold medals by winning the 100- and 200-meter dashes and anchoring the winning team in the 400-meter relay. Wilma, whom the Russians dubbed "Queen of the Olympics," has indeed contributed to the present high place of women in track and field and has helped dispel the misconception that athletic participation lessens femininity.

In the 1964 Olympics there was a high level of performance by women from all countries, and new records were set, many of which were surpassed during the 1968, 1972, and 1976 Olympics.

International competition is extensively planned today, with championship meets being held in many countries of the world. There are the European Championships, Pan-American Games, British Commonwealth Games, Polish-American Meet, and numerous invitational meets, both indoor and outdoor. One of the most recently added events in the Olympic Games is the 1600-meter relay, included in the 1972 Olympic program in Munich and the 1976 games in Montreal. There is currently impetus to include long-distance and marathon (approximately 26 miles) running in the Olympic events. The 1970 decade has seen successful domestic competition in longer races, but only time will tell if the advocates of the inclusion of this event are successful in their quest.

MODERN-DAY PARTICIPATION

Contributors of today. There are many girls and women who have helped to establish the place of women in track and field events; furthermore, they have helped to show that participation in track and field contributes to the all-around development of women. Some of these young women are Kathy Schmidt, America's bright young javelin champion; Marie Mulder, who at 15 years of age set a national record in the 880-yard run for United States women; Tamara Press, the Russian weight champion, who was at one time the most outstanding woman to hurl the discus and put the shot; Poland's brilliant sprinter, Irena Kirzenstein, who set a new world record in the 200-meter run in 1965 and tied the world record in the 100-meter; the outstanding high jumper from West Germany, Ulrike Meyfarth, who dominates this event by jumping 6 feet 3½ inches; Pat Connolley, a seven-time winner of the U.S. National Pentathlon; Wyomia Tyus, world record holder in the 100-meter run; Doris Brown, National AAU 800-meter run outdoor champion; and the incomparable Olga Connolly, a five-time Olympian, who made a tremendous comeback in the 1968 Olympics by placing sixth in the discus throw and in 1972 establishing a new American record of 189 feet. Further recognition must be given to the great woman athlete from Taiwan, Chi Cheng, who broke world records in the 200-meter sprint and the 100-meter hurdles and gained great recognition as the 1970 World Athlete of the Year.

In the past, the greatest women performers in the United States were sprinters and hurdlers, but now American girls and women are excelling in almost all the events in international competition. On tracks in the United States, records are being improved every year, indicating that an ever increasing number of talented girls are participating in track and field activities. The 1972 Olympics found Kathy Schmidt from California winning a bronze medal for her effort in the javelin, a feat that had not occurred since 1932, when another American, Babe Didrikson (Zaharias), won the event.

In 1975 Jackie Hansen from southern California set a national record in the 26-mile marathon. A pioneer in distance running, Ms. Hansen frequently competes in men's races to prove that women are capable of running the marathon. Women are now permitted to run marathon races, and women's records were established in 1975.

Far-reaching implications. The implications of women and girls performing in a superior manner in track and field activities, whether it be in an Olympic arena or on an improvised play area, are many. Young girls everywhere may think: ''If Wilma Rudolph and Wyomia Tyus can be gold medal winners, why can't I?'' Physical education teachers are looking for ways to teach track and field skills to their students properly, and colleges are offering courses and conducting clinics and workshops to prepare teachers of track and field.

As stated previously, there is an upsurge of interest in track and field for girls and women all over America as well as in other parts of the world. Our culture is a competitive one, and women are finding themselves more and more in places of leadership and in challenging pursuits. Track and field is an area in which women leaders and competitors are needed. It has become a challenging endeavor for women.

Girls love to run, jump, and throw just as boys do, and they are finding out that they can learn to do so very well. The medical profession supports the need for girls to participate in vigorous physical activities, and girls who participate in track and field athletics know what it means to be physically fit.

Another healthy trend is the fact that public school officials are beginning to provide programs for girls who like to take part in track and field sports. Female participation in track and field activities is no longer a controversial issue, and more women physical educators are making provisions for highly skilled youngsters to enjoy participating in these exciting activities.

Special programs. The National Institute of Girls' and Women's Sports, held in 1963 at the University of Oklahoma and sponsored by the United States Olympic Development Committee and the National Association of Girls' and Women's Sports (NAGWS) of the American Association for Health, Physical Education, and Recreation (AAHPER), was evidence of the desire of many to improve sports and games programs, especially track and field, for the American girl. Another similar institute was held at Michigan State University in the fall of 1965, with the instruction and information presented on an intermediate level. In January, 1969, the fifth National Institute of Girls' and Women's

Sports was held at the University of Illinois. The emphasis was on advanced track and field coaching techniques and officiating. Never before has so much effort been expended by the United States Olympic Development Committee, or by any group, to help physical education teachers improve sports programs for girls. The results from workshops and clinics held on this subject have influenced 1.5 million people to become interested in track and field programs for girls and women (Fig. 1-3).

Recently a track and field film library on women performers has been established at Indiana University, Bloomington, Indiana, for teachers and competitors. These films are available for rental at development cost or can be purchased at production cost.

The outgrowth of this impetus for track and field for girls is found in the track and field programs offered by the following groups: recreation departments, schools at all levels, track and field clubs and associations, and the junior Olympic programs and other activities of the Amateur Athletic Union (AAU).

Recreation departments will often set up a single area meet for girls of specific age groups. Often the leaders will request assistance for conducting the meet from AAU officials, physical education teachers, and coaches who have had experience officiating at track and field meets. These meets usually do not require the participants to follow a highly organized system of training and conditioning to compete. The girls often appear irregularly at the recreational areas to work out, and it is difficult to convince them to participate in regular practice sessions. However, the number of young girls who do participate in these meets is astounding. It is not uncommon in a large metropolitan area such as Los Angeles to have so many entries that it is necessary to hold several heats in each sprint race for each age group. The younger girls (under 14 years of age) usually

Fig. 1-3. Practice session in starting. These girls are taking practice starts right along with the boys in a clinic held at Slippery Rock College, Pennsylvania. Notice the relaxed head positions and good hand positions.

comprise the largest age group entered in the meet. However, more and more young adult women are training and participating in organized meets.

In 1970 a group called Senior Sports International, styled after the Olympic format, was formed. Annual competition is open to all interested competitors, and there are no rigid requirements about amateur status, and so on. Women must be at least 40 years of age to be eligible for competition in track and field events, although there are younger age groups organized for other sports. Each year the number of entries has increased, and it is presumed that interest in this competition will increase.

Throughout the nation there has been large growth in the number of track and field programs offered in schools, particularly at the junior high school level. Many cities and counties now sponsor track meets open to all the schools within their district or area in late spring. Usually the schools that enter have just completed their own track seasons, and the girls are in the very best condition. Several states conduct state meets for high school girls.

The AAU has developed the junior Olympics track and field program for girls (and boys) and has made this program available to recreation departments and schools. Other interested civic organizations may also sponsor this program, and often Chamber of Commerce groups conduct it for the girls in their towns. Civic groups frequently sponsor track and field programs for physically and/or mentally handicapped youngsters. Such meets include boys and girls.

In many areas there are clubs created solely for the purpose of promoting girls' track and field programs. These clubs usually register their members with the AAU so that their athletes can compete in AAU-sanctioned meets. Most of the girls who enter AAU competition, both locally and nationally, are affiliated with some athletic club, but this is not a prerequisite for participation.

Colleges are now sponsoring track meets for women, sometimes of an invitational type, but greater numbers experience conference competition. Also, the Association of Intercollegiate Athletics for Women (AIAW) national championships are held on an annual basis.

As one views the many organizations that sponsor programs in track and field for American girls, it becomes apparent that there will be more and more opportunities for all interested girls to participate. It is hoped that these activities will be conducted in such a manner that the girls' experiences will be of the highest order.

CHAPTER 2

Principles of conditioning and training

This chapter presents some general and specific information regarding individual conditioning and training. Attainment of the proper level of conditioning should be the goal of every girl, not just of those who wish to participate in track and field events. However, training must suit the individual, and each girl's program will be different even though it will include some general procedures used by all girls with the same objectives (Table 2-1).

The girl with a naturally strong body, who conditions herself properly by improving her bodily functions through exercise and good health practices, will soon learn that she responds well to competitive stress and shows improvement in track and field activities.

Each girl should have a complete physical examination to be certain she has no organic defects that would interfere with her participation in strenuous competitive activities. The development of any serious or prolonged illness would make subsequent examinations necessary to ensure that she is healthy enough to compete again.

When girls first take part in running, jumping, and throwing movements, they must be careful not to injure their leg and arm muscles. They must be in proper physical condition to perform effectively and safely. Proper conditioning of the body consists of doing stretching, relaxing, and strengthening exercises and participating in speed and endurance-producing actions. Muscles that are stretched and body parts that have eventually been extended through their full range of movement are less likely to sustain injury. Stretching should be done in a gradual and continuous manner until the full range of movement is reached. A body part should be put on a stretch, but it should not be overstretched. A good rule of thumb for a coach to follow in early season is to have a girl work up to her pain zone but not beyond it.

SUGGESTED CONDITIONING SCHEDULES

Preseason conditioning (2 weeks). Basic preliminary preseason conditioning or the development of basic fitness must precede any specific conditioning for an event. Such general fitness development is accomplished in a myriad of ways and is necessary for optimal healthful living for all persons. However, the girl who has only a recreational interest in running, jumping, and throwing does not have the same need for specific conditioning as does the serious competitor. The serious athlete will begin early to get her body in a state of readiness for all-around development. She will do a lot of easy running,

13

Table 2-1. Exercises grouped according to primary use in specific events

	Sprints	Hurdles	Weight events	High jumps	Long jumps	Middle-distance runs	Distance runs
Endurance							
Fartlek	X				X	X	X
Spurt sprinting (three-fourths sprint, then all-out spurt)						X	X
Wind sprinting	X	X	X		X	X	
Circuit	X	X	X	X	X	X	X
Logging miles						X	X
Timed running						X	X
Interval running						X	X
Paarlauf	X					X	X
Strength							
Back, arms, shoulders			X	X		X	X
Legs	X	X	X	X	X	X	X
Hands	X		X				
Abdomen		X	X	X	X		
Flexibility							
Legs, hips	X	X		X	X		
Back		X	X	X	X		
Trunk		X	X	X	X		
Speed							
Repeat running	X	X			X	X	X
Wind sprinting	X	X	X	X	X	X	
Interval training	X					X	X
Spurt sprinting	X	X		X	X	X	X
Loosening	X	X	X	X	X	X	X
Weight training	*	*	X	X	X		

*Used to a limited extent.

perform stretching exercises, and do strength-building exercises in the preseason period of conditioning. Fartlek, interval running, and weight training are systems of exercises that are of special benefit during this period of training.

Early season conditioning (8 weeks). The early season conditioning period is the time for the athlete to focus on perfecting form and properly executing the various moves while still aiming for the development of the needed strength, endurance, and flexibility required for success in an event. Early season is the time for participation in drills, which become progressively more intense as the athlete is exposed to longer and more strenuous training routines.

Competitive season conditioning (6 weeks). The competitive season conditioning period is the time to maintain physical condition and to sharpen mental attitude toward the competition. Practice periods will become shorter and generally less intense. The athlete will concentrate on getting adequate rest, doing proper warm-ups, maintaining a high level of physiologic fitness, and perfecting the mechanics of form.

Daily training aspects

Warm-up period. During this period the mind and body are getting ready physiologically and psychologically for competition. The preparation should include movements that will use all the muscles involved in performing the various events. It may be done in a group or individually. The benefits derived from preparation are raising the body temperature to improve performance, preventing muscle soreness and injury, and setting the stage for competitive psychologic readiness.

The following is a suggested warm-up routine.

1. The athlete does easy *jogging* on a soft or grassy surface for a period of 10 to 15 minutes. The body should be covered with a warm-up suit, and tennis shoes should be worn.
2. The athlete performs slow stretch *exercises,* such as trunk twisting, sitting toe touches, hurdle exercises, arm circles, trunk rotating, back stretching, and side stretching, in which the entire body is stretched until the individual feels she can move suddenly without any danger to joints and muscles. She should feel relaxed and loose with an absence of tenseness on completion of the routine. Longer periods of stretching may be required for some girls and on cooler days for most of the girls.
3. The athlete runs *wind sprints* for a short distance at three-fourths or all-out speed, walking between sprints for a quick recovery and running all out again. This effort is repeated for a distance of a half mile to a mile.

Daily workout. This period of 30 to 60 minutes or longer is the time for each girl to work on the specific skills involved in her event. The workout may be entirely individual or may be shared with a partner or small group if certain girls have the same need. It may involve distance or speed work or practicing jumping or throwing.

Warm-down period. This tapering-off period allows the body to return to a more normal physiologic functioning level in which the respiratory and circulatory systems return to near normal. The warm-down is an important part of the daily training period. The athlete does an easy jog of a half mile and then finishes the period with a walk followed by a warm shower.

CONDITIONING FOR GENERAL STRENGTH DEVELOPMENT

The general strength of the body may be increased by the provision of a training stimulus greater than the normal daily load to which a particular muscle or group of muscles is subjected. Increments of strength that will not cause girls to develop undesirable bulging muscles can be developed. Strength is developed by utilizing the overload principle, in which the training stimulus is greater than the daily activity demands. Overloading may be applied through self-resisting exercises, weight training exercises, and isometric exercises.

Self-resisting exercises. In these exercises the athlete's weight forms the resistance as the body or body parts work against gravity (Fig. 2-1). The well-known traditional ones are push-ups, pull-ups, dips, leg raises, and back lifts. These exercises can be performed anywhere, and needed loads may be realized by varying the number of repetitions and the number of sets.

Weight training exercises. Exercising with weights according to a prearranged plan under competent direction can add definite strength benefits for all athletes (Figs. 2-2 and 2-3). In the off season the use of weights is for all-around strength development.

Fig. 2-1. Arm strengthening exercise. Pull-ups on the horizontal bar are a good resistance exercise for developing arm strength. Even distance runners and field event girls should participate in this exercise. This position should be held for 10 seconds and repeated several times to build strength.

Fig. 2-2. Wall pulley exercise to strengthen the muscles of the arm.

Fig. 2-3. These three photographs of a young woman performer indicate the desire of women to use strength development devices, such as these exercise machines, to help gain strength for better performance.

Dumbbells, barbells, and special body weights may all be employed. In the preseason conditioning program the purpose is to concentrate on the particular muscle groups that contribute the most to the performance of the different events. This type of program is particularly suited to shot putters and discus and javelin throwers. The hurdlers, runners, and jumpers work with lighter loads twice a week. During the early season training for field events, girls will continue to make use of weight training on alternate days. During the competitive season, use of reduced weights or no weights may be desirable.

Isometric exercises. Isometric movements are those in which the body part involved remains static but the muscles contract. Arm, shoulder, neck, and back muscles (deltoid, rhomboid, trapezius, and pectoral) may be strengthened rapidly through the use of some isometric exercises. It is current opinion that isotonic exercises should be used to a greater extent than isometric exercises. In fact, most athletes use isometric exercises only to supplement their isotonic exercise routines. (See Appendix B for exercise suggestions.)

Specific strengthening exercises

Arm and shoulder girdle exercises. The shoulder girdle area needs special attention because these muscle groups are usually underdeveloped in women. Hanging by the arms, chinning, doing push-ups, and performing dips on parallel bars may help to increase the strength of arm, shoulder, and back muscles (Fig. 2-1). The athlete should begin with light weights and progress to heavier weights.

1. Modified push-ups (Appendix B, Fig. B-4). This exercise is done with the body held perfectly straight. It is performed in a sustained and slowly executed motion and should strengthen arm and shoulder muscles.
2. Bent arm hang. Hanging on a bar with palms forward and arms bent at the elbows and the level of the bar placed at the height of the performer's nose, the performer remains suspended in this position as long as possible. This is good for shoulder girdle development.
3. N seat and L seat. These exercises are good for abdominal muscle development as well as arm, wrist, and finger strengthening. The performer sits in an N position, knees, bent, feet on the floor, and places her weight on her hands while lifting her buttocks and feet clear of the floor. For the L seat the legs are held straight out as the lift is made with buttocks and legs lifted off the floor.
4. Handstands done on low parallel bars. In the balanced position the athlete alternately flexes and extends her arms.
5. Arm curls. Using dumbbells and barbells of appropriate weight that will permit ten to twelve repetitions, the performer pulls the weight to her shoulders by bending her arm at the elbows and using the biceps muscles.
6. Overhead press. Using 50% of body weight as a selector, the performer brings the weight to her shoulders, using an overhand grip, and then pushes the weight directly overhead.
7. Bench press. Using 60% of body weight as a selector, the athlete lies supine on a bench and takes weights from the support, using an overhand grip. She lowers the weight to her chest and pushes it back to full extension with her arms. The athlete should do this exercise under supervision.

Hand and finger exercises. Fingers must be strengthened. Strong fingers make it possible for runners to hold a set position in the sprint start. The increased strength that helps throwers better their performance is developed by wrist and finger flexion, not by merely handling throwing equipment. A good exercise is one in which the performer assumes a sitting position, then lifts and supports her body weight on the first joints of her fingers for from 6 to 10 seconds. This exercise should be repeated two or more times. Performers may also increase strength by doing finger push-ups.

Back exercises

1. Rocking chair. Lying supine, the performer bends her knees, catches hold of her ankles, and pulls her knees and upper body off the floor as her body rocks back and forth.
2. Trunk lift. Lying supine, the performer extends her arms forward with her legs stretched out and relaxes. She raises her arms from the floor as her upper back is bent backward. Holding this position for two counts, she returns her body to the floor for a two-count rest. The same exercise is performed with the hands laced behind the neck. Keeping her feet on the floor, she raises her chest from the floor.
3. Back-lying arch. Lying on her back, knees flexed, with body weight on shoulders and feet, the performer raises her hips as high as possible by arching her back. After holding this position for five counts, she lowers her body to the floor.
4. Back leg-lift. Lying face down, head resting on folded arms, the performer raises her left leg high with movement taking place at the hip, and holds this position for two counts. She repeats the procedure with her right leg.
5. Barbell rowing. Using 50% of her body weight as a poundage indicator, with an overhand grip on the barbell, the performer flexes her trunk forward parallel with the floor. Keeping her head and trunk still, she brings the barbell to her chest and performs a circular motion with it.

Abdominal strengthening. Abdominal strength, which is needed particularly in long jumping, hurdling, and throwing events, can be developed by doing sit-ups and leg-lifts.

1. Sit-ups. Lying on her back with knees flexed, the performer clasps her hands behind her head and very slowly rolls to a sitting position. This exercise should not be done with a jerky motion. Only a few repetitions are required.
2. Leg-lifts. Lying supine, the performer bends her knees to her chest, straightens her legs to a 90-degree angle, and slowly lowers her legs to the floor. When her feet are about 4 inches from the floor, she holds the position for five counts.
3. N seat and L seat (previously described). The L position or L hang can be performed in a suspended position from a bar. In a simpler progression the performer first hangs with her arms extended, then brings her knees to her chest and holds this position for five counts. As her strength improves, she attempts the L hang.
4. V sit. Sitting on the floor with knees flexed, the performer lifts her feet off the floor. As her body leans backward, she balances on her buttocks. Extending her arms and legs in same direction, she makes a V of her body and holds the V position for five counts.
5. Upper body raise. Holding a dumbbell in an underhand grip, the performer raises

her upper body to a half-sitting position off the floor, keeping her lower back on the floor, and holds this position for five counts.

Thigh muscle development. The quadriceps muscle group (front thigh muscles) can be strengthened by lifting weights of progressive poundage strapped to both feet. The legs move through the full range of movement up to angles of 90 and 170 degrees. Resistance may also be accomplished isometrically. With a pad placed under her knee and her leg hanging down, the performer should attempt to extend her leg while her partner applies force to the front of the leg just above the ankle. Strength and muscular endurance of the leg may be increased by the performer's wearing light weights strapped to the ankles during running and jumping practice sessions.

Legs, ankles, feet strengthening. These exercises help to improve running.

1. Toe walking. Walking on tiptoes stretches the performer's foot, ankle, and leg muscles.
2. Heel walking. The performer alternates walking on the heels with toe raises. It is good for strengthening the leg area or overcoming shin splint difficulty.
3. Stair hopping. The performer hops a flight of stairs on one foot and repeats with the other foot.
4. Demi-plié. In various ballet positions the athlete performs demi-plié exercises.
5. Ballet jumps. The athlete performs the moves done in ballet, such as jeté, changement, pas de chat, cabriole, and sissone.
6. Knee bend. The performer bends her knees as deeply as possible but keeps her entire foot on the floor and extends her arms forward. Her knees should be turned out and placed over the feet.
7. Buttocks kick. The athlete performs high hopping, kicking herself on the buttocks with the hopping leg.
8. Leg curl and raise. Using an iron boot or leg weights, the performer curls her foot backward, then raises her leg high to the rear as her body is bent forward. She repeats the process ten to twelve times with each foot.
9. Leg lift with heavy foot. Using an iron boot or leg weights, the performer raises her leg upward and bends forward with both arms extended. She repeats the process ten to twelve times.

ENDURANCE CONDITIONING

Muscular endurance. Muscular endurance is the ability of muscles to repeat a task or hold out against tension without giving in to fatigue. Naturally strong muscles can do more work than can weak ones. The skeletal muscles, heart, and lungs must be strengthened for athletes to turn in maximum performances. Strong girls have a greater ability to resist fatigue (endurance); this increases the time they can work effectively.

Muscular endurance is improved through the use of weight training, circuit training, and all kinds of running. Participation in rope skipping, running in place, trampoline bouncing, and vigorous exercises such as squat thrusts and jumping jacks and other means of developing muscular endurance.

Weight training concepts. Girls need to participate in weight training to develop the strength needed to perform at their best, which is especially true of the weight-event participants. Perhaps the best initial procedure is to have the girl lift as much poundage as possible in one action and then take two thirds of this weight and have her lift it eight times. Later, as she gains strength, increase the number of lifts to twelve and then more. The weight may be increased later on, but it is probably the speed with which she lifts the weight that will help her gain the strength she needs (Appendix B).

Cardiorespiratory endurance ideas. This type of endurance enables the heart, blood vessels, and lungs to catch oxygen and take it to the muscles as often and as effortlessly as possible. This ability is best developed by participation in activities that make for breathlessness but do not permit the athlete to stop right away. Endurance is increased by doing cross-country running, running up and down stairs, performing timed step tests, and doing buddy running and interval running. In buddy running, one of the partners runs a prescribed distance and tags the other partner, who then runs this same distance while the first buddy is walking about in recovery. Many repetitions of this buddy running in competition with other partners will motivate students to sustain their efforts, and a degree of endurance will result. Repeating runs of short distances (75 to 110 meters) for about 10 minutes three times a week is a simple, quick, and excellent way to attain and maintain cardiorespiratory or cardiovascular fitness.

Endurance can be acquired only gradually, whereas skeletal muscles can be strengthened more quickly. In attaining endurance or strength, a girl will be surprised to find that each succeeding preseasonal conditioning session is easier than it was the year before. She will find that she can go through the workout schedules with much less fatigue than she experienced previously.

A girl will also find that while her height and weight remain about the same and muscle bulk does not change appreciably, her performance in speed, height, and strength events will improve. This improvement will be caused by her maturation and primarily by the development of endurance. Perhaps secondarily, this improvement will result from the more efficient use of oxygen by the muscles along with an increased ability to incur oxygen debt. This means that a girl will have learned to push herself further into oxygen debt, but she will have attained the physical and mental level necessary to experience this pain without permitting it to make her quit.

Oxygen debt pain is a result of the accumulation of chemical waste products brought about by muscular contraction; it will always be felt when an athlete pushes herself to her limit. This fact must be accepted realistically. There need not be conscious acceptance of this idea; the muscles will have "learned" that they can exceed previous exertions without intolerable pain resulting from fatigue. When this is realized, the trained performer will have crossed a significant threshold in the development of self-discipline and will have learned that she can perform well even on days when she does not feel her best.

Training methods. Some of the methods used to increase endurance, which are referred to in this and other chapters, can be described as follows.

Fartlek. A method of training used originally by the Swedes, Fartlek, roughly translated, means "speed play." The girl using this type of training should run at her own pace over an undetermined distance; for example, she may run cross-country on a golf course or even back and forth on a football field; she may run at a slow pace, then sprint if she wishes. This is a very flexible training program because it leaves distance and speed up to the runner. However, for a girl to get into condition she must run fast enough to cause physiologic changes in her circulatory system; therefore it is recommended that she use this method of training only during the first few weeks of the season. The disciplined athlete who has a strong desire to improve performance and the ability to push herself to increasingly challenging feats will find this method of training to her advantage.

Interval running. In interval running a girl is required to run a specific distance a definite number of times at a given pace and walk or jog a definite distance after each run, as a recovery measure. If she starts off running 200 meters in 45 seconds, she should then walk 200 meters or just rest, repeating this procedure three times. Each time she is ready to repeat the run, her pulse and breathing rates should have returned to near normal. As she gains strength, she should increase the distance of the run to about 300 meters negotiated in 60 seconds, and either rest or walk 100 meters. Gradually the time of the run may be reduced and the distance of the run increased.

The four variables of interval training are (1) the length of the distance to be run, (2) the time in which to run the distance, (3) the number of repetitions to be run, and (4) the duration of the recovery interval. A good procedure is for the girl to run shorter distances at a faster speed and longer distances at a slower speed than her competitive distance.

Wind sprints. Another method of training to increase endurance involves wind sprints. The runners jog a certain distance and then, at a command, sprint a specific distance. This procedure may be repeated as many times as is thought feasible, taking into consideration the physical condition of the girls. This method is also referred to as *repetition running* (used more by sprinters than by others). Fast running is interspersed with recovery periods of 4 to 6 minutes. A workable plan for wind sprinting is for the girls to run the straightaways and walk the curves a definite number of times. This plan may be reversed, with the curves sprinted and the straightaways jogged or walked.

Timed running. In timed running a girl runs a given time without stopping. Usually she selects a reasonable pace and time—perhaps 10 minutes—gradually increasing her time. This method is best for the girl who is in good condition. Another approach is to establish a predetermined time for running a given distance. An attempt is then made to run the distance in the prescribed time. Each week the time is lowered, and a record of accomplishment is kept. *Continuous running* at race speed may be used to get the girl accustomed to the "blue haze" feeling that causes pain because of the accumulation of lactic acid in the muscles. Each time the girl should run until she cannot run any more to develop tolerance and to have "mind triumph over matter."

Circuit training. In circuit training a girl moves as rapidly as possible from one station to another, performing the prescribed exercises at each station before moving on to the next one. The requirement at a specific station may be to run a specific distance in a given time or to perform a certain number of push-ups, lift a specific weight so many times, or chin herself a predetermined number of times. New requirements and new goals can be established as desired when using this method (Appendix B).

Logging miles. Increasing endurance by means of logging miles requires that a girl simply run as far as is feasible at a reasonable pace. It appears that this is the best method to use in the later stages of training. The novice could begin by jogging 400 meters. Gradually she could increase the distance (for example, a 3000-meter run at a 14-minute pace) and later the distance and the pace could be increased up to 9000 meters at 30⅔ minutes.

Overdistance. It has been common practice for runners to run full speed beyond thier competitive distances to gain endurance. The following overdistances are listed for the various competitive distances:

Competitive distances	Overdistances
100 meters	150 meters
200 meters	300 meters
400 meters	500 or 600 meters
800 meters	1000 or 1320 meters
1500 meters	2000 meters

Paarlauf. Paarlauf is a type of interval running used to stimulate interest in competing in an all-out effort. Two runners compose a team running alternately against the runners on other teams. The object is to carry a baton the farthest distance. The runners may be given the opportunity to decide how they will alternate. No distance is established; usually the coach decides to have the runners compete for a certain total length of time, for example, 30 to 45 minutes (or less), depending on the age and condition of the runners. One runner may run a given distance, such as 400 meters, and rest while his teammate runs the same distance. Often a 1-minute warning whistle is given before the race is terminated. More than two runners may be on a team, and the distance each runs may be considerably shorter or longer than 400 meters.

Flexibility development. Women are generally more flexible than men. However, there are varying degrees of flexibility among women. Static stretching exercises are those considered the most desirable for use in increasing range of motion of joints and for lessening chances of muscular aggravation and pain. A girl should warm up the body by walking rapidly, jogging, and performing some systemic exercises such as running in place, skipping rope or doing jumping jacks, and performing stretching exercises progressively. The same type of stretching exercises used in dance and gymnastics are excellent for use in track and field. The girl should perform the stretching exercises slowly, working at her own ability level to extend her range of motion to increasingly greater degrees. She should involve all parts of her body in the exercises.

OTHER FACTORS

Diet. The diet of the track athlete is no different from that prescribed for any active healthy girl. There should be a balance of all the essential foods. The athlete can accomplish this balance by eating a variety of fruits, vegetables, milk products, bread, cereals, and meat products. Breakfast should consist of cereal, fruit or juice, an egg, toast and jelly or honey, and milk. Young athletes should normally avoid the use of coffee because of its stimulating effect on the intestinal and urinary tracts. In certain individuals there is an unusual sensitivity to caffeine, sometimes resulting in diarrhea or bladder irritation. This produces discomfort as well as a bad psychologic effect on the athlete, who already may be experiencing considerable difficulty in connection with the competitive experience.

Sleep and rest. Sleep and rest are necessary for the growth and development of young people, especially young athletes. Sleep should be regular, sound, and long enough to satisfy the demands of the individual. Competitors should have a good night's sleep and spend a restful day preceding the day of competition.

Muscle tone and readiness posture. A relaxed, effectively moving body will be evident in the person who has strong well-toned muscles. The track athlete who has practiced stretching and strengthening exercises during her training periods will show evidence of an improved posture of readiness. If a girl shows a tendency toward too much toeing out, side-arm swinging, neck straining, or other ineffective movements while running, these should be called to her attention so that she may correct them as soon as possible. Good running, jumping, and throwing postures demand erect and balanced bodies that are as rhythmic and relaxed as the activity allows. This means that specific exercises should be performed by the participants to increase their ability to perform these movements. Great strength and speed are needed at the moment of explosive release of the body (jumping events) or of the object (weight events). This is clearly evident at the moment of gathering just before the takeoff in the long jump and high jump and in releasing the shot and discus. In these latter events added force and speed at the moment of release will automatically result in added distance.

Suitable clothing. Correct clothing for athletes is as important as their participation in effective practice sessions and emotional readiness for competition. Girls should wear low-cut gym shoes with built-in arch supports during participation in all warming-up exercises and distance running. Track shoes should be worn during actual training runs, timed runs, and competitive runs. Warm-up suits should be worn during training sessions and between events in a meet. Girls should wear short shorts that do not bind the thigh muscles during participation in the competitive events. Shirts made of knitted material are better than those made of broadcloth, since they cling to the body, are more comfortable, and do not whip in the wind.

Hair styles and cosmetics. Girls should arrange their hair in a style that will not impede them in any way during training and performing. If hair is long, it should be pulled back and held securely in place. A short attractive cut may be easier to manage, but girls should be allowed to decide this for themselves. The use of little or no cosmetics is generally preferred during the competitive athletic periods.

SOME TRAINING AND LEARNING DETAILS

All girls need to participate in progressive practice programs to build their speed, stamina, and power. Girls may wish, under guidance, to develop their own exercise routines to suit their specific needs and to overcome their individual weaknesses. After general conditioning exercises are performed en masse, athletes will usually practice the moves required in the performance of their specialties. An event leader may drill a small group in the performance of special conditioning exercises necessary for a particular activity and conduct the training session for individuals practicing for competition in special events. The individual and small-group practice sessions may be followed by strength-development exercises for those who need them. The practice periods should be challenging, exciting, and varied.

The human body is a wonderful machine and will respond in a remarkable way when it is well trained, especially if attention is focused on the correct application of sound mechanical principles. Techniques performed in accordance with the laws of physics will produce the best results with the least expenditure of energy. A coach's careful study of and adherence to these laws, coupled with her promotion of a program involving such factors as challenge, encouragement, training, and development, should result in the girls' performing at their maximum, showing noticeable improvement, and often becoming champions.

Many times the force necessary to initiate and sustain a motion in an effective manner is dependent on the strength of the girl. She often needs greater strength momentarily than that developed during participation in a particular activity. Sometimes the most important variable is not how great the force but how quickly it can be applied. The proper utilization of force is also dependent on the direction it takes and its point of application.

The coach should understand the necessity for harmonization of certain laws of motion with body structures; she should realize that most human movements are involved in the principle of third-class lever action; and she should know where the center of gravity is located during a particular action. Furthermore, the proper application of forces in an angular motion involves special concepts and learning that, when properly mastered and applied by the performer, will contribute greatly to the development of championship form (Appendix B).

ATTITUDES OF THE PARTICIPANT

Practice for competition. In establishing a favorable attitude toward competition, it is important for the coach to instill confidence and to help develop mental readiness in the girls. Officials should be trained to avoid handicapping athletes by making harsh remarks and giving inadequate instruction.

The athlete can develop confidence in several ways. She should concentrate on a definite plan of action in training for her event. This will help divert her attention from imagined weaknesses or fear of failure. The coach may call the athlete's attention to a particular weakness in a rival, again focusing attention away from the athlete's own weakness toward those of others. This should help her realize that other competitors have their problems too.

Some coaches have found it helpful to unobtrusively change an athlete's particular obstacle. For example, a coach may shorten the distance between hurdles without informing the girl who is having trouble getting in the proper number of strides between hurdles. Likewise, to aid a shot-putter, the coach may have her throw down a slight incline without being aware of it, thereby enabling her to exceed her previous maximum throw, a distance she felt could not be bettered. The coach should not scoff at such tactics, for it has been known to help athletes achieve good results. It is psychologically important to the athlete participating in such events to strive for a successful first attempt at a given height and succeed or to get a measured jump on the first try. This helps relax her so that her subsequent jumps will be more effective. The first attempt is not always the best, but it is important for the athlete to have a measured mark so that she does not fear that she may foul on every try.

A girl must learn to point toward each meet during a season to be at the peak of her physical and mental ability for her current level of development. The performances attained in the most important meet at the end of the season, in the competition between two girl athletes of comparable natural ability, will be determined in large part by the degree to which each one concentrates on the proper actions, adheres to her scheduled workouts, and devotes attention to the improvement of details.

Many races, throws, and jumps are won by inches, and these inches are gained through attention to details in technique, development of proper emotional control, maintenance of mental readiness, and attainment of good body conditioning. To key oneself up to the exertion of maximum effort at any one time, it is important that no stone be left unturned to the preparation for this effort. The coach must be able to encourage, stimulate, motivate, and educate to the highest degree to make the girls believe in what they are capable of doing.

Competition. Proper mental and emotional readiness are very important for the track athlete because she has such a small margin of time in which to make her maximum exertion. The hours and weeks of practice will culminate in a single effort made in a few seconds or minutes—all the time that is required to compete in an event. Therefore adequate time should be devoted to the development of mental and emotional controls so that the athlete can learn to maintain a competitive edge and increase her energy potential to its maximum for a controlled release during competition. This phase of conditioning is too often minimized. Development of such control should result in the athlete being able to concentrate on executing the desired action. It will allow her to take victory in stride; or, rather than being crushed by defeat, she will be even more determined to improve her preparation for the next time. Therefore the coach must convince the athlete that there is almost no limit to what she can do and must instill in her the desire to always do her best.

There are two important elements in preparing the athlete for top performances: she must be provided with opportunities to compete against top performers, and she and her coach must make a constant study of her performances. The highly skilled athlete is spurred on to better performances whenever she is forced to push herself beyond previous efforts during the heat of competition. If possible, this should be done on a gradual and progressive basis. One way of ensuring continued top effort is to make use of the results of the tape and stopwatch in practice sessions. The performer should maintain an awareness of her ability as compared with that of other competitors she may expect to meet during the season.

Another method of helping a performer continue to improve is to use the times, heights, and distances made in time trials prior to each meet as a means of selecting girls who will compete in the forthcoming meet. This method will prevent a girl from becoming overconfident and developing lazy habits. Each girl will realize that she does not have a permanent place on the team but must earn her place every week. This procedure will serve as an incentive for girls who have not been on the team to continue working toward a team position.

SUMMARY

Conditioning, like learning, is specific and individual. However, there are certain general statements that may be made and that should be given consideration by most performers.

1. If speed is the objective, the runner must work on speed; if endurance is the objective, it must be attained through running long distances. Most runners, regardless of their speciality, need to work on acquiring speed and endurance. They need to practice running overdistances and underdistances and to learn pace. The longer the running distance, the more endurance is needed. It appears that the best way to train long-distance runners is to have them run for a given distance or in a given time.

2. When strength is needed, it appears that a girl has to use supplemental means, such as training with weights, to attain it.

3. Practicing the moves that are part of a skill is necessary for the attainment of top performance. Weight training cannot be substituted for, but should augment, such practice.

4. The mental attitude of a performer is perhaps the single most important factor in determining how she performs. She must want to do well to perform at her maximum ability.

5. There is no substitute for continuous effort over a long period of time if a performer desires to realize her potential.

CHAPTER 3

Beginning a track and field program

GENERATING INTEREST

An energetic and interested teacher or coach can easily get a track and field program started in a community. The first step is to get some track and field action under way. The scheduling of an all-school track and field sports day composed of many relays and jumping and throwing activities, including novelty and fun events, will help generate much interest in this area. All-comers meets are extremely popular with many performers during the late summer months as well as during the cross-country season. Usually these meets have several different age groups involved, and the athletes simply show up in time for the meet and sign in on the field. There are no official records kept, since there are seldom qualified officials on hand and the purpose is for training and conditioning only.

The attendance of the teacher and the girl students at track and field clinics and at boys' track meets is valuable in developing interest as well as increasing knowledge of the sport. Watching college meets is also most beneficial to the prospective participants. The inclusion of a good instructional unit in track and field in the physical education program is of vital importance in helping to stimulate interest and in providing good experience for the students. The fast runners and good jumpers discovered here and in the intramural program, who are encouraged to compete in track and field events, will prove a good source of potential top level performers. The competition held in running, jumping, and throwing events between class squads, separate hourly classes, and separate grades should help the teacher discover potentially good track team members.

If the teacher has had no experience with track activities, she should use all means available to the present-day coach to become informed, so that she can learn along with the girls. She should read guides, periodicals, and textbooks, attend clinics conducted for men and women coaches, attend boys' and girls' meets, and contact persons active in track and field (such people are often glad to lend their assistance in getting a track program started). She should also read scientific articles on track and field.

The track teacher and coach may want to visit the elementary and junior high schools to encourage the development of children's interest in track and field activities by giving talks, putting on demonstrations, showing films, and promoting meets for this age group. Potential performers may be discovered as the result of scores made on physical fitness tests, and they may be asked to join the track squad. High school girls may enjoy working as student leaders for the junior high and intermediate grade school girls in their various track and field events. Through such training sessions the older girl is challenged to become more informed about her event while helping younger girls become more skilled. Track team members will often encourage others to participate if the program is attractive, stimulating, and self-satisfying.

Good track and field movies and interesting bulletin board displays of girls performing various events, especially pictures and records of national and Olympic performances, challenge and motivate students. It is believed, however, that the best motivation results from participating in a well-planned and properly promoted program in which proper competition is offered. This may be in physical education class contests, intramural activities, and/or scheduled meets.

CONDITIONING THE GIRLS

One of the first steps to take in initiating a track program is to properly condition the girls. Relatively little participation in the events should take place until there has been a period of conditioning to attain the top level of physical fitness that is so necessary for the proper functioning and development of growing girls. This conditioning may be accomplished in a variety of ways. Strength may be developed through a progressive weight training program, flexibility may be improved through dance exercises, and endurance may be increased through vigorous and sustained running (Figs. 3-1 and 3-2).

A good approach to use is to get the girls involved in many activities. They may run cross-country, barefoot on the grass, or in the gym on rainy days. They can be encouraged to walk rather than ride. They may even run to school or to the store, or they may just run for the sheer pleasure of being able to run. With today's interest in bicycling, girls should be encouraged to ride bicycles to and from school, to work, on weekend jaunts, and whenever possible.

Fig. 3-1. Stadium-stair running to develop thigh strength. (Photograph by Gary Dahle.)

Fig. 3-2. Small wooden hurdles are used to gain confidence and help develop high knee action and step consistency. (Photograph by Gary Dahle.)

A complete physical examination must be given to the girls to ensure that they have no physical defects, so that they can be worked far beyond the point where they think they are "too tired."

After the preliminary conditioning is accomplished, the girls should be encouraged to participate in the various events to find out where they show potential and which types of activities they prefer. However, the girls must first be physically ready for competition.

In the beginning the better competitors will be those with the better previous performance records, but no one should be dropped from the squad. The coach also will discover that some girls with no experience will be far better performers after some training than others with previous experience. Those who are willing to work hard in practice sessions may not win any races or receive great acclaim, but they usually improve their general health, strength, and coordination. Also, many of those who score no victories for 1 or 2 years may be the girls who find themselves becoming champions after 3 to 4 years of training. All participants should be encouraged to read all they can about their events to become better informed and more able to employ the technique of self-improvement.

During each practice session there must be warm-up activities, including jogging, stretching exercises, and wind sprints, followed by participation in the regular practice session. Later a warming-down procedure should be followed for a gradual return of the girls' circulation to normal.

BEGINNING TRACK AND FIELD ACTIVITIES

One good way to get competition started is to schedule a few girls' events as a part of the program of a boys' meet. This helps acquaint the girls with the proper procedures to follow, teaches them important lessons about being in good condition, and lets all connected with the meet realize the values of promoting such competition for girls.

The track squad will continue to show eagerness and enthusiasm if practice sessions are kept interesting by being well organized and varied. Girls may be trained separately, or boys and girls may be trained simultaneously. If the latter plan is used, each will gain from the other by seeking social approval and acceptance. The girls learn a great deal about a given event by observing the superior performances of the boys; this will challenge them to extend themselves to learn and excel. The boys in turn work harder because they recognize an appreciative audience and want to perform well for it. They will also come to recognize that girl athletes have the ability to perform at high levels.

Early workouts should be relatively easy and fun for the participating girls. The essential equipment should be provided, although track is an activity that can be enjoyed with a minimum amount of equipment. All girls should try out for all events to learn about them, to find out where their strengths and weaknesses lie, and to discover which events they enjoy participating in the most.

Good performances can be rewarded through the establishment of track honor rolls attractively displayed, through the use of pictures and write-ups in the school newspaper, and through the keeping and displaying of the best school records. It is a good procedure to include school track and field records in the school handbook to call attention to the outstanding performances of the past. Movies made of the athletes make it possible to effectively study individual performances while calling attention to excellence of performance. A list of meet records attractively displayed with pictures of the squad and various record holders helps to stimulate interest at a school. Special honor rolls of those who have performed in an outstanding manner in various events, such as putting the shot a certain distance or running the 100-yard dash within a certain time, may be posted as motivating devices within track and field classes.

For team members to perform to the best of their ability, there must be a careful and constant evaluation made of their performance. This evaluation may be accomplished by keeping records of performances in timed and measured practices as well as meet performances. Individual progress records should be kept by the coach and by each girl. One technique to follow is to have each girl keep a personal record book that would include personal data such as height, weight, medical record, and performance scores and, for later use, a place to add ribbons, awards, news clippings, and photographs.

The scheduling of a dual meet with a nearby school will provide encouragement to those who have been training for track and field participation and will supply the impetus needed to really get a track program started. It is good to follow up dual meets with a county-wide meet so that all the interested girls in the area are involved in track competition. A number of dual meets, coupled with some triangular meets and finally a large invitational meet scheduled at the close of the season, will offer the competition needed by most participants and will help increase their levels of performance and raise the motivation for most meets in the future.

PART TWO

Running

CHAPTER 4

Sprints

HISTORY

Humans have been running—for survival and for pleasure—since the beginning of time. Styles of running for competition have changed; those used today bear little resemblance to those used during the time of the ancient Greeks and the early Olympic Games. However, the racing concept in itself has remained constant. During the ancient games, women were not allowed in the stadia even as spectators, and the idea of permitting women to compete in races before an audience of men was simply not considered. At times, however, they did have their own separate races.

Shortly before the turn of the twentieth century, however, women's schools and colleges in the United States initiated field days for their students with running as a main feature. Ever since then, girls as well as boys have engaged in foot races at their school and recreation areas. However, track activities for older teenage girls in American schools were neither accepted nor emphasized until recently. European schools for many years have included track meets as an integral part of the experience for their girls, and for this reason young European women have taken for granted the idea of participation in competitive running as proper and worthwhile.

Modern Olympic Games have included running events for women ever since the introduction of track events in the 1928 Amsterdam Olympics. Yet just a few women have been truly great athletes in track; quite possibly the lack of continued interest is the result of social factors, home responsibilities, and the repression of track programs for women that has existed in the United States. There appears to be a change in the making as evidenced by the great acclaim extended to many female track and field stars in the 1976 Olympics. There have been prominent examples of outstanding female track athletes in the past; for example, the late American, Babe Didrikson (Zaharias), set several Olympic records in the 1932 Games at Los Angeles. There have also been outstanding performances given by Fanny Blankers-Koen, the "Flying Dutch Housewife"; Wilma Rudolph, the queen of the 1960 Olympics; and Wyomia Tyus, a great performer in the 1968 Olympics. In the 1976 Olympics, the United States did not have an outstanding woman performer.

Considering how difficult it is to improve on an existing world record in the sprints, special notice should be given to the performance of an athlete whenever this feat is accomplished. Chi Cheng of Taiwan displayed this outstanding ability when she bettered the world record in the 200-meter race in 1970 by running it in 22.4 seconds. The 1972

Olympic champion, Remate Stecher of East Germany, set a new Olympic record and tied the world record by running 200 meters in 22.4 seconds. She also won the 100-meter race in 11.07 seconds. Chi Cheng holds the 100-yard record of 10 seconds. Wyomia Tyus of the United States holds the 100-meter world record of 11.1 seconds. The former world record in the 100 meters is 11.04 seconds, held by Inge Helten of West Germany. The new world record is 11.01 seconds and is held by Annegret Richter of West Germany. All these remarkable women were mentioned in Chapter 1.

SPECIAL CONSIDERATIONS

Prospective girl runners are great in number because almost all girls can run to some extent and many like to run. It is quite another matter to run fast enough to become a *good* sprinter. It is also difficult to predict sprinting ability by body type because there is no "typical" body build that a coach can identify as the most suitable physique for fast sprinting. Speed comes from the fast driving power of the legs—the main qualification for fast running. However, possessing fast moving muscles (fast twitch type) is the key.

Long lower legs with powerful muscles are necessary for the tall girl sprinter; her height must be accompanied by strength in the lower leg muscles for her to have the driving power needed for fast sprinting. The short girl must have strong, fast-contracting muscles to compensate for the shortness of her leg length.

Naturally, since explosive driving power with fast leg action is essential for speed, it would be reasonable to think that sprinting is an event for younger women. Today girls are running in organized competition as young as 9 years or even less. As a result, girls such as Charlette Cook (400 meters), Susan Brodock (race walk), Kathy Hammond (400 meters), and Pernetta Glenn (50 yards) set the top United States marks while still in their teens. Many people think that older women (beyond the age of maximum physical efficiency for greatest speed) are better suited for running longer races, which require more endurance. However, if a woman keeps herself in good condition and practices sprinting continually, she should be able to run fast for many years. It is unusual, furthermore, for a teenager (14 to 17 years of age) to qualify as a sprinter for the Olympic team of most countries. It is the somewhat older athlete (20 years of age or more) who breaks the record marks and makes the Olympic team in the sprints as well as in other track and field events.

Essential qualities. A girl who wishes to step up from the ranks of the average performer into the good sprinter class must possess certain attributes. The better-than-average girl sprinter will have fast leg speed, long stride, and ability to relax. She must have the skill mastered so that she responds automatically and is able to concentrate completely on reacting to the sound of the gun and racing to the finish line.

Fast leg speed and long stride. Since the distances of sprints are short (50 to 200 meters), the athlete who reacts most quickly and efficiently to the command to run will obviously have a great advantage over girls who react slowly. The faster the reflex action takes place in response to the stimulus, the faster the reaction time and the faster the girl will start to sprint. However, there is a difference between the ability to react quickly and the ability to move the legs quickly. The successful sprinter must move a few strides forward rapidly, but she must also be able to continue to move her legs rapidly during the specified distance. It is the leg speed that will cause her to run fast, not just the fast break out of the blocks. It is a matter of simple mathematics that a girl having fast leg speed and a long stride should be a top sprinter. A happy medium must be found so that the long stride is not assumed to the extent that leg speed is reduced appreciably. (Speed equals leg stride frequency times length of stride.)

Relaxation. It is common knowledge that the key to becoming a top sprinter lies in the athlete's ability to relax while running with all-out effort. Girls must learn to relax while expending as much exertion as they can in the sprinting effort. This ability to relax is a result of much practice and experience.

Automatic actions. The good sprinter is so well trained in the required sprinting movements that every action is done routinely. This helps her make the greatest possible use of her effort. She must know automatically which foot should be in the rear block without the confusion of going through a period of trial and error to determine which feels best to her. Trial and error at this point would result in a confused mind and physical ineffectiveness. The more natural an action is to an athlete, the greater will be her efficiency; for example, in hurdling a girl should be so familiar with the hurdle distances and with her stride measurements that approaches and proper takeoffs are done automatically, without conscious thought of foot placement. Likewise in sprinting she must perform every action with no thought to what she is doing at the precise time of performance; a sprinter's actions must be reflexive in nature, based on practice, prior analysis, and present concentration on results rather than on the technique of body actions to be made during the performance.

Concentration. Absolute concentration is essential to success in sprinting as it is in all other track and field events. The sprinter has to block out all outside stimuli, except those of the start and of the race itself. This is apparent when, after assuming a set position, a sprinter leaves her blocks on hearing the sound of any sharp report, even though it is not the noise of a gun being fired. The sprinter is concentrating on the start at this moment rather than on a specific sound, and she is reacting to a stimulus (noise) by leaving the blocks. During a sprint she must not hear the crowd, see the tape, or in any other way permit outside distractions to interfere with utter mental and physical dedication to the running of the race at hand.

ELEMENTS OF SPRINTING

Types of starts. All starts in the sprints should be taken from starting blocks, with the athlete using one of the more common techniques. The starting positions are different and, based on previous results and the proper "feel" of the position, individual athletes will chose one in preference to others. However, most of today's top sprinters use about the same starting foot placement position. A girl will often automatically assume her best natural driving position from the blocks when told initially to get down in the blocks. Only when she stops to think about which leg to place in a certain position will she suffer confusion. Some coaches advocate placing the stronger leg in the front block for support because by so doing the body is over the forward foot longer. The longer span of time always occurs with the front foot. Other coaches believe the strong leg should be in the rear block for driving purposes. Most sprinters use a crouch starting position, but recent research results seem to indicate that the use of a stand-up starting position promotes a faster pace during most of the early part of a race.

Bunch start. Using the bunch start, the sprinter kneels with the toes of the back foot opposite the heel of the forward foot (Fig. 4-1). The blocks are placed close together, usually about 8 to 10 inches apart. According to many researchers the use of the bunch start allows the sprinter the fastest starting time from the blocks. There was some doubt in the past, however, that this initial speed could be maintained long enough to assure the fastest sprinting times for distances over 30 meters. Then, too, the hips are held high in a bunch start, causing the sprinter difficulty in holding her position during a particularly long set position and in some cases making her stand upright after leaving the blocks and before beginning the sprint.

However, with the advent of the starting rules permitting the starters to fire the gun in less than 2 seconds after the sprinters have come to a set position, the bunch start has again become popular for many sprinters.

Medium start. The medium start (Fig. 4-2) is popular among men and women sprinters, since it is somewhat more comfortable than the bunch start yet allows enough gathering of muscle force for explosion to take place from the blocks. The runner places the rear knee beside the toe and the arch of the front foot. To ascertain the spacing needed for this start, a girl will have to experiment to find the exact foot placement that suits her leg length and results in her attaining the best speeds for particular distances. The blocks will be set at a distance of from 10 to 13 inches apart when the medium start is used.

Elongated start. Few sprinters may want to use the elongated start because the distance between blocks is too great. The runner determines the spacing needed for this start by finding the distance between the rear knee and the forward foot from a kneeling position. Tests conducted by many investigators indicate that this type of foot spacing

Fig. 4-1. "Take-your-mark" position as viewed from the side at the start of a sprint. This girl is using the bunch start.

Fig. 4-2. Correct medium start position as viewed from the front.

Fig. 4-3. Set position. The runner is using an elongated start for the sprint race. Note that her head is not elevated; if it were, it would cause tension in the neck muscles.

results in the slowest starting times. It is not recommended for this reason unless the girl is unusually tall with long and rather heavy lower limbs (Fig. 4-3).

Techniques of starting. As a result of working with girls and studying their performances and time results, we recommend the following techniques to girl sprinters.

Set blocks. The sprinter should place the blocks at the back edge of the frame, which is set a very wide handspan behind the starting line. She should take a bunch or medium starting position, push the blocks forward until they are pressing against the balls of her feet, and then set the blocks tightly. The sprinter should run out of the blocks a few times to see if the settings are comfortable and if they give her the thrust she wants. She must remember the desired block settings so that she will not have to go through a great deal of block adjustment just before participating in a meet.

Standing position. Sprinters take a standing position behind their blocks as the starter gives the instructions for the race. He will generally tell them: "Runners, go behind your blocks." Next he will tell them to remain in their lanes and avoid false starts. He will remind them that he will hold them for almost 2 seconds in the set position before he fires the gun. He will also remind the girls of the distance of the race they are running.

Starter commands. The starter commands the sprinters: "Go to your marks" or "Runners, take your marks." With either command each sprinter steps in front of her blocks and places her hands on the ground so that her weight rests on the thumbs and fingers, making a "bridge" of her hands just behind the line. Hands are placed at about shoulders' width apart or somewhat wider, depending on the strength of the sprinter's arms. The sprinter then stretches her rear leg and places it against the back block first, after which she places her front leg properly against the other block. (At this point sprinters usually dust off their hands to get rid of any unwanted dirt or lumps.) Her arms are left hanging straight down and fully extended, and her head and neck should be relaxed, with her head hanging down to avoid the development of tenseness. Her hands

Fig. 4-4. Sequence of movements in a sprint start are shown here from the set position through the first step. Observe arm and leg action.

are placed in the desired position, and her rear knee is on the ground. At no time should the sprinter look around to see the starter (Fig. 4-4).

Set. On hearing the command ''Set!'' the full concentration of the sprinter takes over and conditioned responses occur. The hips are raised slightly above the level of the shoulders; the body moves forward and up, with the shoulders moved ahead of the hands; the head is held down and relaxed; the eyes look downward rather than down the track to avoid having tenseness occur (Fig. 4-4). Even as the girl is leaving the blocks, she should look down the track only far enough to ensure that she maintains good body direction. She should be in perfect balance, with the feeling that if her hands were moved, she would fall forward. There should be greater body weight over her forward foot than over her rear foot. The runner should take a quick deep breath just before coming up to the set position. Complete concentration should now be focused on the start, and any noise should cause the sprinter to leave the blocks as if it were the sound of the gun being fired. To be sure of getting good thrust from the blocks, she should lean forward enough to feel her body weight on her front foot and hands.

Starter's gun report. The reflex action of the sprinter begins with her response to the sound of the pistol. (This gun sound should occur about 2 seconds after the ''set'' command is given.) As the girl leaves her mark, she executes a tremendous drive and thrust with her legs and a vigorous quick motion with the arm of the side opposite the back leg (Fig. 4-5). The rear leg leaves the blocks, taking the first step—not a short choppy step, but one that is reasonably long and close to the ground. The sprinter's body is low to the ground at this point. The opposing forces take over the body action, with the arm pulling sharply backward as the other leg thrusts forward, both working in opposition to the legs' driving action. The body weight should be kept in front of the feet. As the runner

Fig. 4-5. This sprinter drives hard out of the blocks in the sprint start.

goes farther down the track, she gradually assumes an upright position; this should occur about 14 meters from the start. There might be some slight forward lean at full stride (Fig. 4-7). Some coaches recommend that arm action at this time be vigorous but of short amplitude—that is, a rapid, short arm action is preferred to long arm action.

Full running strides. On leaving the blocks the rear foot (usually the right) strikes the ground at the same time that the forward (usually the left) foot leaves the block (Fig. 4-6). Terrific effort must be applied by legs and arms during the initial strides. After the sprinter has run four or five strides, full running stride is assumed, with the head gradually raised to a normal upright position. The first steps out of the blocks will be somewhat shorter than the full running strides used in the final phase of the sprint. Arm action is diminished from the vigorous action used when leaving the blocks. The arm should not swing higher than the shoulder level on the forward swing and no farther behind the body than where the hand comes even with the rear of the hip—or even shorter, perhaps the front of the hip. Arm action is pistonlike, with the fingers curled as though holding a rod and the thumb placed against the forefinger. Sprinters will be running on the balls of their feet during the first five or six strides after leaving the blocks, with a little heel support used during the full stride phase of the run (Fig. 4-7).

Fig. 4-6. Sprint start. **A,** Notice the relaxed head position of the sprinter. **B,** This girl's starting position is considered good; however, her hips may be a little too high. **C,** She is getting a good start. Both feet are pushing against the blocks. **D,** A low body position is still being maintained. **E,** The first step is relatively long. **F** through **L,** This girl is gradually coming up to a full running stride position. Note that the arms and legs begin to move rapidly, and that the knee lift of the front leg becomes evident in **K.**

The leg kick to the rear should be a bit higher than the knee, but the knee lift to the front should be trained to be high, not unlike the prancing of a horse. Of course, the sprinter should try for as much speed as possible in moving her legs, taking as long a stride as she can without sacrificing speed of leg action for increased length of stride. She should point the knee of each swinging leg straight ahead, but she may rotate her foot slightly outward as it strikes the ground.

Smoothness in stride. The sprinter should keep her head straight while running. Some sprinters keep their heads down too long after leaving the blocks, and others throw their heads back, seemingly to give them a feeling of greater speed. These actions result in a loss of mechanical functioning. Total action of the body at this point should seem smooth, with absolutely no extraneous body motions that could cause the sprinter loss of efficiency. Some common faults of sprinters are throwing the arms across the chest, kicking the legs or feet or both outward or inward, disrupting the rhythm of the stride by a hitching and galloping motion, and tensing of the head, neck, shoulders, and arms. It must be kept in mind that a sprinter does not accelerate further after 6 seconds have elapsed after leaving the blocks. It is merely a matter of maintaining velocity as long as possible.

The runner should have learned to run relaxed at this point, realizing her greatest

Fig. 4-7. Full speed sprinting action. These drawings show a fine sprinter running at top speed. Notice the long stride and high knee lift. There is considerable hip action, which aids in increasing the stride length. Her arm action is very good.

efficiency with the least effort. Usually a breath at about 70 meters increases the ability to finish the sprint easily in a 100-meter race. Those running shorter races do not breathe during the race. Sprinters running 200 meters will breathe on demand and undue instruction need not be given them. Sprinters should not concern themselves with breathing (beyond the 100 meters), since they will breathe normally and without conscious thought. To try to follow a pattern of breathing for any race beyond 120 meters may unnecessarily confuse them and make their entire running thrust less than automatic. Knowing the optimum running rhythm to use for peak performance is a great aid in helping the sprinter to run smoothly and get the most from her efforts (Fig. 4-8).

One will sometimes see sprinters shaking their hands in the attempt to keep their arms from becoming tense. This motion should not be necessary if the sprinter is relaxed. Some girls must learn to relax their facial muscles during a race to prevent the tension that results in a loss of speed at the end of the race. One way some sprinters learn to remain relaxed during a race is to drop their lower jaws into yawn positions during the sprint, thereby releasing facial tension. Breathing is individual, and there are no special rules to follow; sprinters will usually breathe when they need to in races beyond 100 meters.

Finish of the race. The conditioned sprinter will finish her top-speed run at a point some yards beyond the finish tape. She will not slow up until after she has crossed the finish line, with her peak performance taking place just as she crosses it. Any unusual actions that she might attempt at the finish line will only impede her movements. Some girls get into a habit of making an extra motion by thrusting their chests forward as they cross the line. This may be done as a part of their running technique, but it should be done only during the last stride before hitting the finish tape. The drive must continue past the

Fig. 4-8. Running the 200-meter sprint. These girls are running at full stride to the finish line. Note the thrust to reach the tape.

finish line for the greatest speed to be maintained, and any actions that would tend to decrease speed should not be used.

RULES

There are a few simple rules established for running of which competitors should be aware. Generally these are the rules governing competition, although they may change from time to time.

1. All competitors must run the full distance of the race.
2. The runner must start the race with her hands and feet behind the starting line. The runner must have her entire torso across the finish line to have completed the race.
3. Each competitor must remain in her respective lane from start to finish in a straightaway race. In races of one or more turns not being run in lanes, she must not cross in front of her nearest competitor until she is at least two strides in advance. At the final turn of the race she must run in a straight line unless there is another runner in her path. In all races run in lanes, each girl must stay in her assigned lane for the entire distance.
4. Any competitor who willfully jostles or runs across her lane to cause another competitor to change lanes or who obstructs another runner so as to impede her progress will forfeit her right to any position or prize to which she would have otherwise been entitled.
5. All competitors must report to the clerk of the course on arrival and be informed of the times of their races, and they must report promptly to the starting point on being called.

COMMON ERRORS MADE BY THE BEGINNER

One of the most common errors made by girls in running is incorrect action of the arms. The wasted motion made by swinging arms across the chest should be corrected before it becomes a habit. At first, inexperienced runners will tend to watch the starter and will not react to the sound of the gun. Furthermore, they may actually turn their heads during the sprint race to see where other runners are, which in turn slows them up or causes them to lose their balance.

Some girls have a tendency to move their heads from side to side as they run. This may cause them to run in a crooked manner, resulting in a loss of speed. Running in a direction other than a straight line is disastrous in any race; not only does it result in loss of forward speed, but it may also cause the runner to be disqualified for cutting into another runner's lane.

Failing to prepare mentally for a race is a common error often made by the beginning competitor. If it is not corrected, she will never attain the mental discipline necessary for success in top competition. The proper habits must be learned early and the proper attitude developed by competitors as soon as possible if they are ever to perform at their best.

TEACHING SUGGESTIONS FOR THE BEGINNER PROGRAM

Running is one of the basic skills practiced by children from the time they are about 2 years old. Thus the teacher's main task is to refine and improve running techniques of older girls. There are several helpful exercises for novices to perform (Figs. 4-9 to 4-11). Several teaching methods and techniques are available for helping the teacher to properly introduce the phases of running to so-called beginners. For example, sprinting should be the first track event taught to the beginning class because success in other events is based on proper use of skills developed in sprints. Other events are taught after the sprints have been learned.

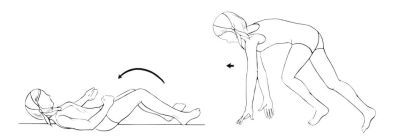

Fig. 4-9

Fig. 4-10

Fig. 4-11

Methods. Some of the common methods used in teaching the running phases are presented here.

Reaction (Fig. 4-9). Participants lie on their backs on the ground. At a command they quickly turn and run 15 meters in the direction opposite to the way their feet are pointed. Participation in this drill helps runners keep their bodies low during the first few running strides.

Resistance by partner (Fig. 4-10). One partner runs 20 meters while the other holds her hips (waist) from the rear. The rear partner must be sure to run to one side or the other of the front runner so as not to interfere with the running action. The front partner lifts her knees high as she struggles against the resistance offered by her partner. The front runner must be careful not to lean forward and lower her body in an attempt to overcome the resistance. She must run as she would in sprinting. The rear runner may occasionally ease up on the resistance or even eliminate it in the midst of the front runner's action. The partners reverse their positions frequently.

Running in a straight direction (Fig. 4-11). The runners attempt to run beside a straight line drawn on the track or field. This improves their ability to stay in their lanes during all-out sprinting efforts.

Running with the knee pointed in a straight direction (Fig. 4-12). Since inexperienced girls tend to rotate their thighs inward when they run in an all-out sprint, a good corrective practice is to run with thighs held in a neutral (straight) position. The girls should run in an all-out effort down a straight line with the knee of one leg pointed in a straight direction so that it coincides with the line.

Up and down the field. Girls following a leader run up and down the field, back and forth over a specific area, or around the track. At a signal from the leader they sprint as fast as possible for about 15 meters, jog for a few meters, and then sprint again. This is repeated as many times as the individual condition of each girl warrants.

A teacher must not wait for the track and field unit to start before she begins conditioning her class. To help prevent muscle injury and undue soreness from all-out effort in track and field activities, intensive conditioning by class members should be a part of daily procedure in the weeks immediately preceding the introduction of the track teaching unit,

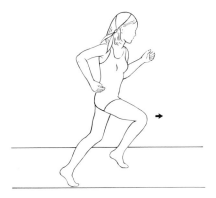

Fig. 4-12

in an early coaching situation, or during squad practice. Top physical fitness and mental readiness are needed for participation at any level of track and field events.

Exercises must be included during the presentation of the track and field unit material. Additional exercises especially designed to develop strength, speed, agility, flexibility, and endurance should be included as the time for introduction of these events to the class approaches.

As stated previously, sprinting should be the first track event taught to girls. It involves the basic actions that must be mastered before other events can be participated in effectively. Short dashes should be used at first, and the results should be given to the girls after they have had some experience in running the distance. They should be prepared for running dashes against established times and encouraged to make all-out efforts in their runs.

A typical reaction of beginners racing against others in a timed race or racing for a place among finishers is to quit when they see someone ahead of them. Teachers must be prepared for this reaction when teaching girls how to compete. The girl who is behind will feel she has lost the race and will see no point in finishing it. It is the duty of the teacher to instill in her the value of completing the run. Girls have to be taught the value of winning second and third places in a race (and the value of such places in relation to the team's outcome in a track meet), as well as the value of finishing every race started no matter how far behind they might be. The psychologic and practical implications are apparent here: if girls were permitted to drop out of a race, the fastest runner in the class would always be running alone, and the other girls would fail to learn the value of improving and putting forth maximum effort.

The crouch start. The crouch start should be taught to the class almost from the beginning—in fact, as soon as girls have learned to run in a straight line down a lane, to run on the balls of their feet, and to use their arms and legs correctly. This start will probably be learned during the first or second lesson on sprinting. Often the beginner will complain of feeling uncomfortable in the crouch position, as though she might fall on her head. This is a typical reaction to a first-time experience with the crouch position and should be expected and mentioned beforehand so the girls will know what to expect.

The starting blocks probably will not be used in the first few days of the sprinting lessons; however, a girl can easily learn to adjust to the crouch start by using the feet of another girl standing directly behind her for her support. It will not hurt the toes of the supporting girl's feet to have someone push off from them.

Blocks should be brought out and their use explained to the class as soon as the girls have learned the principles involved in the crouch start. They should be taught how to set and adjust the blocks, how to fasten them into the track surface, how to remove them, and how to put the equipment away carefully. Proper attention to these details will make a program function successfully.

The standing start. There is some thought among today's sprint coaches that using the standing start in sprints will bring about as good a result as using the crouch start. In the standing start the runner uses the blocks for support as in the crouch start. However, the blocks should be constructed so that the forward support is inclined slightly; the rear block support should be almost perpendicular to the ground so that the rear foot will have only the toe on the ground and the push will come against the transverse arch.

Teachers should experiment with the crouch and the standing starts to find what seems to be the most successful stance to use with students. The one obvious disadvantage in using the standing start is that there is a great tendency for the runner to get "set" before she receives the command from the starter. Then she cannot hold the set position long enough to push adequately against the blocks, and she has a tremendous tendency to "jump the gun." This occurs especially when runners in the same heat are using the crouch start as well as the standing start. It takes the runners in the crouch start much longer to take their marks and get steady in the set position than it does the runners who are using the standing start.

Motivation. Motivation is the key factor in teaching a new event. The teacher can motivate the girls by telling them the times they make in running races of various distances. This will help each girl judge her progress in terms of herself as well as in relation to the other girls in the class. Progress charts should be kept daily and should be made easily available to the students. A student could be assigned to keep the records up to date on the progress charts. The girls should be informed of the good times for the various short dashes and the top records for the various sprint distances in their age group. A comparison of times among members of the various classes is also a good motivating factor.

Class-teaching techniques. In teaching large classes composed of fifty or more girls, the teacher has to use mass practice procedure. One efficient way to provide practice for a large group of girls in a short period of time is to make use of heats—running one group right after the other in a wavelike manner. The girls could be lined up at the starting line one behind the other, filling each lane on the track. The front line should be composed of as many girls as there are lanes on the track. The second group of girls should be ready to run as soon as the first group leaves the blocks, the third group should be waiting behind the second, and so on, depending on the number of girls in the class.

In this way, if the waiting girls pay attention while instructions are given to the front line, they will profit from hearing the instructions and from observing the errors made as well as the good techniques displayed by the preceding groups. The teachers should point out the good and bad techniques of performance seen as a group finishes its dash and returns to its position behind the last group of waiting girls. At this point the teacher could also inform the class about proper safety measures to use in returning to the group and the value of staying in one lane while running the races. All these things may be mentioned as the girls in the front group are adjusting their blocks prior to running the race.

The fast runners are easily identified by the best times posted and by those who win the practice races. These girls should be encouraged to display their abilities in some after-school competition. A novice track meet can be easily organized and is of great interest to the girls toward the end of the track and field unit. Not only does this serve as a fitting climax to the class unit, but it provides the incentive for a highly skilled girl to seek avenues of competitive expression beyond those found in class participation. (Details concerning the planning of a meet are found in Chapter 16.)

Finally, it is good to plan for the girls to attempt to equal school records in each sprint

Table 4-1. Standards of performance for the 50-yard dash*

Age	Type of competition	Expected time†
10-11	School beginner	7.8
10-11	School experienced	7.2
10-11	National record	6.3
12-13	School beginner	7.5
12-13	School experienced	7.0
12-13	National record	6.1
14-18	School beginner	7.2
14-18	School experienced	6.8
14-18	National record	5.8

*It is very difficult for a girl who has begun her sprinting experience by running the 50-yard dash in a fast time to improve very much in this short race.
†These times can serve as a guide to the beginner in anticipating degrees of success. Times are in seconds.

Table 4-2. Standards of performance for the 75-yard dash*

Age	Type of competition	Expected time†
10-11	School beginner	10.3
10-11	School experienced	10.0
10-11	National record	9.0
12-13	School beginner	10.2
12-13	School experienced	9.6
12-13	National record	8.9
14-18	School beginner	10.0
14-18	School experienced	9.2
14-18	National record	8.1

*Some years, within a given school or track group, there are not very many fast sprinters. At those times the girls may not be running under 10.0 seconds for this distance.
†These times can serve as a guide to beginners in anticipating degrees of success. Times are in seconds.

Table 4-3. Standards of performance for the 100-yard dash*

Age	Type of competition	Expected time†
10-11	School beginner	13.2
10-11	School experienced	12.8
10-11	National record	11.9
11-12	School beginner	13.0
11-12	School experienced	12.6
11-12	National record	11.9
14-18	School beginner	13.0
14-18	School experienced	12.0
14-18	National record	10.3
Women	College beginner	12.6
Women	College experienced	11.6
Women	National record	10.0
Women	World record	10.0

*As in the other short sprints, girls who are truly beginners and who have had no experience—perhaps do not even own track shoes—should try for 13 seconds or less in running the 100-yard dash. If this is done, they can readily be called adequate sprinters.
†These times can serve as a guide to beginners in anticipating degrees of success. Times are in seconds.

Table 4-4. Standards of performance for the 100-meter dash*

Age	Type of competition	Expected time†
10-11	School beginner	15.0
12-13	School beginner	14.5
12-13	School experienced	14.0
14-17	School experienced	13.0
14-17	National record	11.6
Women	College experienced	12.0
Women	National record	11.1
Women	World record	11.04

*As in the other short sprints, girls who are truly beginners and who have had no experience—perhaps do not even own track shoes—should try for 13 seconds or less in running the 100-meter dash. If this is done, they can readily be called adequate sprinters.
†These times can serve as a guide to beginners in anticipating degrees of success. Times are in seconds.

Table 4-5. Standards of performance for the 220-yard and 200-meter dashes*

Age	Type of competition	Expected time†	
		220 yards	200 meters
10-11	School beginner	40.0	
10-11	School experienced	35.0	
12-13	School beginner	38.0	
12-13	School experienced	34.0	
12-13	National record	25.2	
14-18	School beginner	36.0	
14-18	School experienced	32.0	
14-18	National record	23.8	22.8
Women	College beginner	33.0	
Women	College experienced	29.0	
Women	National record	22.6	22.6
Women	World record	22.6	22.1

*A beginner may greatly improve within one season of participation in this distance. Because of the length of this race, it is very rewarding to see times go down greatly as a girl gains confidence during the season. There is a wide variance in the times winners post at any given meet.
†These times can serve as a guide to beginners in anticipating degrees of success. Times are in seconds.

distance for each age level (or to attempt to set new ones) and to post these records for all the girls to see. They should be kept up to date and in a convenient location so that the girls can refer to them frequently.

Exponent system for young girls. Because of dissimilar growth patterns, the physical differences and varying abilities of girls of junior high school age are astounding. For this reason it might be well worth the time and effort to classify girls in this age group according to height, weight, and age, not unlike the exponent system used in most interscholastic athletics for boys. A young girl will often respond well if she knows she will be competing against girls of like age, weight, and height. A teacher can convert the exponent system points used in computing boys' ratings into a similar system for girls. Some modifications will be necessary because of the weight and height differences of boys and girls of the same age, but these can be worked out by trial and error after some thought and a little experience. There is evidence that height and weight (but not age) can be used for classifying high school girls and college women.

Demonstrations for beginners. The careful teacher will make good use of all available teaching techniques in helping her beginning and her more experienced students learn to perform the various sprinting skills. Boys who are good sprinters in the physical education classes or who are on the school track team make excellent demonstrators, and they should be called on for this purpose. All physical education teachers should be qualified to teach the basic fundamentals of running, but not all teachers are aware of the finer points of running used in competitive situations. (However, they should make a determined effort to become knowledgeable in this area.) Therefore these teachers might ask for assistance from the track coach or from members of the boys' team so that correct information may be given to the members of the beginners' class or squad.

Conclusion. In summary, these points should be remembered:

1. Intensive and thorough physical conditioning should precede the teaching of the track and field unit at least a month in advance of any all-out running effort.
2. Progress charts and records are essential to properly motivate students.
3. Some means of classifying students—for example, the exponent system—is recommended for young girls of varying sizes, ages, and grade levels to equalize the competition.
4. An after-school beginner meet should be scheduled at the conclusion of the track and field unit.
5. Demonstrations of good form in running should be presented to the members of beginner groups frequently to keep the proper mental image before them.

Table 4-1 shows standards of performance for the 50-yard dash. A teacher may use the information in Tables 4-1 to 4-5 to present some idea of what other girls have accomplished in sprinting different distances. The girls will be able to compare their own times in relation to the times listed for all levels of competition.

TRAINING SUGGESTIONS FOR BEGINNING AND EXPERIENCED RUNNERS

Most girls do not take part in a fully scheduled season of competitive track meets. The training prescribed for schoolgirls under these circumstances is quite different from that recommended for athletes who compete each week during a planned season. However, it is assumed that the runners, regardless of the situation, will be competing to some extent and should be properly prepared for contests. Teachers and coaches may easily adapt the proposed schedules to suit the specific needs of athletes and their specific situations.

Early season training. The time to build endurance in the girls is in preseason training. General body-building and conditioning exercises should be done previously to ensure that preparation for explosive effort is adequate. Specific muscle groups must be exercised to ward off the possibility of injuries, especially to the thigh muscles.

Shin splints may be avoided by having the girls run on grass until their legs are in condition for the pounding they will receive from the track surface. Girls must not practice starts or do top speed sprinting when they are very tired at the end of a practice session. Instead, they should do light exercises or jog to finish off their workout.

Racing starts with the gun should be practiced regularly throughout the season but not during the first 2 or 3 weeks. Maximum efforts should be expended during these starts to build the proper habitual responses. However, maximum effort exerted too early in the season before the muscles are ready for an all-out effort can easily result in injuries to the key leg muscles.

A preseason conditioning program should include individually designed warm-up exercises because each girl has a specific metabolic rate, and daily expenditures of energy are individual. The highly nervous, quick-moving girl probably needs less time to warm up than does the languid athlete who reacts more slowly. These differences must be taken into account when preparing a training program.

Jogging. Girls jog 50 meters and walk 20 meters or run the straightaways and walk the curves for a total of four laps. They should end each workout by jogging a lap.

Running repeat distances. A girl can run from three to five repeat distances of 100, 200, and/or 300 meters at about three-quarters speed. Timed rest intervals between runs should be adhered to until recovery is complete; this usually takes about 10 to 15 minutes. In preparation for the longer speed races, the girls should run the longer repeat distances.

Preparing starts. After participating in running for 3 weeks, the sprinter should practice starts and run off the blocks using her correct block settings. These starts should be run at three-quarters speed at this period in the girl's training. Perhaps eight of these starts could be done in one session, with the girl running about 20 meters after each start.

Taking a tepid shower. After a workout or competition is completed each day, the girls should each take a tepid shower to finish off their day's activities. However, before the shower a warm-down period should follow each practice session.

Midseason training. If the sprinters are competing regularly, it is easy to have them follow a prescribed workout pattern and practice routine. However, when they compete infrequently, there is a problem of keeping mentally "up" for participation in practice sessions. The wise teacher or coach in such a situation will supply the girls with progress reports of some kind to help keep their interests at a high level.

Technique perfection. Analysis of the running form displayed by each girl, as based on the coach's observations and as seen in available films or pictures, is valuable in helping the girl perfect her running technique, starts, and finishes. Each day she should work on perfecting her form in one or more phases of sprinting. The sprinter may also have to spend 10 to 15 minutes a week working on the techniques of performance of other events if she plans to compete in events other than the sprints.

Weekly schedule. The following is a sample weekly midseason competition schedule for girls who are in continuous training. Each girl should probably follow an individual schedule that fits her condition precisely. However, in case there is no schedule individually established as yet, the program could be used as a takeoff point.

MONDAY
1. Jog one lap.
2. Do stretching and loosening-up exercises.
3. Run repeat distances of 200 meters four times at the speed prescribed by the teacher or coach. A rest period of 10 minutes should follow each of these runs.

4. Run six 60-meter sprints.
5. Jog 400 meters. Run 300 meters in a relaxed manner.
6. Take a shower.

TUESDAY

1. Jog one lap.
2. Do stretching and loosening-up exercises.
3. Run six wind sprints of 60 meters.
4. Take ten running starts, going the full distance on the last start. Five starts should be run out to one-third distance and four to one-half distance of 60 meters.
5. Participate in three or four passing trials with relay team.
6. Jog one lap.
7. Take a shower.

WEDNESDAY

1. Jog one lap.
2. Do stretching and loosening-up exercises.
3. Run six 40-meter wind sprints.
4. Take three or four starts, running the full distance on the last start.
5. Run the straightaways and walk the curves for the entire distance around the track. The straightaways should be run at three-quarters speed. (If she is a 200-meter runner, the girl should repeat Monday's schedule.)
6. Take a shower.

THURSDAY

1. Jog one lap.
2. Do stretching and loosening-up exercises.
3. Run three repeat distances of 200 meters at timed intervals.
4. Take three or four starts.
5. Jog one lap.
6. Take a shower.

FRIDAY

1. Do stretching and loosening-up exercises.
2. Take a shower.
3. Eat a good dinner and get plenty of rest and sleep in preparation for a Saturday meet.

Running heats. On the day of competition, when heats and perhaps semifinal races are required, the sprinter will often run a 200-meter sprint fast enough to defeat her competition and qualify, but not at maximum speed. She must save her energy for the all-out effort to be made during the finals of the race when her competition will be the strongest. Running shorter races, from 50 to 75 meters, requires that optimum effort be expended in all heats because of the shortness of the race and the quickness with which the girl may recover from the effort.

Mental preparation. It is essential for competitors to walk the track prior to a race to familiarize themselves with the surface, lane width, wind, and any other conditions that could affect running performance. In addition, competitors must check the number of heats and allow themselves adequate time to complete their warm-up routines prior to participation in their races. Then the athletes should concentrate completely on the race ahead of them, getting a good start, running at maximum speed, and shutting out all extraneous thoughts and stimuli.

CHAPTER 5

*Relays**

BACKGROUND

Relay running, in which four sprinters combine their efforts to function as a single unit, is an exciting experience for viewers of and participants in a track meet. Relays traditionally are scheduled so that they close meets, and they are indeed "thrillers."† Indicative of the interest shown concerning relays is the increasing number of relay meets, or "relay carnivals," conducted for girls and women as part of a regular track and field schedule.

For some time relay teams for women have been included in international competition as well as in school meets. Since 1932 the United States has consistently placed high in Olympic competition—winning the women's 400-meter relay in six of the eleven games. Fast sprinters are usually members of relay teams; therefore one can expect to find names of well-known sprinters on lists of famous relay teams. In the United States the 400-meter relay teams have always included top women sprinters. The world record for the 400-meter relay, 42.8 seconds, was made by the Olympic sprint team from the United States in 1968 and equalled by the team from West Germany in the 1972 Olympics. The 1972 team from the United States was fourth, with a time of 43.39 seconds. In 1976 the 4 times 100-meter relay was won by East Germany, with a time of 42.57 seconds, a world record. The 1600-meter relay (4 times 400), a new event in the 1972 Olympics, was won by West Germany, with a new world record time of 3 minutes 28.5 seconds. The United States team was second, with a time of 3 minutes 28.6 seconds. In 1976 the United States team was again second, with a time of 3 minutes 22.81 seconds.

The fastest sprinters and middle distance runners make up the various relay teams. Most relay races involve teams with four members. These are the girls with the ability to run fast on the curve, maintain fast leg speed, generate explosive power, and be able to relax so that they have staying power. Each girl runs a designated distance. In some relays the girls run the same distance as in the 400, the 800, and the 1600; however, in medley relays different distances are run (220, 110, 110, 440 yards).

The relay events feature an outstanding individual effort and an outstanding team effort. The coordination of all these elements into a smooth-working total member effort

---

*Wherever possible, metric distances are listed. Some relay distances are purely American and are listed in yards only.

†Relays are also scheduled near the beginning of some track meets.

is of major importance. In fact, a team of average individuals may defeat a team of superior performers, especially in the shorter distances, because of superior baton passing ability. The coach will need to spend much time working with the relay team members to bring about smooth team performance.

PURSUIT AND SHUTTLE RELAYS

Most relays are of the pursuit type. The first runner of a team carries a baton to her second position runner, passing it to her within the passing zone. The second runner passes the baton to the third runner. Finally, the third runner passes the baton to the fourth (anchor) runner, who runs the last segment of the race. The pursuit relay segments may be the same length. However, there are certain types of pursuit relays that do have segments of different lengths within the same race.

In the shuttle relay, the runners move back and forth between two fixed distances. A baton may be exchanged, or the next runner may be tagged on the right shoulder by the incoming runner. The following discussion is concerned with only the pursuit relay, whose distances are provided in meters. Some schools may still be using yards and miles, but it is believed that the United States is or will soon be committed totally to the use of the metric system.

The length of relay races varies from 200 to 1600 meters. The number and kind of relays are set by the local games committee. The relay races that appear most frequently on track and field programs follow:

Elementary school

1. 200-meter shuttle (4 times 50)
2. 400-meter pursuit (4 times 100)

High school and college

1. 400-meter relay (4 times 100)
2. 800-meter relay (4 times 200)
3. 800-meter medley (200, 100, 100, 400)
4. 1600-meter relay (4 times 400)

International (Olympic)

1. 400-meter relay (4 times 100)
2. 1600-meter relay (4 times 400)

Young girls, after learning to sprint, enjoy the team competition associated with running shuttle and pursuit relays. The shuttle relay is usually participated in first. As their skill increases, the total distances should be increased from 100 to 200 meters. In higher level competition the junior high school girls can easily run a 400-meter relay if their training has been in running the 100-meter dash. Elementary school girls competing in dashes of 100 or 200 meters would also run the 400-meter relay.

TYPES OF BATON EXCHANGE

Baton passing in the sprint relay must be made within a 20-meter zone. A run zone of 10 meters leading to the passing zone may be used in races up to 800 meters. In other words, all members of the team other than the first runner may start running 10 meters outside the passing zone. This added distance ensures increased velocity and faster acceleration for the outgoing runner (Fig. 5-1).

Fig. 5-1. Correct baton exchange in a sprint relay. Notice that this is a nonvisual pass. The two runners here are the second and third relay members, respectively. These runners are taking full advantage of the 20-meter passing zone, and they are timing their exchange so that their speeds are equal. The rear runner should never pass the front runner because it will slow down the exchange. This is an overhand downward exchange.

Blind or nonvisual pass. The exchange used in the sprint relays (400-meter, 800-meter, and 800-meter medley) is called a blind pass. The baton may be carried in the right hand or in the left hand, depending on the choice of the coach. This choice may be made relative to the age and experience of the runners. The incoming runner passes the baton to the outgoing runner, who is looking ahead in the direction of the run and moving at the fastest speed she can manage at the time of exchange.

The burden of the baton exchange rests on the incoming runner to make a good pass to the outgoing runner so she may focus her full attention on getting a fast start. Usually the incoming runner runs to the inside of the lane when passing the baton to the receiver, who is extending the left hand to the rear and outside portion of the lane when passing to an extended right hand.

Underhand pass. A popular method of exchange used particularly with young girls and beginners is the underhand pass (Figs. 5-1 and 5-3). The outgoing girl stands or crouches 10 meters short of the passing zone with her right side turned to watch her incoming teammate. Her feet are in a stride position, with toes turned straight ahead. If the crouch start is assumed, the hands are touching the ground and the head is turned so she is looking back over the right shoulder. As the incoming girl, carrying the baton in her left hand, crosses the predetermined check mark, the outgoing girl drives ahead as if she were sprinting from the blocks. She moves as quickly as she can, building up speed and anticipating the pass. When she is about halfway through the passing zone, she extends her right arm rearward, with the palm facing diagonally down and back. The four fingers are together and extended, and the thumb is spread and pointing toward the trunk. A reverse V is made by the fingers and thumb. The receiver holds the arm extended and as steady as possible in preparation for grasping the baton. The incoming runner swings the baton in

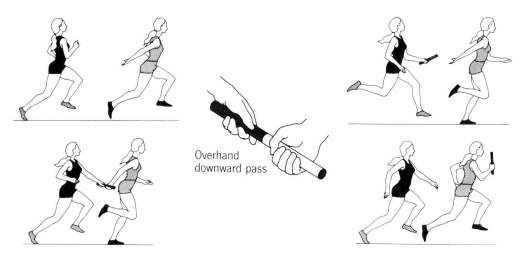

Fig. 5-2. Nonvisual relay pass. The overhand downward pass is executed in this instance from runner number three to runner number four.

Fig. 5-3. Nonvisual relay pass. The underhand pass is performed in this instance by the first runner, who exchanges the baton with the second runner.

between the spread thumb and the first finger of the receiver's right hand with an upper-cutting action. This is accomplished with a forward and upward reaching motion.

The underhand pass is an easy-to-learn, rather natural exchange method that assumes a right-left-right-left exchange. The above directions are reversed if the lead runner starts with the baton in the left hand. To make it easy for girls to know when to extend the arm rearward for the precision timing required for a good exchange, a line located midway between the two lines marking the zone may be drawn on the track.

Overhand downward pass. The first runner holds the baton in her hand and takes her normal sprint position (Fig. 5-2). The receiver (second runner) is crouched in the outside of her lane, watching the incoming runner over her shoulder. When the predetermined check mark is crossed, the receiver sprints away, building up speed as quickly as possible. She will have accelerated for approximately 20 meters until she is at the midpoint of the passing zone, when in coordination with her stride she extends her arm rearward, holding it as steady as possible at about the level of her hip. The elbow and palm of the hand are held up, with the thumb pointed toward the body. At this same instant the passer should be near enough to reach forward and place the baton firmly down in the outstretched upraised palm.

Visual pass. In the mile relay (1600 meters) the visual exchange is used. The outgoing runner in this relay has the responsibility for seeing that a good pass of the baton is made. The incoming girl may show fatigue, resulting in an unsteady stride and inability to control eye-hand coordination for good baton placement. Thus the receiver standing in the passing zone watches the incoming runner. If the incoming runner appears very tired, the pass should be made in the rear half of the zone. If she is able to finish strong, the exchange may be made effectively in the forward half of the passing zone. The method of receiving the baton in this type of relay may vary but is usually done as seen in Fig. 5-4, with one arm extended to the rear and the palm turned downward. The receiver must keep her eyes on the baton until she has grasped it securely. The passer's responsibility is to

Fig. 5-4. This runner is waiting for the incoming runner. She will use the visual type of baton exchange in receiving the baton.

finish her leg of the race as strongly as she can and to put the baton up in a steady position for the receiver. In the actual exchange there should be some free space existing between the two runners. The receiver should move away from the incoming runner, being careful to time her takeoff speed with that of the approaching girl. The baton is usually carried in the left hand and taken with the right hand. After receiving the baton, the runner switches it from the right hand to the left as soon as she has progressed out of the passing zone.

ELEMENTS OF RELAY RUNNING

The start. The same start employed by sprinters is used for relays, but it is done with the baton grasped in one hand (Figs. 5-5 and 5-6). Sprinters should practice their starts by carrying a baton part of the time; undoubtedly the same sprinters will often be the runners in the various relays. So that the holding of even a light baton will not bother the sprinters, they must practice often to ensure stability and to dispel awkwardness and uncertainty. The recommended procedure is to start with the baton in the right hand and pass it to the

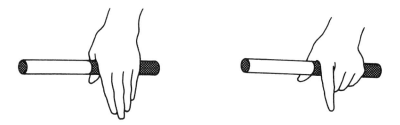

Fig. 5-5. Common hand positions for holding the baton at the start. Each is acceptable. A runner's personal preference for one of these or several other positions determines selection.

Fig. 5-6. Relay lead-off runner grasping the baton.

left hand of the second runner, then to the right hand of the third runner, and then to the left hand of the anchor runner. At the start the baton is held securely by the second and third fingers and thumb, the second finger and thumb, or the third and fourth fingers and thumb. The important point is that the baton should be held securely against the palm. The baton may extend over the starting line, but it must be kept clear of the ground. It cannot touch the track surface beyond the start. The lead-off runner needs to get away quickly, but she surely wants to get away with the baton in her possession.

Passing the baton. The right-left-right-left palm-up passing method is recommended, and it requires a lot of practice to master. The receiver extends her arm and hand rearward, holding the hand steady at about hip level. The elbow and palm are kept up, with the thumb pointed toward the body. The passer extends her arm forward and makes a downward pass, placing the baton diagonally across the outstretched, upward-raised palm. The speed of the incoming runner must not decrease on the exchange; the incoming and outgoing runners must be moving with as much speed as possible at the exchange but at the same individual speed.

The finish. There is no difference in finishing a relay race than there is in any other race. The last runner will run through the tape with as strong a finish as possible. As each segment of the race is finished, the first three runners should remain in their lanes until they can leave the track safely, without causing any interference. (See Fig. 5-8.)

STRATEGY IN RELAY RUNNING

The margin for error in sprint relays is very small, and a tiny error can be disastrous. The selection, placement, and coaching decisions concerning the runners are all very important in relation to the final outcome. Four outstanding sprinters do not necessarily constitute an outstanding relay team. Getting a coordinated team effort from the best individual efforts of four fast runners is what makes the sprint relay a success. The method to use in the exchange of the baton, the use of the free distance concept, the use of the inside passing procedure, and the distance margin to safely allow in the passing zones are major decisions that will be determined partly by the degree of skill of the members of the team and the strategy to be employed in a given situation.

Free distance or free space. The ideal pass in which every inch of zone space is utilized is rarely attained in a race. Yet it is an ideal to strive for, since the margins by which relay races are won are very small. Getting the incoming runner to stretch her arm out and place the baton in the rearward, extended, upward hand of the outgoing runner at the correct zone distance is a goal to strive for in every race. Equally important, however, is that the incoming runner and the outgoing runner are moving as fast as they can at the time the exchange is made.

Safety margin. The pass is usually made in the last half of the exchange zone. This is based on the premise that runners are of equal ability. In the event that the incoming runner is much better than the outgoing runner, there may be a motivational advantage in having the pass made at the far end of the zone. The slower runner would hand off in the first half of the next passing zone; thus she would not have to run as far as the other runner. Again, the important thing is to have a fast exchange made, with both girls moving at maximum speed.

Starting with the baton. Runners need to practice carrying the baton and letting it become a part of them. They should also practice starting with the baton. All members of the team need to practice starting with each one carrying a baton. The holding of the baton at the starting line ought to be done repeatedly to overcome awkwardness, uncertainty, and insecurity.

Order of running. The placement of the runners is not a haphazard or hastily made decision. Since baton speed is the main objective, the coach should time the four runners in all the various positions over a long period of time to reveal without doubt who is consistently the fastest runner for the various legs (segments) of the races. The combination of runners that will give the fastest time around the track is the one to use. Once this combination is determined, the runners should spend concentrated practice in polishing the fine details of making fast exchanges.

The check mark. Runners must work at top speed, repeatedly adjusting the check mark that will be used to guide the starting of the outgoing runner. The check mark is the exact point at which the receiver allows the incoming runner to touch her foot before the receiver begins her sprint start. In establishing the location of the check marks, a tentative spot marked with masking tape or chalk is chosen about 6 to 9 meters short of the receiver's starting point. When the incoming runner hits this mark, the outgoing runner sprints at full speed and extends her arm backward at the midpoint of the passing zone. The two runners must practice the exchange repeatedly to ensure that they have correctly placed the check mark. After a satisfactory mark is determined and verified, the exact distance is measured off and used until improved performance indicates a needed change.

The outgoing runner assumes a crouch start position, looking back over her shoulder to watch the check mark. The instant the incoming runner reaches this mark, the outgoing runner, looking straight ahead, begins her run, building up speed as quickly as she can. As she passes the midpoint of the 20-meter passing zone, she continues to drive forward but extends her receiving hand to the rear in coordination with her stride. It is at this moment that the incoming girl reaches forward and places the baton downward in the outstretched palm. The outgoing runner then closes her fingers securely around the baton and continues sprinting at top speed to the next runner.

Specific responsibilities of the passer

1. The passer should be moving at her fastest speed when the baton pass is made.
2. The passer must place the baton downward against the palm of the receiver. The success of the exchange is primarily the responsibility of the passer.
3. The passer lays the baton across the palm with a moderate amount of pressure so that the receiver will automatically grasp it. The passer must not relinquish her hold until it is received by the outgoing girl.
4. The passer must extend the baton forward at the opportune moment to ensure that the receiver grasps it.
5. The passer continues running in her own lane until the opponents have passed her and she is free to leave the track.

Specific responsibilities of the receiver

1. The receiver is positioned in a crouch start on the outside of the lane if she receives

with the left hand, on the inside of the lane if she receives with the right. She is crouched 10 meters outside the zone.

2. She watches the check mark until the passer reaches it; then she builds up speed as quickly as she can. She has about 20 meters (10 outside the zone plus half the 20-meter zone) before extending the hand rearward. Once she starts to move, she wants to build up speed as quickly as she can.

3. The outgoing runner watches the check mark, but she does not fail to also watch the incoming runner to note if she is moving at her usual speed.

4. The instant the incoming runner hits the check mark, the receiver turns her eyes and body straight ahead and starts sprinting to develop the greatest acceleration.

5. The receiver extends the correct hand rearward, coordinating it with her stride as she continues to build up speed. She will have 25 to 30 meters in which to accelerate. The hand is extended backward at the time she crosses the midpoint of the passing zone.

6. The outgoing runner should never look back. Also she must run with great confidence in an all-out effort.

RULES

The rules governing sprinting apply to relay running as well. There are, however, some additional rules that apply especially to the passing of the baton.

1. The baton must be passed, not thrown or dropped by one competitor, and must be received by the succeeding runner within the marked passing zone. The baton must be carried in the hand throughout the entire race.

2. No girl may run in more than one leg of a relay.

3. Any of the last three runners in a relay may take her proper position on the track and commence running before she receives the baton, but not more than 10 meters outside the passing zone; however, the baton must be passed only when both athletes are within the 20-meter passing zone.

4. The order in which the members of a relay team run may be changed from trial heat to succeeding rounds except in the case of the members of the distance medley relay (where runners of a team do not run the same distance). This latter group must run in the same order from heats to finals.

5. The membership of a team may not be changed from heats to succeeding rounds unless illness or injury of a member occurs, in which case the request to substitute another runner must be approved by the referee. If the substitution is approved, the ill person is not allowed to participate in any further events during a particular meet.

COMMON ERRORS IN RELAY RUNNING

The runner may have too much tenseness in her hands, arms, chest, and neck. She needs to consciously relax hands and arms, breathe naturally in and out of the nose and the mouth, and make an effort to relax neck and jaw muscles.

A grave error often made in running a relay is for the receiver to ''run away'' from the passer; that is, to incorrectly judge the incoming runner's speed or her fatigued condition and start too soon. In this case the transfer is not made or is poorly made because the incoming runner simply cannot catch up with the would-be receiver. This is a common occurrence among beginners.

Another fault typical of beginners is the tendency for the receiver to stand perfectly still when the transfer of the baton takes place. The entire passing zone should be utilized, and the receiver should gain full speed before the exchange is made. Participation in many practice sessions is essential for runners to learn proper timing, to gauge the speed of their teammates, and to be accurate in making passes.

TEACHING PROGRESSION FOR THE BEGINNER

After girls have been taught the correct fundamentals of sprinting, it is time to introduce relays. The following unit of instruction, involving teaching sequence and progression, might well be used for a physical education track class. It could also serve as a basis for developing teaching progression in other areas.

Baton pass. Handling the baton properly and knowing how to pass it successfully are

Fig. 5-7. Relay runners in action. One relay runner is holding the baton in her right hand; the other is holding the baton in her left hand. They both are members of a 4 times 400-meter relay team.

the essentials to master first. To help students do this, organize the members of a group or a class into squads of equal number and arrange them in columns. Give a baton to the last girl in each column (squad) and have her, from a stationary position, pass it forward to the next girl in line, the receiver. The baton may go from the passer's right hand to the receiver's left hand, with each girl changing the baton from her left hand to her right hand after receiving it. This procedure should continue until the front girl is reached, whereupon the girls should reverse their direction and repeat this procedure in the opposite direction. In the right-to-left and left-to-right exchange procedure the baton is carried by the receiver in the hand in which she received it from the passer (Fig. 5-7).

Girls can easily learn to pass the baton correctly, becoming familiar with the feel of it and accustomed to changing it from one hand to the other while in a relatively stationary position. It is best to arrange the squads in groups of four and repeat this exercise as many times as is necessary to ensure that the baton is passed and received properly.

The members of each squad should walk through the passing procedure, each girl starting at a distance of about 2 meters from the girl in front of her. The receiver should not look back after she sees the passer start to move forward. This practice should be repeated enough times to ensure that all squad members develop a smoothness of motion.

Running exchanges. Next, the squad should run the exchange distance at half speed with the girls stationed about 12 to 18 meters apart. At this point the purpose of the check mark is explained. Instruct the receiver to cease watching the passer at the check mark and begin her half-speed run. Several repetitions are necessary for the girls to learn to exchange the baton and to time the takeoffs correctly.

To continue the progression, the squads of four to a team should run the given distances of the relay at full speed. If the girls are not yet in peak physical condition, a relay distance of 160 meters (4 times 40) is a good practice distance. Also at this time

Fig. 5-8. Relay runners in action at a large meet.

Table 5-1. Standards of performance for the 440-yard and the 400-meter relay races*

		Expected time †	
Age	*Type of competition*	*440 yards*	*400 meters*
12-13	Experienced	58.0	56
14-17	School beginner group	59	57
14-17	National record	46.7	45
Women	College beginner	57	55
Women	Experienced	51	49
Women	National record	46	43.4
Women	World record	45.2	42.5

*With time this race will become an important part of track and field programs.
†These times can serve as a guide to the beginner in anticipating degrees of success. Times are in seconds.

Table 5-2. Standards of performance for 880-yard relay and medley relay races*

Age	*Type of competition*	*Relay type*	*Expected time†*
14-17	School beginner	4 × 220	2:00
14-17	School experienced	4 × 220	1:50
14-17	National record	4 × 220	1:39.7
Women	College beginner	Medley	2:14
Women	Experienced	Medley	2:00
Women	National record	Medley	1:43.9
Women	World record	4 × 220	1:36

*In the 880-yard medley relay the distances that are run are 220, 110, 110, and 440 in outdoor competition.
†These times can serve as a guide to the beginner in anticipating degrees of success.

define passing-zone limits and explain that all exchanges are to be made within those limits. In the next phase have the girls run the full distance of the specific relays.

Running for time. The final phase in the progression is the establishment of teams to compete against each other and against time. Arrange the girls in positions according to the suggested running order after explaining this order to them. Trials and practices in short distance running (that is, shortened segments of the relay) should have been performed by all teams; this will give them practice in passing and receiving from each other and the feel of total team effort. Such practice should also help them eliminate disastrous "drops" that might otherwise occur during exchanges.

Finally, teams should run in competition against each other and be timed. Running in heats of two or three teams will usually ensure their receiving better times than they would make if they ran one team at a time. Furthermore, it will be possible to have a recorded time on each team, which could not be done if all teams ran at once (Tables 5-1 to 5-4).

Practice. After relay teams are formed and running in the established order, team members must practice passing the baton. This is easily arranged by having two people involved in a particular exchange practice running and exchanging on the infield or on the track; in practice have them use a shorter running distance than their regular segment. This shortened distance will give them a good deal of practice in passing and receiving before

Table 5-3. Standards of performance for the 220-yard relay races*

Age	Type of competition	Relay type	Expected time†
10-11	School beginner	Pursuit	34
10-11	School experienced	Pursuit	31
10-11	National record	Pursuit	28

*There will be a wide variation in the times made in these races at a given school meet, since many teachers and coaches may place their slower girls in the shuttle relay and the faster ones in the pursuit relay.
†These times can serve as a guide to the beginner in anticipating degrees of success. Times are in seconds.

Table 5-4. Standards for the mile and 1600-meter relay races*

		Expected time	
Age	Type of competition	4 × 440 yards	4 × 400 meters
Women	College beginner	4:10	4:00
Women	Experienced	3:50	3:42
Women	National record	3:38	3:27
Women	World record	3:38	3:19.23

*These relay races are not usually run by young girls.

fatigue sets in. Members of the teams should run at least one complete relay distance with all teams competing against one another at least once during each period designated for baton practice.

TRAINING SUGGESTIONS

Members of a sprint relay team follow the early season and competitive season training programs used by sprinters. In addition, the regular relay team members will concentrate on passing the baton twice a week during practice sessions. A sample mid-season work schedule follows:

MONDAY
1. Warm up and jog two laps with baton-passing practice.
2. Do sprinters' work schedule.
3. Warm down.

TUESDAY
1. Warm up and jog two laps with baton being passed.
2. Do relay practice. Make three passes at the three exchange zones.
3. Warm down.

WEDNESDAY
1. Jog two laps with baton being passed.
2. Work 20 minutes on starts.
3. Do 30 minutes of baton-passing work.
4. Do 10 minutes of finish work.
5. Warm down.

THURSDAY
1. Jog two laps with baton being passed.
2. Do relay practice. Make three passes at the three exchange zones.
3. Warm down.

FRIDAY
1. Warm up and jog 2 laps with baton being passed.
2. Do relay practice. Run continuous relays for three laps.
3. Warm down.

SATURDAY   Competition.

CHAPTER 6

Running the 400 meters

BACKGROUND

It was a comparatively short time ago that men athletes thought of the quarter mile or 400-meter as something other than a sprint. The concept was that the 400-meter was a middle-distance event, and the ideal way to run it was to cover the first 200 meters as close to top speed as possible, stride or float along for the next 100 meters (to conserve strength for the finish of the race), and then sprint the rest of the way. It is not too irregular then to admit that women 400-meter runners also thought it important to go out fast but to save energy for the finish of the race. When women first began competing in the 400-meter, it was thought of as a middle-distance event, and the slow running time indicated that it was being run as an endurance event. It was not until 1966 that any DGWS records were reported for the 440-yard run, as it was then called. The 400-meter dash was first made an Olympic event in 1964. The gold medal winner was Betty Cuthbert, running the race in 52.0 seconds flat. Sim Kim Don of North Korea had run the 400-meter dash in 51.9 seconds in 1962. The winner of the 1972 Olympics was Monika Zehrt of East Germany, with a time of 51.08 seconds. Kathy Hammond of the United States was third at 51.64 seconds. In the 1976 Olympics Irene Szewinska of Poland set a new world record of 49.19 seconds. Rosalyn Bryant of the United States was fifth, running the distance in 50.65 seconds. These faster times are indicative of the vast improvements that have taken place in the women's competitive 440-yard or 400-meter dash and also strongly suggest that unless a girl wants to be outrun rather badly, she is going to have to sprint this race for the entire distance. (See Table 6-1 for standards of performance.)

SPECIAL CONSIDERATIONS

The quarter miler or 400-meter dash athlete is a sprinter who has done a lot of running. Height is of little consequence. The important qualification is that she have good speed, strength, and endurance and can tolerate a lot of work. She must be able to get optimum speed out of little energy and be able to apply maximum effort for the entire 400 meters. This race requires a girl with a strong personality. She has to have a lot of determination and desire and be willing to bear self-imposed pain. Dedication and concentration are also necessary ingredients for success.

ELEMENTS OF RUNNING

The start. The same starting techniques for the sprinter apply to the 400-meter dash athlete (Chapter 4). A fast start is important to her but not as essential as it is for the

A B C D E F

G H I J K L M

Fig. 6-1. The 400-meter (440-yard) run. **A** to **F,** Compare the similarity of body actions used here with those of a sprinter. This girl appears to be running at a fast speed, yet she seems relaxed. Her driving leg shows she has good knee lift. **G** to **M,** This girl's arms are carried in a good position. She is using a ball-heel-toe action with her feet. Her shoulders and arms are relaxed.

Table 6-1. Standards of performance for the 440-yard and 400-meter dashes*

		Expected time†	
Age	*Type of competition*	*440 yards*	*400 meters*
12-13	School beginner	75	73
12-13	School experienced	70	68
12-13	National record	58.2	58.2
14-18	Experienced	65	67
14-18	National record	53.6	51.6
Women	Experienced	62	59
Women	National record	52.2	52.2
Women	World record	50.4	49.29

*Note the wide variation in times for this distance. Since this is a long sprint, it is easier to improve the time from the beginning efforts than it is in the shorter races.
†These times can serve as a guide to the beginner in anticipating degrees of success. Times are in seconds.

sprinter. However, a very good way to run the 400 meters is to get out in front and stay there.

Running form. The running stride is long, with a skimming rather than a pounding action. The runner has lots of bounce without any uneven bounding. Her arms may be hanging slightly lower than the sprinter's, but the same forward-backward, relaxed driving motion is observed. The runner accelerates as quickly as she can and then runs as fast as she can to maintain this built-up speed.

Relaxation. The flowing and graceful runner must be loose, with almost an absence of tension. The demand for great speed over a gruelling distance places a strain on the mental and physical conditions of the runner. The runner must be so trained that she is able to settle into a comfortable fast pace and maintain this pace without losing speed or building up tension.

Facets of the good runner. The runner must think and feel that she is running loosely, yet she must be under control. She will not be surprised to find that her fastest time for this distance will be taken when she feels that she is running almost effortlessly.

The finish. As the runner comes down the stretch toward the tape, she should continue to maintain her stride as best she can and stay as relaxed as possible as she runs through and beyond the finish line.

STRATEGY IN RUNNING THE 400-METER DASH

The 400-meter runner wants to run the first 200 meters of the race as fast as she can and still be able to maintain this speed for the rest of the race.

The 400-meter dash is generally run in lanes the entire distance. The competitor will

Fig. 6-2. A 400-meter runner in full stride near the finish. Leg action appears to be good, but open rather than closed fist-hand position is recommended.

want to remember that running near the inside of her lane means covering a shorter distance around the track. Also, she must be keenly aware of the importance of running the curves properly. She should accelerate on the curve and lean into it, rather than pull away from it.

RULES

1. Each contestant should stay in her respective lane from start to finish in the 400-meter dash.
2. In races involving turns on the track, the starts have to be staggered to make up for the variations in lane lengths caused by the curve of the track (Table 16-3).
3. All other rules that apply to the running of sprints also apply to the running of the 400-meter dash.

COMMON ERRORS

Overstriding is a common error of beginners. It creates fatigue and tends to slow the forward progress of the body.

Running too wide on the curves means running a longer distance.

Failing to maintain nearly full sprinting speed for the entire distance of the race can cause a runner to lose to a more consistent competitor.

Failing to accelerate to optimum speed for fear of not being able to run the entire distance is an error made by runners who do not have confidence. Participation in a training program designed to build endurance and speed should help develop this confidence.

Floating on the curve instead of accelerating may be disastrous to a potential winner.

TEACHING SUGGESTIONS

Girls need to find out what it means to run a distance in a set period of time. After being thoroughly warmed up, girls may jog a 200-meter distance and then run 200 meters in a definite period of time. The teacher or coach may set this time at whatever she thinks best for beginners. It may take some trial and error to find the appropriate time (Table 6-1). For example, the girls may jog 200 meters and then run 200 meters in 36 seconds. This process is repeated three or four more times. The teacher will call out the time at 100 meters so the girls will know if they are hitting the specified time for that distance. At the beginning the girls may not be in good enough condition to recover by jogging and may need additional rest periods. This process of running repeated paced distances will take time, but it can be introduced into the regular physical education class program.

Girls who are discovered in physical education class as good prospects for running the endurance spring of 400 meters should be encouraged to do additional training in the after-school program and try out for the team.

Group practice. It is best to have a small group practicing together for the 400-meter dash. They need the presence of each other for encouragement and challenge.

Building speed. The main objective of the work-out sessions is building speed. Assuming that the girls are already conditioned by participating in the off-season and early season workouts, they can then devote the practice sessions to improving speed. The use of various interval speed training progressions is the best way to increase speed. One or two days each week need to be devoted to the running of several 200-meter races.

A good learning progression and a useful training device is to instruct the girl to run the first 80 meters with an easy long stride and then to hit 400-meter speed for the next 130 meters. Then the girl should walk back to the starting point and repeat the same action three more times. After a period of 15 to 20 minutes of rest, another set of the same running procedure is done.

TRAINING SUGGESTIONS

As previously suggested, girls should work in small groups and run 200's twice a week. The 400-meter sprinter may also find it advantageous to work out with the 100- and 200-meter sprinters. All runners should spend approximately 20 minutes in a progressive warm-up period before undergoing the training schedule. Following is a good warm-up exercise: (1) do an easy jog for 800 meters; (2) stretch the legs and body for 10 to 15 minutes; (3) run wind sprints for 800 meters or twice around the track. The runners should warm down by doing easy jogging for 800 meters after the workout.

The following suggested training schedule is for those girls who plan to compete at a high level; however, the times and repetitions may be altered to conform to the various abilities and backgrounds of other girls who may not be as highly skilled.

Weekly schedule

MONDAY
1. Warm up for 20 minutes.
2. Run two sets of four 200-meter distances. Run the first 80 meters with an easy long stride and then run 400-meter speed for the next 130 meters. Walk back. Repeat three more times. After a 20-minute rest, do another set.
3. Warm down.

TUESDAY
1. Warm up.
2. Run 400 meters six times. Run the first 300 meters at a 400-meter speed and then control deceleration for the next 100 meters (14 to 15 seconds). Walk back. Repeat four times.
3. Warm down.

WEDNESDAY
1. Warm up.
2. Run two sets of four 200-meter distances, as on Monday.
3. Run 300 meters three times at full speed. Walk back.
4. Warm down.

THURSDAY
1. Warm up.
2. Take a running start of 50 meters and then run the next 50 meters as fast as possible while staying relaxed. Repeat six times.
3. Run four 200-meter distances, each in a time of 32 seconds.
4. Run a progressive relay four times. Rest and repeat.
5. Warm down.

FRIDAY
1. Warm up.
2. Run a progressive relay four times. Rest and repeat.
3. Warm down.

SATURDAY
Meet day.

CHAPTER 7

Running the 800 meters

BACKGROUND

Women athletes are becoming quite proficient at running the middle distance of 800 meters or 880 yards. The half-mile run (800 meters or 880 yards) is a paced run for women; each 200-meter or 220-yard distance is run at a practiced pace. However, the 800-meter run is rapidly taking on sprintlike qualities for top runners.

Since the inclusion of the 800-meter distance as an event for the female athlete, American women have rapidly improved their middle-distance running marks. School-girls are now better prepared to run at a faster pace and have become accustomed to the practice periods necessary for developing excellence in running these races.

Two outstanding American 800-meter runners from the past are Madeline Manning and Doris Brown. Marie Mulder exemplifies the new interest on the part of American girls and women in running longer races. At 15 years of age Marie Mulder ran 800 meters in 2 minutes 07.2 seconds. Times change rapidly in this distance as a result of improved training techniques and increased interest. Although European women have been ahead of American women in running this distance, this changed for a short time when Madeline Manning won the 1968 Olympics in a new Olympic record time of 2 minutes 0.9 second. However, the 1972 Olympic time was 1 minute 58.6 seconds, set by Hildegard Falck of West Germany. The former winner, Madeline Manning, had a time of 2 minutes 06.4 seconds and failed to make the finals. In the 1976 Olympics in Montreal, the 800-meter was won by Tatiana Kazankina, U.S.S.R., in 1 minute 54.94 seconds, with Eastern European women dominating the event.

SPECIAL CONSIDERATIONS

There seems to be no true "800-meter" physique to be found among women. That is, one cannot look at an athlete and determine by her build whether she is a sprinter or a middle-distance runner. The great difference between middle-distance girl runners and sprinters is, of course, endurance, but reasonably fast leg speed is rapidly becoming essential. Some fine middle-distance runners were originally good sprinters who trained to build up the necessary endurance. Usually, a very heavy girl is at a disadvantage in events that involve running, except in very short races in which speed is an all-important factor for success. This would also include the middle-distance runs because the last part of the race involves a sprint to the finish line. Girls with long slim legs should be successful at any distance, provided they have good led speed and have developed endurance. Sprinters can often become middle-distance runners if they place additional emphasis on acquiring endurance while still working on speed.

A primary factor to consider in developing endurance is the increase of muscle strength and greater oxygen utilization; respiratory action must be capable of adjusting to the fatigue aspect of the strain that prolonged running brings about in such a race. Synchronization and smoothness of stride action are essentials in developing the ability to run in the most efficient manner, with the greatest degree of success and the least amount of energy output. The middle-distance runner must learn to spread her energy throughout the entire race, making allowances for her own ability and the efforts made by her opponents.

Fatigue is more of a consideration in the 800-meter run than it is in the 400; therefore, the 800-meter runner must be able to perform under the strain of fatigue. The unexpected spurt of an opponent may cause a runner to exert extra energy at the finish or to maintain her position relative to the other runners during the middle portion of the race. A runner's body must be in condition to put forth this extra effort after she is fatigued.

ELEMENTS OF RUNNING

The start. In the 800-meter race a girl does not have to concentrate on effecting the same tremendous "getaway" from the blocks that the sprinter does. Generally, 800-meter runners do not use the starting blocks at all. They usually start from a standing position; that is, they lean forward ready to begin their rhythmic running cadence instantly (Fig. 7-1). Therefore the start does not have the same importance to the runner in the 800-meter run as it does to the runner in the sprints.

Running form. In the 800-meter run, because of the greater distance, endurance is of more concern to the runner. Thus development of proper patterns of running is an impor-

Fig. 7-1. 800-meter runners just before gun is fired.

tant part of training. These patterns must be adequately applied during competition. The following factors will influence the acquisition of good running form in the 800 meters.

Stride length. Usually the running stride should be long, with the runner using a free-swinging hip action. However, a runner should not sacrifice speed for an elongated stride.

Body relaxation. A runner's arms should be relaxed with the hands held loosely and slightly flexed. Tension should be evidenced only when the thumbs are pressed against the index fingers, and it should never appear in the entire forearm. The arm should be carried lower than in sprinting and without the vigorous arm action used by the sprinter. The mouth should be kept open for ease in breathing. This also helps relax the entire upper body of the runner.

Leg action. Knees are lifted high enough to allow for easy extension of the foot forward, but not as high as in the sprints (Fig. 7-2).

The finish. At the finish of the race (the last 20% to 25% of the distance) optimum effort is expended until the run is completed. This final spurt done with full stride action is referred to as the "kick," meaning the runner must use greater effort near the end to increase her running speed. It is actually a sprint executed at full speed.

Middle-distance strategy. When running a paced race the runner should plan her race in light of her own ability, her opponent's ability, and good racing techniques. Following are some points of strategy.

Fig. 7-2. The 800-meter (880-yard) run. **A to G,** This girl is running a relaxed race. Her front driving leg moves forward yet does not seem tense. Her stride is adequate. The head, neck, and trunk are kept in proper alignment. **H to N,** This girl's arms are carried at about the right position. Note the relaxed position of her wrists. Her rear foot is raised, perhaps a little too high, in the rear kickup.

Leading or following. The runner must not be fooled into trying to keep up with a very fast leader at the start when the pace is much faster than her usual starting pace. The athlete must know how to pace each 200-meter section of the race in accordance with her practiced time. Extremely fast running at the beginning of the race usually cannot be maintained throughout the entire distance.

Knowing the opponents. These comments are intended for experienced runners who have competed more than once against another runner or have previously studied a particular runner's style. A girl should plan her racing strategy by learning how her opponent runs. She should know if her opponent has a good "kick," if she likes to lead the pack, if she can psychologically stand to be passed, and for how long a distance she can maintain the sprint. In situations where an opponent attempts to set too fast or too slow a pace, a girl should just run the race to win. Athletes should run their races based on their own ability first and then capitalize on their knowledge of their opponent's ability.

Passing an opponent. Runners usually pick up cadence to draw around or pass an opponent. The straightaway passings generally require less energy output than do curve passings. Usually the trailing runner runs on the right shoulder of the leader rather than directly behind her. This position will eliminate her being boxed in and will allow her the space to easily pass an opponent if she desires.

Maintaining stride and energy. The runner must keep in mind concepts concerning stride and energy output when running long races. She must remember to hold her body erect and over her feet, the base of support. It is better for a girl to run on the outside shoulder of the pole runner and immediately in front of her than to run at her heels. She may then run at an even, steady pace instead of having to break into a faster run or use a slower speed and shorter stride, depending on the leader's pace. Scrambling for the pole position causes many runners to use short choppy strides and even to experience body contact that results in a loss of stride, rhythm, and speed. Once a girl has started her final sprint during the last hundred meters or so of the race, she must continue to put forth maximum effort until the race is over.

Maneuvering for position. A runner must not sacrifice strength and energy to secure a desired running position. This is too great a price to pay in terms of lost energy. The front runner's distance must be kept to less than 10 meters if the second position runner wishes to close the gap in an 800-meter race. Naturally, the shorter the distance to overcome, the greater the chance of accomplishing it, keeping in mind that the distance one is able to sprint is a key factor.

Mental attitude. The winning runner is usually convinced that it is possible for her to defeat any of her opponents in a particular race being run on a given day. She is confident that she can follow her planned pace for the first three fourths of the distance and that she can sprint the last one fourth at near top speed to the finish line. She also has a knowledge of her opponents' habits and is able to capitalize on any weaknesses—a tremendous psychologic edge for a competitor.

RULES

It is permissible in races of 800 meters or more for an official timer to call out lap times.

A "scratch" start in races of over two turns (over 400 meters) is now allowed. The scratch start line curves gently outward from the inner edge of the track to the outside lane, conforming to published rules. The runners are to break for the pole (inside lane) as soon as possible but still adhere to the rules of noninterference.

When a girl is permitted to move into another lane to get in front of another runner, she must be not less than two full strides ahead of the runner she is passing. She is not allowed to willfully jostle or cause the runner behind her to break her stride.

All other rules that apply to the running of the sprints also apply to the running of middle-distance races.

COMMON ERRORS

No matter how great her natural ability, at one time or another every athlete is likely to commit certain errors.

Matching strides. In the 800-meter race some runners become hypnotized and match their stride and cadence with that of their closest opponent, thus destroying weeks of practice on individually designed running. This situation often happens to beginning runners, and it may be of some value to them to run at a faster pace, but this is often disastrous to the experienced runner. Middle-distance runners should run at a certain pace and time during prescribed sections of the race; in fact, a girl must know her race so well, that with the passage of a specified number of seconds she will be at a predetermined location on the track. Another way of expressing it is to say that she will have counted her strides and matched them to specific distances if she runs at the correct pace. Only repeated experiences in timed distance training give a girl a feeling for the habitual pace needed for success in the middle-distance races.

Going out too fast. A runner who starts off a middle-distance race at too fast a pace may falter later on. Such a situation usually results from a runner trying to keep up with a "rabbit," one who deliberately sets a fast pace for the pack so that a teammate can run a steady pace and thus win. Sometimes inexperience causes a girl to try to lead the group at all costs; she will run at a pace far beyond her endurance capacity, causing her to fade badly at the finish.

If inexperience is the principal reason for a girl running too fast at the start, she must train diligently in her practice sessions so as not to go out too fast during the first part of the race. Repeated practice runs with another girl who sets an irregular or a faster pace than she does during the first part of the distance should help a girl to run at her own starting pace during a meet. The beginner should learn through these experiences that she may not be able to lead the pack at all times, and that she may have to run behind one or more runners if the pace is faster than she is able to maintain for the entire distance.

Unrhythmical cadence. In an effort to prevent an opponent from passing or attempting to pass a leader, a girl may easily alter her cadence and stride action and begin to use irregular and uneven steps in running. This is costly in energy, since successful running of middle-distance races depends on a smoothly executed, well-paced, carefully thought-out race. A girl should usually run each segment of a race as she practiced it. Deviation from her practiced pattern may result in undue expenditure of energy and may prevent her from even finishing the race because of fatigue.

Indiscriminate passing. Inexperienced runners often think that they must be in the lead, and so they pass the leader regardless of their relative positions on the track or the cost in loss of rhythm and stride. Runners must be able to evaluate whether passing the leader at a particular moment is an advantage or a disadvantage in terms of energy output.

Getting boxed in. If a runner drops immediately behind the leader and runs in second or third position on the inside lane, she may be boxed in by other runners who come up to a position parallel with hers in the second lane. She may be unable to get out of the box at all, possibly losing a race she should have won. Therefore she should run slightly behind and at the right shoulder of the leader until she is ready to assume the lead.

TEACHING PROGRESSION FOR THE BEGINNER

Many girls enrolled in physical education classes have had no experience in running middle distances. Even if they have had some training, the minimum training for girls who expect to compete in the 800-meter race is believed to involve more days of practice than are usually available in a 3-week daily unit. Girls who are found in class to be good prospects for running longer distances must be encouraged to do additional training after school and on weekends.

In general, instruction in sprinting and running is presented as part of the track class program; therefore novices need to learn distance running in a paced manner rather than learning to perform with the all-out effort they learned in sprinting. First, it should be understood that not all girls will make good prospects for running the longer races. Although all girls should be able to jog the 800-meter distance, not all can run that far in a race. A young girl may approach her physical education teacher with a remark similar to this one: "I cannot run very fast, but I feel as though I can run a long time and would like to run farther." This may be an opportune time for her to try running longer distances (Table 7-1).

The first thing a teacher should do is have the girls who are distance running prospects run the 200-meter distance in a specified time so that they will learn to pace themselves. She should set this time at whatever she thinks best for beginners; it might take some trial

Table 7-1. Standards of performance for the 880-yard and 800-meter runs*

Age	Type of competition	Expected time†	
		880 yards	800 meters
12-13	Beginner	3:00	2:48
12-13	School experienced	2:45	2:44
12-13	National record	2:17.6	2:17
14-17	Experienced	2:40	2:39
14-17	National record	2:14.6	2:14
Women	National record	2:05	1:59.8
Women	World record	2:05	1:54.94

*Note the wide range of difference between the beginner's time and that of the world record. Beginners should be aware of the many months and even years of training necessary to become a good half miler.
†These times can serve as a guide to the beginner in anticipating degrees of success.

and error to find the appropriate starting time. As a suggestion she might select 40 seconds. The girls could jog 200 meters and then run the second 200 meters in 40 seconds. Using this technique, girls should learn to pace their runs. The teacher should call out the time at 100 meters so that the girls will know how their speed compares to the desired speed at this point. At first girls will probably not be in good enough condition to recover by jogging; therefore a teacher should plan additional rest periods. Naturally, this process of running repeated paced distances will take time; that is why it is not always feasible to include longer races in the physical education class program.

Prior conditioning. It is absolutely essential for girls to have some endurance conditioning prior to participation in a running program. Because of the short time that is often involved, it is impossible to commence a conditioning program for girls immediately prior to instruction in the track and field events.

Group practice. It is best to have a group of girls practice together, pacing themselves while they are learning to run the distance of 800 meters. It is not good for a beginner to work alone because she needs the presence of others to help her discipline herself to practice and to give her encouragement. A teacher could have the sprinters run alongside the distance runners during a part of their workout, not only to encourage the distance runners but also to provide the sprinters with additional training.

The teacher should train someone to accurately call out the times the girls make as they learn to pace themselves, and this person should be allowed to give the information to the distance runners while the teacher works with the participants in the other events. This helper should be able to start the girls off in a run by a wave of the hand, the use of a whistle, or some other signal. She should also give the time to them at the halfway point and at the finishing line as each runner crosses it. It is helpful to have the track pegged at 50-meter intervals for interval and pace work.

Increased distance and faster pace. As soon as the girls are ready, their pacing distances should be increased from 200 to 300 meters, to 400 meters, to 600 meters, and finally to 800 meters. The time required for these runs may or may not be lowered, depending on the abilities of the girls. Times should be called out for the girls at the 200-meter or 300-meter distance, as desired. The teacher will notice that some girls progress faster than others. The training of girls for these longer races is individualized and must be geared to the needs of each girl. A beginning time of 85 seconds for the 400-meter run is acceptable. Then as the girls progress, the time should be dropped a few seconds—say to 80 seconds. The beginning time of 3 minutes in the 800-meter run is to be expected; then after much training, a girl may try to run it in 2½ minutes or less.

Competition. Each time the beginning middle-distance athlete runs a race in competition, she should profit from the experience. The teacher will be wise to plan frequent races among these girls. Because they do train and practice alone and are somewhat away from any one station (unlike high jump practicers), it is necessary to convince them of their importance and let them know someone cares about what they are doing. The teacher should keep in mind that these girls are the ''workhorses'' of the track team and that it is sometimes boring for them to run distances.

Conclusion. In summarizing the presentation of the running of the middle-distance races by the beginner, the following should be included.

1. At times, a girl can be the best source of information concerning her ability to run distances. Girls who have good endurance and like to run but are too slow to participate in sprints may be good potential middle-distance runners.
2. The technique of interval running should be taught early to middle-distance runners.
3. Prior conditioning is essential if girls are to learn to run properly during the time allotted to the teaching of track in a physical education class.
4. Group practice is better than individual practice for beginners because girls will try harder for improved performances.
5. Running speeds or distances should be increased periodically as girls progress in their ability to run faster and longer.
6. The middle-distance runner can profit from frequent competitive experiences, and under such conditions she can learn to pace herself properly.

TRAINING SUGGESTIONS

The following sample program is presented as a guide for girls who are training to run 800 meters and those who are planning other programs for competition at a high level. This program may be changed to conform to the various abilities and backgrounds of other girls who might be using the same practice pattern but are not as highly skilled.

Weekly schedule*

MONDAY
1. Jog 2000 to 3200 meters (1½ to 2 miles).
2. Do interval work: run four 200-meter distances, each in 40 seconds; do two sets of interval running (600, 400, 300, and 200 meters); run two 100-meter distances, each in 16 seconds.
3. Warm down.

TUESDAY
1. Stretch for 5 minutes.
2. Run 45 minutes of Fartlek.
3. Warm down.

WEDNESDAY
1. Jog 1600 meters (1 mile).
2. Do 30 minutes of weight training.
3. Run hills for 20 minutes.
4. Warm down.

THURSDAY
1. Stretch for 5 minutes.
2. Do 60 minutes of Fartlek.
3. Warm down.

FRIDAY
1. Jog 1600 meters (1 mile).
2. Do 30 minutes of weight training.
3. Warm down on the grass.

SATURDAY
Competition.

A more vigorous workout schedule may be devised by a coach if the preceding appears not to be strenuous enough. In fact, to be a world champion, a much more rigorous program must be devised and followed.

---

* Since middle-distance training schedules should be individually designed, the pattern presented here is suggestive and not meant to be an absolute regimen. However, hard workouts should be conducted only 2 days a week at midseason, and very early in the week when there is a meet. As the meet day draws closer, the training should become lighter in nature.

CHAPTER 8

Distance running

Running distances varying from 1 to 3 miles (1500, 3000, 5000 meters) including cross-country distances and up to a marathon distance (26 miles 385 yards) requires courage, stamina, and discipline. There are women who are short on speed but long on stamina, who should look to endurance running for their laurels. These women can be successful if they train diligently.

One mile, or the slightly shorter Olympic 1500 meters, has been the most common distance run by women as part of a regular track program (Table 8-1). The 1500-meter run for women is gradually becoming a combination speed and endurance race. In the very near future, it will be a separate specialty for the average-to-good runner as it now is with the world class runners. It is included in this edition only because the average-to-good women performers still think of this distance as an endurance race. However, the distances now are 2 to 5 miles for college and open competitors, with the high school competitors running 1½ to 2 miles. Many programs have cross-country competition involving race distances of 3 or more miles. In addition there are more and more women participating in marathon races (approximately 26 miles). Some women athletes who are strong and light in weight like to be challenged by running these long distances, which will all soon be standard races for women.

SPECIAL CONSIDERATIONS

How tall or short, how sturdily or slightly built an endurance runner is may not be of great importance, but often the girl who is successful in distance running has a slight build. What matters most is the mental and emotional makeup of the runner and whether she is strong and in top physical condition. Runners must have the dogged determination to work hard and the desire to gain the necessary endurance they will need. A girl's life must be so organized and so regimented that she has a chance to run many miles every week. She must possess the mentality to devise a workable running plan and then have the

Table 8-1. Standards of performance for 1500 meters

Age	Type of competition	Expected time*
Women	Beginner	4:45
Women	National record	4:05

*These times can serve as a guide to the beginner in anticipating degrees of success.

character to make the plan work. She must enjoy running and run hard enough to get into top condition. Good running is truly an accumulation of excessive running. It does not matter where the running occurs or when it occurs, as long as it is done under safe conditions and often enough to allow for progress. "A mile is covered by taking about 1,000 strides, one stride at a time, in rain or snow, in the dark before supper can be eaten or in the earliest morning before the sun is up—one stride at a time."* There is no mañana for the endurance runner—today is the best time to do what must be done.

Cross-country running is becoming very popular with more and more women across the United States. Girls 9 years old and under are running the mile cross-country race in just under 6 minutes. High school girls are running 2 miles in just under 12 minutes, and women are running 2½ miles in under 15 minutes. The number of participants taking part in more and more long-distance meets is increasing by leaps and bounds. Recently more than 800 participants took part in a five-division race with the largest group, the 12- to 13-year-old division, having 220 entries. Some girls are running in marathon races, which are approximately 26 miles in length. Cheryl Bridges, a 23-year-old schoolteacher from San Luis Obispo, California, set a new world record for women in the 26-mile 385-yard marathon race, running it in 2 hours 49 minutes and 40 seconds.

Another popular distance in the United States is the 10-mile race. The record is held by Davida Jackson, with a time of 1 hour 13 minutes and 44 seconds. Such a race was held in Canton, Ohio, in 1975 and was won by Kay Flatten, a relatively inexperienced runner, in 1 hour 15 minutes and 31 seconds. Such athletes signal the entrance of women in this event in greater and greater numbers in the future.

RUNNING THE MILE (OR 1500 METERS)

A variety of different styles of running will be observed when one sees a miler in action. The runner's ability to stride at a rapid pace with a minimum output of energy is the critical determinant of success. Her actions must appear smooth and relaxed; there is no bobbing of the head, and the arms and legs swing rhythmically as they move forward and backward. A miler appears to move along a straight line freely and efficiently.

Body position. There is an upright position of the trunk except at the start. The head is carried erect, with the eyes focusing down the track, and all movement appears to be directed in a straight line. Good running form consists in having a strong relaxed body and in taking easy strides, with arm and foot action making a rhythmic smooth pattern of movement.

Arm action. The arms should hang loosely from the shoulders, the elbows should be bent slightly, and the wrists should be relaxed and swinging toward the chin. There is no pumping action made by the arms. The arms should come forward in synchronization with each leg step to add rhythm to the running motion and swing smoothly from the shoulders in a forward-backward, relaxed motion. The fingers are slightly cupped, with no effort made to clench them or hold them open.

The arm and leg action should be as effortless as possible so that the motion flows freely and easily, with no extra shoulder or hip swinging to increase fatigue, slow the

---

*Wilt, Fred: Track techniques, Track and Field News **15**:459, 1964.

A   .B   C   D   E

Fig. 8-1. Distance run. This distance runner is using the correct running form for the 1-mile or 1500-meter run. The short stride, low knee lift, and small arm action will enable her to conserve her energy to last the distance.

action, or offer resistance to the body movement. The arms are caried low and are not swung vigorously.

Foot placement. The landing of the foot on the ground is made low on the ball of the foot. Then the heel touches down, and the push-off is made from the toes. This is a ball-heel-ball action. The heel should never slap the ground or hit it first. The faster the runner, the more the body weight comes down toward the front of the foot.

After a runner is under way, she should maintain an upward stance, and there should be little or no forward lean of the trunk. There is little forward knee lift but a rather high rear leg kick. The stride is short, natural, and unexaggerated, with the toes pointing slightly outward; the hips are kept loose and relaxed; the body is driven forward in a straight line; the chest is held high, and the head is carried in line with the rest of the body (Fig. 8-1). The longer the race, the shorter is the leg stride distance and the lower the arms are carried. The least possible tenseness of muscles must be maintained. Breathing is done naturally, with a slight forcing out of air through the mouth and nose, making it easier for the runner to take in needed oxygen. Relaxation must be part of the running action. It is a quality that cannot be taught in a few sessions or learned in a few weeks; rather, it comes gradually to the accomplished runner who through year-round training and much experience has gained the confidence of knowing what her body can do.

RUNNING CROSS-COUNTRY*

Cross-country running is on the increase as a popular sport in this country for women at all levels. In the past, cross-country has often been considered primarily an off-season conditioning program for runners, as have other winter and spring sports. It is now more often recognized as a separate sport, with many women distance runners placing as much emphasis on their training in cross-country and road running as on track running.

Cross-country and road running require the woman to have the ability to run efficiently for long periods of time—similar to distance racing on a track. An additional requirement,

*Many of these concepts were presented to the authors by Dr. Philip Hensen, Head Track and Field Coach, Central Connecticut State College.

however, is the ability to adapt this efficient running method to positive and negative variations in grade or slope (hills and valleys) along with possible accompanying variations in pace. These, along with changes in the running surface, are the primary differences between cross-country racing and track distance racing.

Some male distance runners have had considerable success in track racing but have encountered difficulty in achieving comparable success in cross-country racing. Some runners adapt more easily to cross-country running than to track running, and others adapt equally to either activity. With the addition of hills as a part of the race course, it is nearly impossible for an individual to maintain a constant pace throughout the race, as she might at an equivalent distance on a level track surface. A distance runner with finite energy-producing capacities must constantly adjust her speed to the variable grades to conserve needed energy for the latter part of the race. In other words, the runner may find it necessary to make adjustments in her running mechanics as the speed and grade change.

In studies conducted in the exercise physiology laboratory at Indiana University, it was found that the energy costs of running at an even pace vary considerably at different grades. The energy requirements increased 10% at a +4% grade and 40% at a +8% grade when compared with level- or flat-surface running. In downhill running the requirements were found to decrease 19% at a −4% grade and 25% at a −8% grade when compared to zero grade. These results would indicate that a runner must reduce her speed when running up a steep incline to avoid extreme oxygen debt, and that she should increase her speed on the downhill grade to make maximum use of her aerobic capabilities. If one is to conclude that the most efficient way to run a distance race is at a steady pace, then the speed must be adjusted to meet the changes in the grades encountered.

Some additional comments are needed here to clarify downhill running. The results mentioned apply to running downhill on a smooth surface. Running on an uneven surface could extract great energy from the runner because of the foot jar and greater body adjustment. This may cause the runner to reduce her speed somewhat while running downhill.

Changes in grade are also accompanied by changes in running mechanics, and it has been found that the better runners decrease their stride length as the incline of the positive grade increases. Placement of the foot should be higher on the ball of the foot at the positive grade, and the time of nonsupport, or flight phase, of the run should decrease. Body lean should be essentially vertical at all grades, which gives one the impression of "leaning into" the hills. On downhill runs the speed of the run, the stride length, and the time of nonsupport should all increase, but the runner should maintain "control" of herself at all times.

The type of shoe worn for cross-country racing depends on the type of surface, but for grass or dirt courses spiked shoes or "waffle" type cleats are essential. On paved surfaces "flats" may be worn, but they should be lightweight and without excess padding. For cross-country running, shoes should be selected that have considerable shock-absorbing capabilities (particularly the heel of the shoe) to avoid foot and leg injuries during the run.

SOME ELEMENTS OF DISTANCE RUNNING

Performance and training. Endurance running for girls and women, which includes long-distance running, 3000 meters, 5000 meters, 10,000 meters, marathon, and 3-mile cross-country distances, is just approaching the point of attracting outstanding runners. Its popularity is also the result of social acceptability, stemming from the national interest in jogging for girls and women of all ages.

Following are certain factors involved in running distances that must be taken into account.

1. It takes time to practice for running in a race, which means that a more rigid daily living schedule must be followed. This may mean running up to 100 miles or more a week and training most of the year.

2. It is possible to run long distances at a very slow pace (10 minutes a mile) and not experience undue discomfort other than blisters on the feet, sore leg muscles, and a fatigued feeling for a while early in the training season. However, as the speed of running is increased, a tolerance to the so-called blurred blue haze of pain must be developed to be a competitive runner. A girl can learn to run 15 to 20 miles in a day, which would be called a ''long-run'' workout, and a total of more than 100 miles in a week. In other words, the development of courage to withstand some pain is necessary for competition.

3. Concentration throughout a race is paramount in bringing about a good performance. What does an athlete concentrate on when she is running in an organized race? Trying to maintain the established pace (which is around 6 mph for the top marathon runner) is one direction in which thoughts should be directed. Also, her mind might dwell on the rhythm of the breathing process and be alert to the strategy employed by the other runners. Another idea might be to observe how relaxed she is by using some of the techniques of a sprinter, such as rolling the lip out and yawning. Changing the position of the arms (lowering and raising) and slight movements of the head are essential to relieve tension and characteristic only of long-distance runners.

4. Having friends present at a race is encouraging and is often important to the runner by helping her navigate the course properly. To know that one's friends will not let one go off course, particularly in the last portions of a cross-country or marathon race, lets the runner concentrate on the elements of effective running.

5. The runner must get enjoyment out of running even during hard and intense workouts. There is an exhilaration that comes to those who run for hours that those who have never experienced it cannot truly appreciate. The feeling of freedom to express oneself in this manner is seldom equalled in the performing arts.

6. Adjustment is needed to be able to run equally well on hard surfaces, grassy areas, rough terrain, smooth terrain, up and down hills, etc.

7. In the really long distances such as marathon racing, conversing in an easy manner can take place, especially in the early portion. It tends to help the runners involved to relax and relieves anxiety. However, it should never be done as a distraction or to cause a runner to lose her concentration.

8. If a hill is encountered, the runner should lean slightly forward and take shorter strides in ascending, to conserve energy and use the hill to an advantage. Conversely, going downhill the runner should lean slightly backward and take longer strides. A hilly course is often scheduled for use in cross-country running.

9. The proper diet for a long-distance runner is somewhat debatable. Many nutrition experts believe that a balanced diet is all that is necessary. Even extra salt in hot weather is

thought to be unnecessary. Race preparation proposed by many coaches is that the runner should eat a protein diet 4 to 7 days before the race and then a diet high in carbohydrates up to 3 days before the race in what is known as ''carbohydrate loading.'' To go on a 1- or 2-day fast does not seem to be supportable.

10. It normally would take about 15 weeks of intensive training to be prepared for an important meet.

11. Normally, a chaser should never try to catch a pacer all at once. A wide gap should be closed slowly unless the race distance left is small.

12. A 6- to 7-minute mile (1500 meters) may eventually be the pace women can maintain, even in the marathon.

13. The last 5 miles (8000 meters) of a marathon race are the most difficult to run. The women who run this last portion must do so faster than the others in the race to win.

14. The training program must be varied to avoid it becoming stale and monotonous.

OTHER CONCEPTS CONCERNING THE MARATHON

The major source of fuel for distance runners comes from glycogen reserves in the muscles, liver, extracellular fluid, and blood of the runner. It is estimated that these sources of glycogen can last for slightly less than 2 hours or 30 kilometers. Races that take more time or cover more distance than this cause the runner's metabolic source of energy to be supplied from fats. This change in energy source requires slightly more oxygen for the same amount of work. This means that once the glycogen reserves in the body have

Fig. 8-2. A race aid station where runners are given fluids during the progress of the race.

been used and fat becomes the fuel, maintaining the same running pace will require more oxygen. In short, this will be harder work for the runner and may result in a slight dropping off in speed to keep the oxygen requirement the same.

In an attempt to find a way to delay the depletion of glycogen reserves during sustained runs, some researchers have studied the concept of ''super compensation,'' ''carbohydrate loading,'' or ''packing.'' All these terms refer to a dietary and running program aimed at depleting the glycogen stored in the muscle tissue prior to the race and then rebuilding these reserves back to an even high level. The general procedure involves a long run of 1½ to 2 hours to deplete the muscle glycogen. After this run the athlete stays on a high-protein, low-carbohydrate diet and continues running but at lower mileage workouts. This prevents the muscle glycogen reserves from being refurbished. Three days on this low-carbohydrate diet are followed by 3 days of a high-carbohydrate diet and no running. During this time the muscle glycogen is restored, and if no running occurs, the body actually overcompensates and stores two and one half to three times more than the normal level. Race day should be the fourth day after reinstating carbohydrates into the diet.

It has been suggested that women may have a biologic advantage in the long-distance runs. Women may be able to store more glycogen naturally in the muscular tissues, and because of hormonal differences, they may be more efficient in mobilizing fats when glycogen reserves are depleted. More research is needed on women distance runners to identify these sexual advantages.

The discussion at the 1976 Olympics on ''blood doping'' raised some ethical and moral questions concerning the extent to which individuals and nations will go to perfect human running machines. The fact that it may be of value in enabling distance runners to utilize more oxygen by having their own blood stored and later injected into their bloodstream may beg the question. On the other hand, officials and society in general may eventually accept this procedure as a worthwhile endeavor; only time will tell. It appears that there should be a limit set as to which artificial means may be utilized by performers in sports events.

Women may also be unique in their tolerance for heat because of fluid balance. Marathoner Jenny Taylor has experienced three cases of heat stroke or heat exhaustion. Since there is little research done on women distance runners, she found it necessary to submit herself to a series of heat-with-exercise stress situations to see if and how well her body acclimatized to the heat. Through this series of tests it was found that oral contraceptives may affect water retention and fluid balance. There is a definite need to pursue the possibility of a relationship, as it is a drug that women can avoid when training and running a marathon.

Finally, it has been suggested that young girls exhibit a natural form for distance runs that is more efficient than that of young boys. They tend to be more relaxed and do not carry their arms as high or lean their trunks forward as much as do boys. Young boys often approach the distance runs with a form more appropriate to the sprints.

Once past puberty some girls may experience a change in form due to their widening pelvic bones and the additional upper body weight of the breasts. Such changes may result in a tendency toward greater leg tendon problems from the increased angle of the femur and crossing the midline of the trunk with the arms to counteract the hip action. Thus the slimmer girl has the morphologic advantage in running the marathon.

DISTANCE-RUNNING TECHNIQUES

As has been stated, the 1500-meter, the cross-country distances, road races of up to 5 miles, and the marathon are the distances used in competition; the 1500-meter is often the longest distance. However, the 3000 meters has recently been run in international competition. In the 1976 United States versus USSR meet the 3000-meter race was won by Ludmila Bragina in the world record time of 8 minutes 27.1 seconds. Francie Larrieu Lutz set a new American record in the same race of 8 minutes 54.9 seconds.

The start. All distance runners choose to use a stand-up position at the start of a race. However, a runner must get away quickly to secure a good position at the pole and avoid running farther than is required.

Full-speed stride. The runner is urged to relax her muscles, stride rhythmically, and make the most of her breathing ability so she can run with power and speed.

The finish. The distance runner must be in a position to make her drive for the tape when she feels she must to win the race. If she is leading in the last eighth of a mile, she will want to fight off any challengers and hold the lead. The miler or 1500-meter runner should run through the tape to a point 5 meters or more beyond the finish line. Runners finishing longer distances may not be able to do more than just hit the finish tape before stopping.

COMMON ERRORS

1. Failure to maintain contact with other runners
2. Failure to have a good position in the pack
3. Going out too fast or too slowly
4. Failure to run fast enough to meet a challenger in the last 200 meters of the race
5. Failure to take the lead at the correct psychologic or physiologic time
6. Getting boxed in after being passed by a runner
7. Relaxing too soon (just before the finish line) and losing the race to a fast-finishing runner

COACHING HINTS AND RUNNING TACTICS

General concepts. Mental readiness is of the utmost importance to the distance runner, who must believe in her ability if she is to excel at distance running. A good runner carefully thinks out what is necessary for her heart, lungs, and skeletal muscles to perform properly. She knows what she must do to gain sufficient speed and stamina and acquire an efficient running form. She knows pace to the extent that she can judge within 0.2 to 0.3 second how fast she runs each 400 or 200 meters, and she can recognize that, in her race, judgment of pace is one of the keys to success. For efficient performance it is usually best for the girl to run her race at an even pace, allowing for only slight slowing down and speeding up during the run; however, a runner usually runs faster than normal during the last 100 meters or so.

Knowing when to make a move, disregarding fatigue, and being alert as to what position to take at a particular instant are some of the most vital aspects of racing. Mental fortitude and dogged determination are necessary qualities for the competitor to outsmart her opponents and also win a victory over herself.

The miler must consider the condition of the track and the number and abilities of the competitors, and she must know who the best runners are and what their strengths and weaknesses are before the race begins.

The runner should have a race plan and believe in it, thus avoiding unnecessary worry. Running in the lead may be more fatiguing than is following other runners. Once a runner has attained the lead, she should realize she is where she planned to be and should concentrate on relaxing and maintaining a smooth running motion throughout the race. When a runner's lead is challenged, she should pick up speed slightly to maintain her lead. An experienced runner can often force an inexperienced runner to stay on the outside of the track and consequently run a greater distance.

The miler always keeps contact with the leader and does not let that distance widen too much. This keeps her in striking distance at all times and keeps the opposition in doubt. If the runner knows she is faster than the other runners, she must take the lead if others are deliberately slowing down the race. When running in second place in a race, the athlete should run on the leader's right shoulder and avoid getting in a position where she cannot make a move to pass the leader and assume the lead.

The start. The use of the stand-up start is preferred because it enables the girl athlete to move fast enough to secure a good position yet does not cause her to expend undue energy. She need only run hard enough at the start to assure herself of a good running position.

A well-conditioned runner with good endurance can take an early lead and set such a stiff pace for the first one half or two thirds of the race; an opponent who sprints will be too far back to catch up or too tired to spring down the homestretch. On the other hand, a good sprinter can beat the girl who has greater stamina by first running a fast 400-meter dash and then slowing the pace gradually while maintaining the lead, thus conserving her energy for the homestretch sprint. Many male 1500-meter runners relax during the third-quarter run without meaning to do so. However, the girl who trains herself in daily work-outs to expend extra energy during the middle third of the long run will often be able to run this portion of an actual race faster than her competitors.

Passing another runner. When passing an opponent, the rear runner should make her move quickly and with surprise because a quick motion will probably upset the opponent's running pattern and help to establish a psychologic advantage for the successful challenger. If possible, an opponent should not be given a chance to retake the lead. If the lead is challenged, the front runner should pick up speed and continue to hold it. Usually a runner cannot continue to accept challenges from the rear because they are too costly in energy.

A first-position runner can be forced by a challenger to run a little faster than she wishes to run during the early stages of the race. She must avoid letting the challenger run too close to her and thus pass her without expending much extra energy. If the pace is too fast, the fact that a runner is closely followed by another one may cause the front runner to become tense, slower, and fatigued sooner than expected. She may want to let the challenger take the lead under these circumstances.

The finish. Near the finish of the race the front runner will be trying to overcome fatigue and—maybe—her nearest opponent's surge at the same time. This is the time for the leader to think about the location of other runners in the race; it will help keep her mind off her own fatigue and aid her in relaxing as she runs. During the finish of a race a runner must give attention to maintaining proper body control and form. She should prepare herself at this time for an all-out effort. In this final move, when she elicits the body's reserve power, care should be exercised to see that body efficiency is maintained and smoothness of rhythm, so necessary for a fast finish, is not sacrificed. A runner should increase speed gradually rather than in a sudden burst because the former is more economical. However, it may be necessary to pass opponents by suddenly bursting forth when others least expect it.

Motivation. Running is fun, but strong self-motivation is required for girls to do repeated amounts of distance running. The warm-up session of a physical education class consists of running a specified number of laps. The coach can create enthusiasm even among the less energetic girls if there is a roster to sign indicating they belong to the 800- or 1500-meter club. Only those who have actually run the distance may belong to the specific club. Ten laps of most high school gymnasiums is a half mile and twenty laps a mile. A gold star or similar symbol can be placed next to the names of girls who have run a mile, then special recognition can be given for running 10 miles, up to an accumulated 50 or even 100 miles to further interest girls in running distances. The accomplishment of a certain number of laps in a specified time will increase the distances run by the girls and help them to improve their speed. The concept of running being a group rather than individual sport aids in creating interest.

If a coach repeatedly makes comments to her girls, such as the following: "How well you look!," "What a nice streamlined, strong body you have!," "How improved your posture is!," and "How healthy you look!," the comments will often serve as a motivational device to make girls conscious of the importance of participating in distance running.

TRAINING SUGGESTIONS

There are many procedures for developing good long-distance running. Perhaps the most logical is to arrange a workout plan that is varied enough to be interesting, yet challenging enough to make girls work at developing needed strength and stamina.

Systems of training. Cross-country running, overdistance and underdistance running, repetition running, Fartlek, continuous running, running a timed period, circuit training, marathon running, Paarlauf, and interval training are methods that can be used for training women to run long distances. (See Chapter 2 for more information.) It is most important that coach and athlete understand fully the effects of all systems of training and make the proper modifications of them to gain the maximum benefits for the specific girl.

Fartlek. Fartlek is a system that many runners employ to good advantage in endurance running. This Swedish system of "play of speed" or "speed play" is used in many different countries. It was given the name Fartlek by Gosta Holmer. According to this method the runner runs on dirt roads, across meadows, up and down country hills, in the sand along beaches, through city parks, and on golf courses. The runner runs hard for part of the time, then rests by slowing down and jogging or walking for a while, enjoying the surroundings, and then runs hard again. This system is excellent for girls and women who appreciate green forests, sandy beaches, and the rolling countryside and for those who enjoy variety in their workouts while experiencing important physiologic benefits. Running should last from 1 to 2 hours each day, and in the workout the runner should alternate easy running with steady hard running every one-fourth to one-half mile.

Fartlek allows the runner a great deal of freedom in choosing how fast and how far she will run, but it also calls for a great deal of self-discipline on her part to effect the greatest good. By using the Fartlek system a runner may run as strenuously as she chooses in accordance with her condition and self-discipline. Fartlek can be a progressive accumulation of endurance as the time spent on it increases, or it may be only a nice experience with little endurance gained. Some of the activities, such as running hills, running in sand and surf, and climbing up and down stairs, will increase endurance considerably. Fartlek as well as overdistances and underdistances may be used by sprinters, middle-distance runners, and endurance runners alike.

Interval training. Interval training is a system developed primarily by Woldemar Gerschler involving repeated runs of fixed distances. This is an extremely valuable system for developing good long-distance runners. Perhaps its greatest value lies in the range of adaptability provided for the diverse needs of the runners. The objective is running repeated distances at a timed pace alternated with the use of recovery periods of easy jogging or walking until the pulse rate is reduced to a level that warrants resumed running. This method is best suited for the sprinter and the middle-distance runner, but it is also useful to the endurance runner in developing speed.

Cross-country running for conditioning. Cross-country running in the fall and winter is an excellent method for establishing a good foundation for all-around fitness for girls as well as for developing stamina, strength, and cardiovascular endurance. This is one of the best methods for obtaining and developing the ability to run long distances. The runner should begin by running at a pace that coincides with her physical condition at the moment. Usually the first 3 or 4 weeks' workout should consist of running at a slow pace from 3 to 6 miles 2 or 3 days each week, with shorter distances run the other days.

The main purpose in using cross-country running is to help the runner gain speed and endurance. A daily workout is preferred to any other plan of training for long distance, and the minimum practice schedule should not be less than 3 days a week.

Repetition running. Repetition running is a more strenuous method of training but deserves to be considered by the serious athlete. This is a type of interval running that requires longer intervals of running at a slower pace with complete rest between the runs to allow for near complete recovery. A 400-meter distance in 70 seconds with 10 minutes' rest between each run is an example.

A teacher or coach can help an athlete plan her workout schedule, train her to use good racing tactics, and most of all lend the needed encouragement to keep her properly stimulated and motivated toward self-improvement. However, it is up to the individual girl to discipline herself to train properly and consistently to become a top distance runner.

SUGGESTED TRAINING SCHEDULE

The following program is suggested for middle-distance and distance runners, whether or not they are actively involved in a competitive cross-country program. This plan calls for practice to take place 4 days each week, with girls being encouraged to do some running on their own the other days of the week. The weeks may be varied by changing and increasing the loads progressively.

Warm-ups (to be done before each training session)

1. Do easy running for 4 to 5 minutes.
2. Do bending and stretching exercises for 10 minutes.
3. Run four 120-yard distances at three-fourths speed.

Fall season   6 weeks

MONDAY
1. Do 3 to 5 miles of slow running at 8½ to 10 minutes per mile.
2. Do 20 minutes of weight training to strengthen trunk and back muscles.
3. Warm down by jogging for 5 minutes.

TUESDAY
1. Run ten 400-meter intervals at an easy tempo. Jog 200 meters between the runs, with a constant motion—no walking.
2. Warm down for 5 minutes.

WEDNESDAY
1. Do 3000 to 5000 meters of slow running at 8½ to 10 minutes per 1500 meters.

THURSDAY
1. Run four 200-meter hill runs.
2. Run 330 yards four times at medium speed.
3. Run 110 yards three times at full speed.
4. Jog for 5 minutes.

FRIDAY
Some coaches suggest that this day be one of complete rest. Others believe that a slow run of a long distance up to 5000 meters is indicated.

Preseason   2 weeks

MONDAY
1. Run three sets of four 50- to 70-meter hill runs.
2. Run five sets of seven 200-meter intervals with 30-second rests between runs.
3. Run three sets of four 400-meter intervals with 30-second rests between runs.
4. Run one 160-meter distance at fast speed.
5. Warm down for 5 minutes.

TUESDAY
1. Do 10 to 15 minutes of long running at one-half speed for 3000 meters.
2. Do 10 minutes of varied slow running, springing from the toes.
3. Do 15 minutes of weight training or circuit training.
4. Warm down for 5 minutes.

WEDNESDAY
1. Do 1 hour of running at various speeds cross-country.

THURSDAY
1. Run three sets of four 50 to 70 meter hill runs.
2. Run two sets of three 100-meter intervals with a 1-minute rest between runs.
3. Do 15 minutes of weight training or circuit training.
4. Warm down for 5 minutes.

Early season 6 weeks

MONDAY
1. Run 1 hour of Fartlek on a golf course or in a wooded area.

TUESDAY
1. Run six sets of ten 400-meter intervals with a 30-second rest between runs.

WEDNESDAY
1. Run two sets of three 400-meter hill runs.
2. Run four sets of six 300-meter repetition runs with 3- to 8-minute recovery periods.
3. Do 10 minutes of weight training or circuit training.

THURSDAY
1. Do 10 to 15 minutes of slow running at three-fourths speed.
2. Run six 600-meter intervals with a 45-second rest.
3. Warm down by jogging for 10 minutes.

Competitive season

MONDAY   1. Run 110 meters three times at full speed.
                  2. Run ten sets of fifteen 200-meter distances at 34 seconds each, with a 30-second rest between runs.

TUESDAY   1. Run six 100-meter wind sprints, 30 meters at a fast pace and 70 meters coasting.
                  2. Run four 400-meter repetition distances with 4- to 6-minute recovery periods.

WEDNESDAY   1. Run 110 meters three times at full speed.
                  2. Run four 1200-meter repetition distances with 8- to 12-minute recovery periods.

THURSDAY   1. Do 1 hour of continuous running.

PART THREE

Hurdling

CHAPTER 9

Hurdles

BACKGROUND

The hurdle race is a thrilling event for spectators as well as performers because it combines the challenge of clearing a series of obstacles with the excitement of sprinting. Races of 50 yards and of 100 and 200 meters are standard distances for girls' and women's hurdle events. Other distances, such as the 60-yard hurdles, are run indoors. Hurdle heights vary, depending on the length of the race and the age group of the competitors, from 30 to 33 inches. However, elementary school girls usually begin hurdling over the 18-inch hurdles. Experimenting is currently being done with the hurdle heights and with the adding of distances to include more hurdles in certain races. This may come about in the future.

American women have hurdled since the event was added to the Olympics in 1932, and the American Mildred "Babe" Didrikson (Zaharias) won the Olympic competition with a time of 11.7 seconds in the 80-meter race. Championship hurdlers today are negotiating the same distance in about 10.8 seconds. With today's distances of 100 and 200 meters being commonly used in international hurdle competition, world class hurdlers such as Chi Cheng of Taiwan, Mamie Rawlins and Patty Johnson of the United States, and Olympian winner Annelie Ehrhardt of East Germany are often running these races in 12.8 and 23.9 seconds, respectively. In fact, Annelie Ehrhardt won the 1972 Olympic 100-meter hurdles with a time of 12.59 seconds for a new Olympic record. In the 1976 Olympics Johanna Schaller of East Germany won the event in 12.77 seconds, with the Eastern Europeans taking the first five places.

SPECIAL CONSIDERATIONS

An outstanding sprinter with good coordination, flexibility, endurance, courage, concentration, patience, and speed has the natural qualities necessary for a good hurdler. Coordination and flexibility are essential because of the body action required in clearing the hurdles, and patience is necessary if a girl is to learn the techniques of good hurdling form and correct stride pattern. Concentration is important to be able to focus on the hurdle immediately ahead. Courage is a prerequisite to avoid being afraid to run through a hurdle if necessary. Speed and endurance are important to good sprinting. Hurdling is a kind of sprint race: the time actually consumed in clearing hurdles is minute compared with the time the runner spends between the hurdles. A hurdler must also have judgment of distance and good vision. Good sprinting shoes will give confidence to the hurdler.

In the 50-yard hurdle race four hurdles are spaced 8 meters apart (26 feet 3 inches),

Fig. 9-1. Good hurdling form is exhibited here.

with the first hurdle 12 meters (39 feet 4½ inches) from the starting line. The distance from the last hurdle to the finish line in the 50-yard race is 31 feet 10½ inches. The spacing in the 100-meter race is 13 meters from the start to the first hurdle and 8.1 meters between hurdles. The distance from the last hurdle to the finish line is 15.57 meters. For other distances such as the 70-yard race or the various shuttle hurdle races, current rule books should be consulted for the proper spacings, as they vary from time to time, depending on the rules made by the various committees concerned with hurdling. Table 9-1 contains a list of the currently approved spacings.

Presently, 80 yards is considered a good distance for the high school age group to run. This race, as seen in Table 9-1, includes seven hurdles spaced 8.1 meters apart, with the first hurdle 13 meters (42 feet 8 inches) from the start. Using a height of 2 feet 6 inches, a girl can be considered a good hurdler if she can break 11.0 seconds in this race.

Whereas a girl's height may be of some importance in hurdling, it does not influence speed, the most important quality for hurdling. However, having long legs could be an important qualification for the girl who also has good speed, coordination, flexibility, and the desire to win.

Table 9-1. Hurdle race distances and spacings*

Race distance	Number of hurdles	Height of hurdles	Distance to first hurdle	Distance between hurdles	Distance from last hurdle to finish
50 yards	4	2 feet 6 inches	39 feet 4½ inches	26 feet 3 inches	31 feet 10½ inches
50 yards	4	2 feet 6 inches	42 feet 8 inches	27 feet 10½ inches	23 feet 8¾ inches
60 yards	5	2 feet 6 inches	42 feet 8 inches	26 feet 3 inches	32 feet 4 inches
70 yards	6	2 feet 6 inches	42 feet 8 inches	26 feet 3 inches	27 feet ¾ inch
80 yards	7	2 feet 6 inches	42 feet 8 inches	26 feet 3 inches	39 feet 10 inches
100 meters	10	2 feet 9 inches	42 feet 8 inches (13 meters)	26 feet 3 inches (8.1 meters)	51 feet 1 inch (15.57 meters)
200 meters	10	2 feet 6 inches	52 feet 6 inches (16 meters)	62 feet 4 inches (19 meters)	42 feet 8 inches (13 meters)

*These distances are reported in accordance with the NF of SHSA and the AIAW and NSPEA rules of AAHPER. When women run the 50- and 60-yard hurdles, the hurdles are designed for indoor competition and the height of 2 feet 9 inches is used.

ELEMENTS OF HURDLING

Basically, the action made in hurdle clearance should be as nearly like sprinting as possible. Smoothness and speed of action in clearing the hurdle bring about good hurdling form. The leading knee—for example, the left—is lifted high enough to assure a close clearance, and there is a slight forward body incline. The arm opposite the lead leg must be thrust forward quickly so that it can synchronize with the fast action made by the trail leg. Because a quick leg snap is essential to the speed needed in getting over the hurdle, the lead leg should reach out and down in an elongated stride rather than just "float" over the hurdle, with height to spare. The right leg (trail leg) must be elevated and flattened enough (with the foot going out sideways) to allow for safe clearance (Fig. 9-2). As the forward arm is retracted, the lead leg is brought down quickly to the ground. The trailing leg whips quickly over the hurdle so that the girl can be ready to move immediately into a full sprinting stride between hurdles. As the balance arm (right) moves forward, the trailing leg clears the hurdle and the girl moves out into a full running stride.

Details of clearing. As the girl clears the hurdle, she should focus her eyes on the top of the next one. She will take off approximately 5 or 6 feet from the hurdle. Actually, the speed at which the individual runner moves will help determine her distance from the hurdle when she takes off; the faster a girl runs, the greater will be the distance. She should take care to thrust her body down and forward onto the lead leg rather than upward as she prepares to go over the hurdle. The trailing leg has to be raised quickly and flattened out, with the knee and toe pointing outward and the thigh almost parallel to the ground at this point. However, flattening the trail leg is not a static position; the whipping downward of the trail leg should take place at the same time as the snapdown of the lead leg. The knee of the trailing leg is held higher than the foot. The toes of the foot on the trailing leg are turned up to keep them from striking the hurdle (Fig. 9-3).

As soon as the lead foot clears the hurdle, the snapdown should start, with the action originating in the hip. The girl must be leaning forward as she goes over the hurdle. The landing should be on the ball of the foot, with the toe pointed forward to avoid any unnecessary sideward movements. The foot of the lead leg should land between 2 and 3

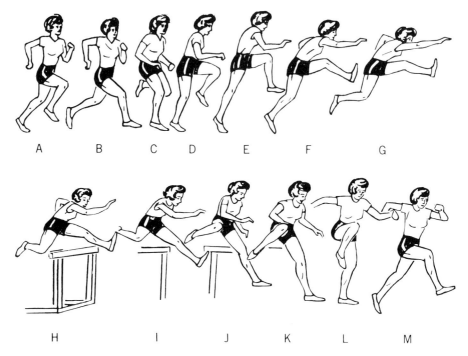

Fig. 9-2. Hurdling. **A** and **B,** This girl is in a full running stride. **C,** Note that she is gathering herself for the hurdling action. **D,** She is leaning forward in preparation for going over the hurdle. **E,** The opposite arm and leg are thrust forward. **F,** Extension of leg and opposite arm is still taking place. **G,** Note how the head is lowered and the back is bent forward. **H,** The correct lead leg position is seen here. The left arm is in the correct position, emphasizing the opposition idea. **I,** The snapdown of the lead leg is accomplished. **J,** Note the position of the trail leg. It is flattened as it should be; however, the foot of the trail leg should also be flattened to avoid striking the hurdle. This is causing her to be too high as she goes over the hurdle. **K,** The lead leg snapdown is completed. **L,** The stride to be made with the trail leg is taking place. **M,** The girl again runs in a full sprinter's stride.

feet from the hurdle. It should land in a normal running position ready to resume sprinting. The trailing leg whipping downward coupled with the extreme arm thrust gives the hurdler a great deal of forward momentum.

The girl is now ready to sprint the distance between this hurdle and the next one. Most young girls have to take five strides between hurdles, but experienced hurdlers possessing good speed are able to sprint with only three strides between hurdles. It is not uncommon for very small girls and novices to take seven strides between hurdles. The snapdown step is not counted as a step in the odd-numbered counting of strides. The girl hurdler should be able to sprint the distance from the starting line to the first hurdle in seven or eight strides, depending on her height and speed. The shorter girl may have to use eight strides. If the number of steps to take is eight, the lead leg will probably be placed against the rear block at the start; this ensures that the correct leg is leading as she approaches the hurdle. If the number of required steps to the first hurdle is odd (seven), the lead leg will be in the forward block. Naturally, many practice starts are necessary to be sure that a girl will get out of the blocks quickly. This is especially true if the girl has to change from her normal sprinting start because she must place a different foot in the front block.

Fig. 9-3. Approach to, above, and over a hurdle. Observe the arm and leg action of this outstanding hurdler.

Intense concentration on the part of the performer is absolutely essential in running hurdles. The competitor must now allow distractions such as falling hurdles or other runners' positions to divert her attention and cause her to run out of her lane. As she crosses a hurdle, she must also focus her eyes on the next one. It is always the hurdle beyond that holds her attention to help her avoid changing the plane of flight. The last few hurdles and the final distance to the finish line should be run as if in a sprint, with maximum effort expended and the hurdler almost forgetting that the hurdles are there. A girl should place emphasis on sprinting as fast as possible in a relaxed manner.

RULES

The rules of hurdling are few and easily understood, even by the beginner. Basically, the same rules used in sprinting apply to hurdling, with the following additions:
1. A hurdler must run over all hurdles; any competitor who runs around or carries her leg or foot alongside but not over any hurdle will be disqualified.
2. Knocking down one or more hurdles does not disqualify a competitor, provided the hurdles are of legal size and weight.

Fig. 9-4. Side view in sequence of a hurdler executing the hurdling action.

COMMON ERRORS

All beginning hurdlers have some faults in common, and they must be recognized to be overcome or avoided. Some of these are mentioned here.

Starting strides. Taking steps that are too short is a common fault. If this is done during the first few strides, the runner will overextend during later strides to get to the first hurdle in the prescribed number of strides. Therefore it is necessary for a girl to repeatedly run to and over one hurdle if she is to perfect her step pattern and clearance action (Fig. 9-5).

Clearing the hurdle. The takeoff spot should not be too close to the hurdle. Repeated runs by the girl to and over three hurdles will help perfect the takeoff and the body clearance techniques. Arm action made as the girl goes over the hurdle must aid the body balance and give added impetus to the leg thrust (Fig. 9-7); any action that deters the speed and smoothness of movement must be eliminated. Imbalance may be caused by the hurdler executing wrong action with one or both arms or by making a sideward swing with the lead leg as she goes over the hurdle. Floating over the hurdle or sitting back while going over the hurdle, or both, forces a girl to land with her body weight toward the rear, causing her to stagger for a moment before she begins to run.

Strides between hurdles. Any deviation from good sprinting form while running

Fig. 9-5. Hurdlers in competition showing excellent form in the 80-meter race.

Fig. 9-6. Good hurdling form.

Fig. 9-7. Clearing the hurdle. This hurdler is using good form.

between the obstacles will reduce speed. If the first stride after clearing is short, the girl will have to overstretch for the next two to make up distance; this is detrimental to her performance. Also, any break in a smooth and continuous stride is an error that must be eliminated. Although five strides are often taken by beginning hurdlers, it must be remembered that a top hurdler should take only three strides between hurdles.

TEACHING PROGRESSION FOR A BEGINNER PROGRAM

The following progression procedures for teaching beginners should be used after they have completed early conditioning sessions and are able to sprint reasonably well. Hurdling involves clearing an obstacle that might appear awesome to the beginner and in her opinion might even result in her being hurt. Therefore the teacher or coach must be very patient in presenting this new event to a group of beginners. She should make an attempt to help the girls overcome any feelings of apprehension of dread. Unfortunately, these feelings exist even though children have been leaping over barriers and jumping from heights as a normal playtime activity for generations. This fear, then, is a learned reaction. The more unfamiliar hurdling is to the girl, the more carefully the presentation must be made to develop confidence and the desire to acquire knowledge and understanding of as well as appreciation for this event.

Demonstration. A class of girls must see the action performed many times to understand what is expected of them in an activity such as hurdling. Almost every school will have someone in it who has had some experience in hurdling, either a student or a staff member, who may be used as a demonstrator. However, if none of the students or staff members (this is most likely to occur in an elementary or junior high school) can hurdle, then it may be necessary for the teacher to select a girl skilled in running and jumping and give her special instructions on how to hurdle so that a competent demonstrator is available. Of course, the teacher should do this prior to introducing hurdling to the class. To see a fellow student successfully hurdle should give beginners confidence that they too can learn to hurdle.

Girls should watch several repetitions of the hurdling action before attempting the movement so that a clear mental image is formed in their minds. An important fact to impress on students is that in clearing an obstacle one hurdles, no jumps; the difference should be made explicit. Films showing a hurdler in slow motion provide an excellent way of pointing out correct hurdling techniques to the girls and might well be used in lieu of demonstrations.

Sequence. As pointed out in Chapter 4, the skill of running must be developed in the girl before other events are attempted. Hurdling is basically a running event, with a leap interspersed at certain spots during the sprint. The running part of the activity should be familiar to the girls by now. However, to establish the feeling of confidence needed for successful hurdling, a girl should have had previous experience in activities that required her to leap through space and go over an obstacle. To learn some actions that may be transferred in learning to hurdle, it is recommended that girls participate in the standing broad jump, the long jump, and the high jump. After these events are successfully learned, beginners are less likely to fear going over hurdles.

Walking beside a hurdle. A girl should first walk alongside a hurdle in the direction that causes her lead leg to be closest to it. At first most girls will not know which leg is the lead leg, so all girls should start their walk on the same side of the hurdle until the teacher mentions that if it is uncomfortable for anyone to perform the exercise from this side, she should change her direction. Another method of determining the lead leg is for a girl to run to a given spot on the ground and jump off one foot into the air (such as the method used to determine the takeoff foot in the long jump); the takeoff foot is the trail leg and the other leg becomes the lead leg (the one to go over the hurdle first). This determination could be used until practice proves otherwise.

As a girl approaches the hurdle in this practice procedure, her lead leg is raised high in the air in an elongated high step motion; then the foot of the lead leg lands on the ground to the side and just ahead of the hurdle as the trail leg swings into rapid motion over and beyond the hurdle. The girl continues to walk a few strides beyond. The arms should swing naturally. This action is repeated until smoothness of motion and good rhythm are developed.

Walking over a hurdle. The same technique is used in walking over a hurdle as was used in walking beside a hurdle. However, a hop is added, whereby a motion is made by the takeoff foot to keep the lead leg straight as it later goes over the hurdle. The trail leg action is the same as that used in the walk beside a hurdle exercise. This action is repeated until smoothness of movement is acquired.

Running through gauze. A piece of narrow gauze is taped to the top of one hurdle and stretched across it to the top of another hurdle one hurdle's distance away and adjacent to the first hurdle. (It is through this space that the girl will make her first run.) The gauze is delicately placed on the second hurdle and held in place with another piece of tape; someone may hold it lightly in place while standing behind the hurdle. The slightest pressure from the body of a hurdler on the gauze should release it from the second hurdle. (This release action should be demonstrated to the girls.) The girl may thus be able to run through the gauze to get a feeling of hitting an obstacle and getting a sense of the height of a hurdle without being afraid. This procedure is used to build familiarity with the hurdles and to develop security on the part of the hurdler. Several hurdles placed parallel with each other should be set up with gauze strips across the top of them to enable the members of the entire class to run through the gauze at least twice in a short period of time to help them gain a feeling of security.

Clearing the gauze. The girl is now ready to hurdle over the gauze, approaching it at a jog rather than at a full run. She should practice going over the gauze many times until her hurdling form and rhythm are considered adequate and smooth enough to enable her to go over an actual hurdle. Only after she can successfully and repeatedly clear the gauze should she attempt to go over a standard hurdle.

Determining hurdle height. The height of a hurdle should depend on the age group of the girls learning the event. The elementary school age child should practice going over 18-inch hurdles. Some junior high school teachers believe that their students should first hurdle 24-inch hurdles and progress to the 33-inch hurdles. Thirty- and 33-inch hurdles are considered the official height for girls and women.

Jogging over a hurdle. Employing the same technique used in clearing the gauze, each girl should now attempt to go over a hurdle from a jog. She should jog up to and clear the hurdle, trying to make her actions as rhythmic as possible.

Running over a hurdle. Once she can jog over a hurdle, a girl should run over it, concentrating on making a snapdown of the lead leg as she does so and getting the trail leg to swing quickly up in a flat knee position as it goes over the hurdle. These moves should be repeated until the hurdling is done smoothly and the girl develops a normal running stride between the hurdles. Using a standing start the girl should determine just how many strides are required to reach the first hurdle—it will probably be seven or eight strides. Then she should run over one hurdle.

Running a flight. A girl should now run alongside three or more hurdles to get an idea of the distance between them. She should then run over correctly spaced hurdles. At first she may have to shorten the distance between hurdles or take five steps between hurdles. This phase must be constantly repeated until the girl is able to run a flight with the correct strides between each hurdle and until she can clear all the hurdles. (Four hurdles should be used for this practice phase.)

Using crouch start and step determination. All starts should now be taken from the blocks and the proper step (stride) pattern developed to be certain a girl is going over the first hurdle on the correct lead foot. If a girl consistently arrives at the takeoff point on the wrong foot, she will have to reverse her starting foot position to be on the correct foot for takeoff.

Recording times. Recorded times are a means of judging progress. This may be done anytime after the girl has developed a smooth hurdling style when running at her fastest speed. She should run in timed races for the full distance, competing against one or more performers. Also, at about the same time, she should run with a full complement of hurdlers to get the feeling of competing on a track composed of six or more hurdlers running a full flight. (Tables 9-2 and 9-3 show standards of performance that will help a novice to anticipate results.)

Repeated practice sessions. The practice sessions in hurdling should be held as regularly as the class or group participates in track and field events, until they have acquired some skill in the event. After this initial phase it is common procedure to permit students to choose their favorite events for specialization. However, participation in from three to five practice sessions is necessary for the average girl to understand hurdling. Naturally, the entire class period cannot be devoted to teaching hurdling; some time must be allotted to reviewing previously learned events and to introducing new events, with the result that it may take a girl as much as 2 or 3 weeks to learn to hurdle with any degree of success.

Conclusions. The following procedures are presented as guidelines for the teaching of hurdling to a beginning group of girls:

1. Acquire good physical fitness prior to participation in hurdling.
2. Introduce the hurdle event after instruction in the standing broad jump, long jump, and high jump events has been given to students.
3. Demonstrate proper techniques involved in hurdling using skilled hurdlers or slow motion films.
4. Walk beside a hurdle. (This is the first step to take in learning to hurdle.)
5. Walk over a hurdle.
6. Run through gauze.

Table 9-2. Standards of performance for the 50-yard hurdles*

Age	Type of competition	Expected time†
12-13	School beginner	8.6
12-13	School experienced	7.9
12-13	National record	7.1
14-17	Experienced	7.4
14-17	National record	6.3

*A girl can see from this chart where her results might place her on a given day in a meet of the caliber listed.
†These times can serve as a guide to the beginner in anticipating her degree of success. Times are in seconds.

Table 9-3. Standards of performance for the 100- and 200-meter hurdle races

Age	Type of competition	Expected time*	
		100 meters	200 meters
14-17	Beginner	16	37
14-17	Experienced	15	34
14-17	National record	13.7	30
Women	Experienced	15	31
Women	National record	12.9	22.8
Women	World record		22.4

*These times can serve as a guide for the beginner in anticipating degrees of success. Times are in seconds.

Fig. 9-8. Hurdler's exercise. This action stretches the leg and body muscles used while clearing the hurdle. Note the arm position as well as the trail leg and knee positions. The exercise should be done in a series of five bobs on each side, repeated three times.

Fig. 9-9. Leg extension and trunk flexion exercise. Hurdlers should use this exercise to develop leg extension (lead leg) and trunk flexion. The exercise, consisting of five to eight bobs on each side, should be repeated three times.

Fig. 9-10. Exercise for hurdlers. This exercise helps the hurdler get proper knee lift for easy clearance; trunk flexion and back leg extension are aided. This exercise should be repeated in a series of three for each leg with a total of five to eight bobs in each series.

Fig. 9-11. Thigh strengthening exercise. The arrow indicates the up and down direction of the leg and outward rotation of the thigh. Hurdlers and high jumpers should use this exercise. Each knee is lifted eight to ten times in one sequence, and the movement is repeated three times.

7. Clear the gauze.
8. Jog over a hurdle.
9. Run over a hurdle.
10. Run flights next, with four hurdles making up a flight.
11. Add the crouch start, with emphasis on the proper stride patterns to the first hurdle and between hurdles.
12. Record times and later compare them to obtain an indication of the progress made by the group.

TRAINING SUGGESTIONS

After participating in early season running and performing calisthenic exercises to gain endurance and muscle flexibility, runners could use the following sample schedule as a midseason weekly workout, with a meet held on Saturday.

Weekly schedule

MONDAY
1. Do stretching and loosening exercises such as (a) hurdler's exercise on the ground (Fig. 9-8), (b) lead-leg stretch on a hurdle (Fig. 9-9), (c) trail-leg stretch on a hurdle (Fig. 9-10), (d) thigh strengthening exercise on the ground (Fig. 9-11).
2. Run six 140-meter distances. Walk 140 meters for resting purposes after each run.
3. Run six 50-meter wind sprints.
4. Take two starts, going over four flights of hurdles.
5. Jog 400 meters.
6. Take a shower.

TUESDAY
1. Do stretching and loosening exercises.
2. Run two 140-meter distances doing 140-meter walks after each for a rest.
3. Take six starts going over two hurdles.
4. Run four flights of hurdles.
5. Jog 400 meters.
6. Take a shower.

WEDNESDAY
1. Do stretching and loosening exercises.
2. Run four 50-meter wind sprints.
3. Take two or three starts with the sprinters; go over two hurdles at full speed.
4. Take four starts running four hurdles, covering the full hurdle race distance on the last trial.
5. Jog 400 meters.
6. Take a shower.

THURSDAY
1. Do stretching and loosening exercises.
2. Run six 130-meter distances, with a walk of 130 meters interspersed after each run.
3. Take four to six starts and go over two hurdles.
4. Jog 400 meters.
5. Take a shower.

FRIDAY
1. Do stretching and loosening exercises.
2. Jog 400 meters slowly.
3. Take a shower.
4. Eat a good dinner and get plenty of rest and sleep the day before the meet.

SATURDAY
Meet day.

PART FOUR

Jumping

CHAPTER 10

Long jump

HISTORY AND BACKGROUND

The long jump, which was previously called the running broad jump, was probably the only jumping event included in the ancient Olympic games. However, women did not jump competitively until the London Olympics of 1948. At that time Mrs. Olga Gyarmati of Hungary won with a very modest distance of 18 feet 8¼ inches. New Zealand's Yvette Williams won in 1952 by jumping 20 feet 5¾ inches. In 1956 at Melbourne, a pigtailed girl from Poland, 17-year-old Elzbieta Krzesinsha won, equalling her own world record of 20 feet 9¾ inches. In 1960 at Rome, Vyera Krepina from Russia jumped 20 feet 10¾ inches. The 1964 Olympic participants and spectators in Tokyo saw Mary Rand of Great Britain jump 22 feet 2¼ inches for a new world record. In the 1968 Olympics the long jump was won by Viorica Viscopoleanu of Romania with a leap of 22 feet 4½ inches, which tied the existing world and Olympic records. Presently the American record is 21 feet 6 inches, set by Willye White in 1964. In 1970 Heide Rosendahl of West Germany jumped 22 feet 5¼ inches to set a new world record. She also won the 1972 Olympics with a jump of 22 feet 2¾ inches. In the 1976 Olympics Angela Voigt of East Germany won with a jump of 22 feet 2½ inches. Kathy McMillan of Raeford, North Carolina, was second with a jump of 21 feet 10½ inches.

The men's distance has increased about 6 feet in 70 years, whereas women have improved their distance by 3½ feet in 20 years. The late entrance of women into competitive long jumping is, for the most part, the fault of men officials and the press, who were slow to accept women as competitors in this event. There were also cultural forces in our society that frowned on women competing in any track activities. Long jumping as an event for women is now here to stay.

SPECIAL CONSIDERATIONS

The long jump area should consist of a landing pit 9 by 15 feet filled with sand, sawdust, or other soft materials. A much wider and longer pit is desirable for teaching and training beginners.

The pit surface should be kept level with the takeoff board, which is painted white and is 4 feet long, 8 inches wide, and 4 inches thick. The 4-inch thick slab is sunk flush with the ground. The distance from the toeboard to the pit will vary with the age group of the people for whom the pit is constructed. Elementary and junior high school girls should have a distance of 8 to 10 feet. High school sites usually have a distance of 12 feet to the

113

pit. Maximum distance is always 15 feet. However, it is recommended that when one is teaching beginners no takeoff board or mark of any kind be used. Rather, each jumper should feel free to approach the obstacle and jump from any point without restriction. A 30-foot pit would aid in the teaching of this event when using this concept. As the girls become able to jump, they should begin using the jumping board or a line marked off on the runway. In many cases beginners will not be able to jump the distance to the pit from the takeoff board. Therefore the teacher should paint another takeoff line closer to the pit to ensure the safety of all the jumpers by making sure they can land in the pit on their jumps.

All girls can perform the long jump—the short girl, the tall girl, the stout girl, and the slim girl, the untrained jumper, and the trained competitor. Martha Watson, the 1972 American Olympic jumper, is a small woman weighing less than 120 pounds. The most important qualities a jumper can have are great speed, for attaining good height to stay airborne for the longest possible time, and the ability to fully extend the knees and legs for a good landing. Long jumping is a relatively simple event that can be performed by girls enrolled in a physical education class, yet it is an extremely strenuous event when performed by top competitors. It demands year-round training to develop the strength, speed, and flexibility required to compete at a high level. The legs and feet of the jumpers must be strong enough to withstand the strain of landing and give explosive power at takeoff; leg strengthening exercises should be participated in prior to competing in this event.

Fast runners usually make good long jumpers. A well-coordinated and flexible girl who possesses good speed as well as good leg spring will usually perform well at long jumping. She must be a hard worker to increase her leg and abdominal strength and develop the general body strength that helps avoid injury. She should possess the emotional and mental characteristics that will enable her to better exercise her jumping power at the proper time. She should also work consistently and patiently on perfecting skill details that help develop confidence.

ELEMENTS OF JUMPING

The long jump, or running broad jump, is, as its names suggest, a run followed by a jump upward and forward. The object is to keep the body up in the air and travelling forward in space as far as possible. The faster the run and the higher the jump, the longer the body will stay in the air and the greater the distance it will travel. It is one continuous action from the start of the run until the landing in the pit takes place. The run, takeoff, and flight in the air are merely terms to describe the action.

The distance of the run for girls should be approximately 100 feet. A 120- to 150-foot distance is used by champions. The more highly trained in jumping and sprinting a girl is, the greater the distance she can run and remain relaxed before making her jump. The ability to be relaxed while running close to top speed comes from combining natural ability with arduous work and experience in competition.

Takeoff. It is best to place a check mark near the beginning of a run because a runner cannot concentrate on hitting numerous check marks with her feet and still be accelerating. However, she needs to have some system of checking her consistency of stride to know when to move her starting position forward or backward to hit the board properly. The runner begins with a standing start at the 100-foot mark and runs at full speed until she is 35 to 40 feet from the takeoff board. From this point she concentrates on relaxing while maintaining her speed without the full driving effort that was evident in the first part of the run. This relaxed running helps develop a smooth rhythm and controlled speed. The championship athlete must attempt to be consistent in her strides over the same distance every time, even though wind and track conditions vary considerably.

The runner's eyes should focus on the angle of takeoff (perhaps a point on a tree or building), but the takeoff board should be seen out of the corner of her eye when she is about five strides away from it. She may lower her body slightly in the last few strides as she prepares herself mentally and physically for the takeoff. The jumper contacts the board with a flat foot, with the heel naturally striking first and the toes pointed straight ahead (Fig. 10-1, *A*). At this point the jumper must concentrate on jumping high. She should try to hold her hips as high as possible so that her eyes, chin, and chest will point upward. As the takeoff foot strikes the board in a flat foot action with the heel striking first, the lead leg is swung vigorously forward and upward with the knee flexed and driven high. The sprint action of the run should be continued at the takeoff, causing the athlete to

Fig. 10-1. The long jump. This is the hitch kick style. **A,** The girl hits the board with her whole foot. **B,** She lifts her body off the board with the aid of her lead leg. **C,** She uses her right arm and right leg to thrust herself upward. **D,** Notice the long stride she takes in the air. **E,** The walk in the air begins here. **F,** The right arm is extended to the rear for balance. **G,** The right leg is extended in preparation for the landing. **H,** The left leg moves forward to meet the right leg. **I,** The left arm moves out to be approximately parallel with the right arm. **J,** Both legs are extended as the landing is made. **K,** The forward body lean, the extended arms, and bent knees enable the jumper to fall forward after landing.

run off the board with a forward and upward lift. The takeoff leg is stretched as far as possible before taking off; this natural extension is important for attaining height.

Techniques of delaying landing. There are three techniques used to delay landing by keeping the feet in the air as long as possible. These are the sail, the hitch kick, and the hang.

Sail. Beginning jumpers tend to depend on the sail technique because it is the simplest and easiest to learn (Fig. 10-2). After takeoff the lead leg is brought vigorously forward and upward. The takeoff leg is pulled forward and both legs are then carried in a partially bent position while the body sails forward. Strong abdominal muscles will help the jumper keep her feet up as long as posible. The jumper should endeavor to keep her heels as high as the hips and to reach forward.

Hitch kick. Some girls can learn to walk in the air (Figs. 10-1, *E,* and 10-3). This is done to increase balance, leg height, and leg extension to give the best possible landing position. This striding in the air, the so-called hitch kick, is very difficult for some jumpers to learn, but since it is thought to give the jumper an advantage it should be taught early. Nothing can be done after takeoff to change the flight path or increase momentum, since an athlete has to be in contact with the ground to exert force; only if sufficient height is attained can the hitch kick help the jumper in landing.

To perform the hitch kick the jumper must extend the takeoff leg fully after leaving the board, drive upward with the lead leg, and keep the trunk erect. In flight the legs must be

Fig. 10-2. The sail. This jumper sails above the pit in the long jump. The jumper should always try for height in her jump. This is a sitting, or sail, position in the air.

Fig. 10-3. Olympian Martha Watson in flight as she walks in air. She will thrust her arm downward in the next action. Her arm action is typical of her style.

in continuous motion forward and backward to limit forward body rotation. All these actions contribute to smooth rhythmic forward action of the legs and improve jumping performance. This alteration of leg action may be explained as follows. If the left foot is the takeoff foot, the right foot goes forward as the jumper drives upward and forward. When the right leg has assumed the full forward position, the left leg is swung forward to remain there as the right leg swings back and then forward again, even with the other leg in front of the body. The two legs must move together in a fully extended position for the landing. Normally the walk consists of one and a half strides (sometimes two and a half are used).

Hang. The hang is very difficult to perform because of the need for extremely strong abdominal muscles and hip flexors. The arching of the back at the height of the jump and the thrusting of the arms and legs forward cause a jolt to the body. The head is also thrown to the rear. To execute the hang after takeoff the lead leg straightens out beneath the body and swings backward with the knee bent. The takeoff leg, which is also bent at the knee, is moved alongside the lead leg. The trunk is slightly arched, and the body appears to hang

Fig. 10-4. Flight in the air in the long jump. This jumper has just thrust her arms and legs forward for her extension and lift forward. She is using a sail style of long jumping.

in the air momentarily. The legs are then thrust forward as the arms and the entire body reach for the landing (Fig. 10-4). This action is similar to the jackknife action in diving.

Landing. The landing is properly executed if it is accomplished in a nearly sit-down position with the legs fully extended forward until the buttocks reach a point almost touching the ground (Fig. 10-5). If the buttocks touch the ground, the distance of the jump will be measured from this spot to the takeoff board, thereby losing distance. This loss is avoided if the jumper moves her head and shoulders forward and puts her chin on her chest. The body should lean forward from the knees on landing, causing it to tip over the feet. If a girl falls forward too forcibly after landing, energy has been wasted and distance sacrificed because the height was not great enough to permit the body to gain distance, and the legs were probably not fully extended. The feet are kept close together and parallel while landing. The landing position is a very important aspect of the jump and should be practiced consistently (Fig. 10-6). Very strong abdominal muscles are required to keep the feet high while the jumper is in the air. As the heels touch the pit, the arms must be

Fig. 10-5. Landing preparation for the long jump. Note that the head is hung downward.

Fig. 10-6. Body action of a jumper while in flight and just prior to landing in the long jump.

lowered, brought forward, and then brought back to tuck the shoulders and head forward over the bent body.

RULES

For a beginning jumper to attain best results, she must be aware of the rule infractions that constitute fouls as well as other rules that govern her actions in long jumping.

1. It is a foul to touch the ground beyond the takeoff board, and such an action counts as a trial.

2. The break in the sand nearest the board made by any part of the body is the spot from which the distance of the jump is measured.

3. The jumper may place any kind of marker beside the runway, but no marker can be placed on the runway.

4. Three preliminary trials are allowed each competitor, and three additional jumps are permitted girls who qualify for the finals.

COMMON ERRORS

A jumper must be confident that she can hit the board without fouling and that she can get a good takeoff from a spot within an inch or two of the front edge of the board. This kind of confidence comes from consistent practicing of full run-ups, careful checking, and learning how to relax while running at near top speed while concentrating on jumping high in the air. It is recommended that full-scale jumping be practiced at least twice a week during the early part of the track season. Later, perhaps, one day a week could be allotted to full-scale jumping. Some coaches believe that no actual jumps should be taken after the season begins and that the performer should use only full run-throughs and pop-ups. Some common errors to avoid are (1) failure to get sufficient lift at takeoff, (2) inadequate extension of the legs on landing, (3) failure to lift the hips (the fulcrum of the body) high enough when attempting to gain height, and (4) failure to secure sufficient momentum from the run.

TEACHING PROGRESSION FOR THE BEGINNER

Track and field events are usually introduced to girls in physical education classes. Participation in the standing long jump is a lead-up to participation in the long jump because of the important similarity of the two forms of landing. Getting the legs out in front of the body, bending the knees to absorb the force of landing as the feet touch the ground, and keeping the body moving forward on landing are similarities that make it possible for an easy transition from the standing long jump to the running long jump.

Where weather conditions delay going outdoors, practice in long jumping can be commenced indoors. A double thickness of mats arranged perpendicular to the length of the gym and about 8 feet apart make good landing areas. This arrangement makes it possible for the instructor to give preliminary instruction to the entire class at one time. She is also able to observe many participants at one time and offer assistance when necessary. Any line painted on the floor that is not more than 3 feet from the near edge of the mats may be used as a takeoff spot. If a line is not conveniently located, adhesive tape applied in strips large enough to be easily seen may be used as the takeoff spot. The first step is to have the students make short runs at moderate speed, jump, and land on a target (a handkerchief or piece of tape) in about the center of the mats. The important points to stress at this time are the jump outward and upward and the execution of a proper landing. The use of a specific takeoff spot is not necessary if the mats are long enough. The speed used in the approach, the length of the approach run, and the distance from the target to the takeoff spot depend a great deal on the skill of the jumpers.

The jumper is now ready to learn how to use "pop-ups" when jumping. A pop-up is a short run made by the jumper to the takeoff board followed by a jump to help her improve her takeoff, action in the air, and landing. The short run is only a run-up into the jump, so there is no stamping down with the takeoff foot.

The following practices will help the beginner as well as the more advanced jumper.

1. Run off the board, working on height when jumping.

2. Do pop-ups for perfecting approach, takeoff, and landing.

3. Use full run-ups to check stride pattern.

The beginner must determine the length of the run she needs. This can be done by placing the takeoff foot on the takeoff board and running as fast as possible in the reverse direction. Place the first marker at the point where the girl cannot run any faster (probably about 100 feet from the takeoff board). It will be necessary to check the location of this marker repeatedly until the jumper and coach agree that this is the proper location for it. The jumper then starts from this point and runs as fast as she can to see if she is able to hit the board when running at top speed. She will need to use at least one more marker, usually placed five or six strides from the board. She must continue to relocate this marker until she strikes this and the first marker with the same foot during her approach run. She may move both markers forward or backward until she is satisfied that they are correct. There will be no effort made to jump on these initial attempts; the jumper will merely run through the pit and practice this maneuver until she is sure of where to begin her approach. When the length of the run has been definitely established, it will give the girl confidence to measure this as well as the second marker's distance to help her establish subsequent beginning marks for jumping on other fields.

She is now ready to give serious thought to ''running off the board.'' The performer must attain height to obtain distance, so her attention must be on gaining height as she leaves the takeoff board. She should run off the board, continuing the sprint action she has been doing on the runway, and her arms should be moving vigorously in an alternating fashion. The takeoff foot is stretched as the knee of the lead leg is flexed and driven high. The extension of the takeoff leg contributes to the height achieved and also increases the leg's range of motion in the air.

It is essential at this point to stress that a girl keep her trunk erect with her head held high, her eyes and chin looking up, and her chest lifted very high. The teacher should stand at the far end of the pit on a raised platform, holding a cane with a short strip of bright cloth tied to the middle of it and urging the jumper to keep her chest up and her eyes focused on the bright cloth. When the jumper can run off the board and get a good chest lift, she should be urged to move her legs under her and land in a heels-rock-forward position.

Athletes may practice running motions in the air while suspended from a horizontal bar or while supporting the body by the arms on parallel bars. Chair backs or two buddies' shoulders will substitute for parallel bars. To facilitate learning this phase, the placing of a gymnast's springboard over the takeoff board will give the performer more time in the air after a jump.

A good teaching progression for learning the hitch kick is to have a girl take a short run, then jump from the springboard, springing high and forward with the jumping leg and landing on the lead leg. The next step is to have her run and jump from the springboard, walk in the air (alternate leg motion), and land on the takeoff leg. Next have the girl try the full hitch kick, taking one and a half strides in the air and landing with both legs stretched forward. If the left foot is the takeoff foot, the right foot is swung forward then back as the left leg is swung forward. The right foot is pulled forward again as both feet are stretched for the landing. The springboard is then removed and the hitch kick is practiced from the takeoff board as the jumper again tries to make her head touch the bright cloth tied to the middle of the cane. Each of these progressions is repeated until the jumper is able to perform the separate acts. Coordination of the complete pattern is practiced until it becomes automatic. The pop-up method is useful for teaching upward-outward jumping for height and good landing, and it should be included as part of each practice session.

Every effort should be made to keep the heels up as long as possible in practicing landings. Landing efficiency is increased if the arms are brought down and thrust backward behind the jumper. Good abdominal strength will help keep the legs stretched forward as far as possible.

The third phase of the learning-training procedure is to use the full run-ups or full-scale jumping. This consists of employing all the elements required in competion—the approach, the takeoff, and the landing.

Some coaching hints. The coach should help the jumper with the following:

1. Running off the board and focusing her eyes on a spot about 45 degrees above the horizon
2. Keeping her heels in the air as long as possible
3. Holding frequent short practices rather than a few practices of long duration
4. Moving the check markers back 3 or 4 inches in practice sessions to make sure of getting a measurable jump in a meet (All-out effort on subsequent jumps with the markers moved back to their original location can then be attempted.) (See Table 10-1 for standards.)
5. Performing some complete jumps each week to gain confidence and alleviate fouling
6. Patiently and continuously practicing approach, takeoff, and landing techniques
7. Exercising to develop leg power during the off-season
8. Landing in a sitting position on mats (In indoor situations, the coach can paint

Table 10-1. Standards of performance for the long jump*

Age	Type of competition	Expected distance†
10-11	School beginner	11 feet 6 inches
10-11	School experienced	12 feet 6 inches
10-11	National record	16 feet 9 inches
12-13	School beginner	12 feet 6 inches
12-13	School experienced	14 feet
12-13	National record	17 feet 2 inches
14-17	School beginner	13 feet
14-17	School experienced	15 feet 6 inches
14-17	National record	19 feet 8½ inches
Women	College beginner	16 feet
Women	Experienced	18 feet
Women	National record	22 feet 3 inches
Women	World record	22 feet 11¼ inches

*There is much room for improvement by the women who perform in this event, especially at the beginning level, as the wide range of distances proves.
†These distances can serve as a guide to the beginner in anticipating degrees of success.

numbers alongside mats so that the girls will know how far they are jumping.)
9. Using the springboard twice a week in early season practice periods to learn the value of getting good height and the feeling of jumping great distances

TRAINING SUGGESTIONS

A year-round program of general conditioning is necessary for the long jumper if she is to perfect the required skills and withstand the strain placed on the body by jumping. However, she can train by using a variety of methods and still have a good time. She can enjoy all the things that high school girls are wont to enjoy while becoming a superior athlete. Her conditioning may include participation in cross-country running, dancing, gymnastics, games, rope skipping, sprinting, jogging, Fartlek, circuit training, interval running, high jumping, weight training, isometric training, hurdling, and hill running. (See Table 10-2.)

Daily practice sessions of 30 to 45 minutes are better for beginners than are longer sessions scheduled less frequently. The more mature jumpers can practice for longer periods. Practice sessions consist of general conditioning exercises, fifteen to twenty short runs to work on form, and full-scale jumping or pop-ups once or twice a week.

Circuit training program. A circuit training program may be used by the long jumper for indoor conditioning before weather permits outdoor action. It may also be used to add variety to the weekly practice schedule outlined in Table 10-2.

The complete circuit A consists of performing the exercises at station 1 two times, station 2 three times, station 3 three times, station 4 ten times, station 5 three times, and station 6 six times. The performer may repeat the circuit twice in the same order, using the same repetitions. A complete circuit is performed three times. Circuits B and C are progressively more difficult, and doing a complete circuit consists of the performer doing the exercises three times each.

Following is an explanation of the procedures to follow in the six station items shown in the circuit training table.

Station 1: Do a run-up to accelerate. A distance of 100 feet is marked off. From a sprint starting position the runner covers this distance as fast as she can. She then runs this distance in the opposite direction, trying to hit her regular outdoor marks with her strongest foot. This action is then repeated.

Station 2: Do widespread leg-lifts. A series consists of lifting the knees to the chest while in a supine position and slowly lowering the legs until the straightened legs are approximately 4 inches off the floor. The legs are spread wide and brought back together

Table 10-2. Circuit training program for long jumpers

Item and station number	A	B	C
Run-up to accelerate	2	3	4
Widespread leg-lifts	3 series	4 series	5 series
Run off springboard	3	4	5
Leg raises	10	20	25
Jump for height over 3 feet in long jump position	3	4	5
Vertical jump	6	12	18

five times before the knees are again brought to the chest. This is repeated two more times, making a total of three series.

Station 3: Run off the springboard. The springboard is placed in front of a double thickness of tumbling mats. The run-up distance is only 40 feet. The performer runs up, springs from the board, and attempts to walk in the air and land with both legs fully extended. This is done three times.

Station 4: Do leg raises. The girl lies supine, bends the knees to the chest, extends them overhead, and slowly lowers both legs to the floor.

Station 5: Jump for height over a 3-foot bar in a long jump position. A takeoff mark is placed 3 feet in front of the bar. The landing area is composed of a double thickness of mats. The jumper attempts three jumps aiming for maximum height each time.

Station 6: Do vertical jumps. The performer measures how high she can extend the fingers of one hand. She then jumps vertically to see how much height she can attain with her outstretched hand touching a mark on a wall. Partners record measurements of each other's jumps. The vertical jump is made six times.

The following exercises are excellent as an outdoor circuit for all jumpers and hurdlers (jogging and stretching exercises should be done prior to performing them):

1. Wind sprints
2. Leg raises
3. Five starts running 100 feet
4. Three flights of low hurdles
5. Five jumps using full runs
6. Fifteen pop-ups
7. Bench step-ups and step-downs (3 to 5 minutes)
8. Horizontal bar leg lifts

Weekly schedule

MONDAY
1. Jog on the grass barefoot 400 meters.
2. Do stretching exercises for 5 minutes.
   a. Hurdle exercises from a sitting position
   b. Toe touch with high knee lift
   c. Leg lifts
   d. Sit-ups
   e. Trunk twisters
3. Run three or four wind sprint series with the sprinters.
4. Check starting marks (work with partner) by running through the distance six times.
5. Perform twelve pop-ups for development of height and leg extension.
6. Run three flights of hurdles.
7. Do horizontal bar leg raises for 5 minutes.
8. Do 50 sit-ups.
9. Jog around the track and go to the showers.

TUESDAY
1. Warm up by jogging around the track.
2. Do stretching exercises.
3. Run several wind sprints.
4. Do six pop-ups.
5. Take six starts; run through the pit several times.
6. Run one 200-meter distance.
7. Do leg lifts and sit-ups.
8. Jog around the track and go to the showers.

WEDNESDAY
1. Warm up by jogging around the track.
2. Do stretching exercises.
3. Run several wind sprints.
4. Do six pop-ups.
5. Do eight full jumps.
6. Run one 300-meter distance.
7. Do several horizontal bar leg lifts.
8. Jog around the track and go to the showers.

THURSDAY
1. Warm up by jogging around the track.
2. Do stretching exercises.
3. Run several wind sprints.
4. Run three flights of 50-yard hurdles.
5. Run 100 meters four times as a part of the relay.
6. Do six pop-ups.
7. Do horizontal leg lifts and sit-ups.
8. Jog around the track and go to the showers.

FRIDAY
Rest if there is a meet on Saturday; if not, do the following:
1. Warm up by jogging around the track.
2. Do stretching exercises.
3. Run several wind sprints.
4. Check on step pattern by running through three times.
5. Do six full jumps (for record).
6. Run 200 meters as a part of the 800-meter race.
7. Jog around the track and go to the showers.

SATURDAY
If meet is held on Saturday, do the following before competing:
1. Warm up.
2. Do exercises.
3. Jog slowly around the track two or three times.

CHAPTER 11

High jump

HISTORY AND BACKGROUND

Women are now jumping a foot higher than they did in the first women's Olympic games held in Amsterdam. There were 121 women who competed in five track and field events in the modern Olympics for the first time in 1928. That year Ethel Catherwood of Canada high jumped 5 feet 3 inches. In contrast, in 1964 in Tokyo, Iolanda Balas of Rumania set a new Olympic record of 6 feet 2¾ inches, which was 11¾ inches higher than the 1928 record. Miss Balas has dominated the high jump event for several years, and she established a world record of 6 feet 3 inches on July 16, 1964 in Sofia, Bulgaria.

In the 1976 Olympics Rosemarie Ackermann from East Germany jumped 6 feet 4 inches for a new Olympic record. The world record is 6 feet 4¾ inches (Table 11-1).

The increased height attained by men and women is probably caused by the participation of more and better trained and conditioned athletes, development of improved training programs, introduction of superior styles of jumping, and the utilization of improved jumping areas. Thus better footing at the takeoff areas and shock-proof landing pits have contributed immeasurably to the efficiency of women jumpers. Furthermore, jump training methods that ultimately involve utilization of greater upward thrust power have helped in the improvement of women's high jump performances.

SPECIAL CONSIDERATIONS

Long-legged rangy girls often make good jumpers, but, like performers in other events, jumpers cannot be typed. When looking for jumpers, watch for the springy girl; she will come in all sizes and shapes. Good jumpers should be hard workers, get a thrill out of jumping, have elasticity, possess strong leg muscles, and above all have a compelling desire to learn, train, and improve themselves. The excellent jumper has the ability to show almost complete freedom from tenseness.

The girl who is a good dancer, has an abundance of grace and rhythm, is well coordinated, and has a good sense of timing will usually improve rapidly in her ability to high jump. A girl needs a strong body, an exceptional spring in her legs, and the stamina to work hard and long to become a really good high jumper. She must also have determination to improve and develop the confidence that is needed to succeed. This confidence, so necessary for good high jumping, can be realized through regular and faithful dedication to training. At the beginning the average girl will be anxious about attempting to clear the bar at almost any height; the confidence and relaxation that are so necessary to success

Table 11-1. The Olympic record for the women's high jump

Year	Athlete	Country	Height
1928	Ethel Catherwood	Canada	5 feet 3 inches
1932	Jean Shiley	United States	5 feet 5¼ inches
1936	Ibolya Csah	Hungary	5 feet 3 inches
1948	Alice Coachman	United States	5 feet 6⅛ inches
1952	Ester Brand	South Africa	5 feet 5¾ inches
1956	Mildred L. McDaniel	United States	5 feet 9¼ inches
1960	Iolanda Balas	Rumania	6 feet ¼ inch
1964	Iolanda Balas	Rumania	6 feet 2¾ inches
1968	Milena Rezkova	Czechoslovakia	5 feet 11¾ inches
1972	Ulrike Meyfarth	West Germany	6 feet 3½ inches
1976	Rosemarie Ackermann	East Germany	6 feet 4 inches

in good jumping are acquired through experience. Good high jumping fundamentals must be practiced until habits are well established. A girl who realizes only one good jump out of every four trials will soon be out of the competition. The good jumper must have a consistency that leads to perfection, and care must be exercised to see that she does not lose her zip or allow her competitive edge to become dulled. This consistency leading to mastery is a result of a training program carefully followed over a period of time. A flexible schedule containing varied workouts that are fun and interesting increases the effectiveness of the training program.

ELEMENT OF JUMPING

High jumping consists of a run, a jump, and a layout over a barrier, a crossbar resting on two upright standards. A proper landing area is of great importance in preventing injury as well as encouraging beginning jumpers to defy gravity and thrust themselves up high over the bar.

If landing is made on a hard surface, a scissors type of jump must be the style used. If landing is made in a sawdust pit, a three-point landing on two hands and one leg may be best; but if landing is made on a soft area, the jumper should learn to roll over the bar and land on her back or side. This roll over the bar may be a reverse rollover, as in the flop.

A safe landing area consists of a foam rubber pit or air-filled surface possessing no hard or dangerous boundaries. A deeply dug pit filled with sawdust and sand can be used and may be constructed safely and economically. The pit should be spaded to a depth of at least 2 feet and filled to an 18-inch elevated height with equal parts of sand and sawdust.

Styles of jumping

Western roll. The western roll is a good style for the beginner to use. It is especially advantageous for developing good takeoff habits for straddle jumpers. However, now it is seldom if ever used in competition. The bar is approached by running to it from an angle of approximately 45 degrees. The takeoff is made from the inside foot; the layout position is on top of the bar, with the jumper clearing it on her side and landing on both hands and the takeoff foot.

The approach is composed of a short run of about five to seven strides and is done in a rather deliberate manner (at about three-quarters speed). The last three strides are the fastest as the girl gathers herself for the takeoff.

The takeoff foot is firmly planted, with the heel being the first to strike the ground. As the heel is planted, the lead leg is swung through quickly, reaching upward in a ballistics-like motion as it stretches to a point above the bar. The weight of the body at takeoff is behind the jumping foot as the girl leans slightly backward. The lead leg should be kicked upward as high as possible as the spring is made from the takeoff foot. The head and chest are kept upright, and the arms are first moved downward then upward as the jumper springs into the air. Her eyes are focused at about the desired jumping height, even if the bar is not as high as eye level. As the body rises upward there is a stretching out, a sort of pause, and then the layout over the bar is made. In the layout position the girl's body is placed alongside the bar, parallel with it, and the takeoff leg is kept in a tucked position with the knees of both legs moved nearly together. To elevate the hips the jumper drops her head and arms downward as soon as they have crossed the bar. By looking down into the pit at a given point the head and hands will be forced downward, and consequently the hips will rise. The landing is made on two hands and the takeoff foot, with the head facing the general direction from which the approach was made (Fig. 11-1).

Straddle roll. The straddle role is used by many high jumpers and is generally recognized as one of the more efficient styles of jumping (Fig. 11-2). The angle the jumper uses in approaching the bar will vary considerably from one jumper to another. It is very important that each jumper try to be consistent in the angle used, the number of steps taken, and the speed of the run. A suggested angle is one between 35 and 40 degrees. The length of the run is about seven strides, and the speed of the run should be very controlled, with the last three strides being the fastest. This increase in speed naturally lengthens the stride.

Fig. 11-1. Going over the bar using the western roll. This girl is using a right-foot takeoff.

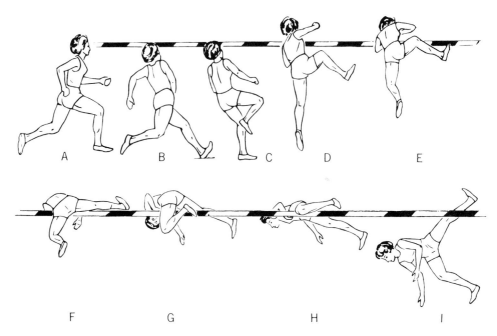

Fig. 11-2. The straddle form of high jumping. **A,** This girl is running easily during her approach. **B,** She is planting her heel well but leaning too much toward the left. **C,** There should be more body lean toward the rear at this stage of the jump. **D,** The arms are not high enough; however, there is good extension in the takeoff leg. **E,** The lead leg is bent at the knee: it should be fully extended. **F,** The body position on top of the bar is good. **G,** The girl's head is leading the descent, which is considered correct. Perhaps her left elbow is too high. **H,** The turn over the bar is almost complete. At this point she should begin to turn her head so it will eventually face the sky. **I,** She is preparing for the landing. She should land more on her back than on her side.

Fig. 11-3. Clearing the high jump bar. This girl is using a straddle dive to successfully clear a good height. This competition was held during the 1968 Olympic trials.

The jumper should have her eyes focused on the point of takeoff and then look at an imaginary target just above the crossbar.

The final stride before planting the takeoff or inside foot is the beginning phase of transferring forward speed into a vertical lift. This is the moment of a brief settling of the body as the hips drop and the body gathers to aid in the upward spring. The toes of the takeoff foot are turned outward to get the most upward thrust as the heel is planted for the lift. A vigorous swinging kick is made with the opposite leg. As the takeoff foot is planted, a very fast lead leg is swung through vigorously kicking to a point above the bar. The knee of the lead leg may be bent, or it may be nearly straight. The important factor is that the leg be kicked high to get the hips high before starting rotation. There is a slight backward lean and slight rolling forward with a heel-ball action to set the entire foot into the spring.

The explosive spring done with the takeoff leg, the upward swinging lead-leg thrust, and the upward action of the arms are the forces that have to be put together for good takeoff action. The tendency for the body to lean toward the bar at the takeoff because of the subsequent face-down layout position assumed on top of the bar must be avoided. The takeoff must be as nearly vertical as possible to raise the body's center of gravity as high as possible before the layout begins. The kick, or lead, leg often reaches a point above the bar when the takeoff foot is still in contact with the ground. As the body is forced upward with head and chest elevated, the arms are alternately thrust downward and then upward at takeoff to bring the body up as high as possible (Fig. 11-3).

Successful clearance is dependent on getting a good lift at takeoff and then rotating around the bar with the greatest efficiency. The takeoff is the important focus, and only as force is applied for the longest possible time will the body be lifted for greatest clearance. When the jumper's head has risen to its full height, she will find that she can safely start to drop her head and at the same time lower her upper body, thus enabling her to raise the lower part of her body. The jumper rolls around the bar, with the right arm reaching across the bar and downward as the left or inside arm is held alongside the body. The rotation of the body is continued right into the pit, with the jumper landing on her back.

Back flop. More and more jumpers are finding success with the use of the back flop style of jumping. The flop is easy to learn, relatively uncomplicated with few technicalities to cause problems, and a great deal of fun because of the sensation of flight engendered by flying backward over the bar. It was introduced by Dick Fosbury and used in the 1968 Olympics. It incorporates and modifies the scissors jump style. The use of better landing pits for safe and comfortable landings has contributed to all styles of jumping, but it has especially increased the confidence of back floppers. The plain scissors jump, a fundamental leap, involves transferring the weight from one foot to another in the action from takeoff to landing and is the style youngsters are prone to learn early in their lives as they clear barriers (Fig. 11-4).

The angle of approach for the back flopper may vary significantly. The jumper may run from the right side of the jumping area, making an inverted J curve; from the left side of the area, making a reverse inverted J curve; or from a position directly in front of the bar in a curved path to end up near the side of the bar, making a reversed C curve. A curve approach is employed to facilitate the rotatory movements of the body needed to clear the

Fig. 11-4. Back flop style of high jumping. Note that the jumper takes off from the ground with her outside leg. Also note that the jumper first executes a scissorlike jump and then twists to roll over the bar on her back. This style is becoming more and more popular with women.

bar. The jumper will predetermine a takeoff spot, the exact number of steps required, and the kind of curved path she will use.

If the left foot is the takeoff foot, the approach will be made from the right side of the jump area. Speed is usually built from an eight-step approach (r-l-r-l-r-l), with the stride being lengthened in the last three steps. The run is made with speed, confidence, and no hesitation occurring along the approach route.

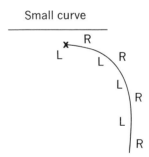

The outside foot is planted in the line of flight, with the knee flexed. The inside bent knee is lifted vigorously upward. The driving takeoff leg forces the body upward. The lift with the arms and shoulders is less than in the case of the other styles. The body is turned to the side as the jump from the ground begins, and then as the body is in the air the jumper rotates so she goes over the bar backward. First there is the upward leap and then hyperextension of the trunk, causing the body to be in a more horizontal position. The head and shoulders are lowered toward the pit, causing the hips and buttocks to be lifted over the bar. The hips are lifted over the bar, followed by the lift of the knees, then the feet. The jumper looks toward her feet as her bent legs clear the bar followed by her ankles. The legs are extended just as they go over the bar. The jumper lands on her upper back as she strikes the pit.

Fig. 11-5. Back flopper in action. Note takeoff position, flight over the bar, and landing.

RULES

To achieve the best possible results from her efforts the beginner should be aware of the rules that govern high jumping.

1. A competitor may begin jumping at the starting height or at any subsequent height. The bar may not be lowered to allow a latecomer to commence jumping.
2. A competitor may choose to pass her turn at any of the heights and try for the next height. Three successive failures, regardless of the height tried, eliminates a girl from further competition. The highest height jumped is the height recorded.
3. It is counted as a trial when a girl, in the act of jumping, knocks the bar off the supports or breaks the imaginary line under the bar in any manner.
4. If a competitor touches the ground beyond the plane of the uprights without clearing the bar (such as going under the bar), it counts as a trial jump.
5. A competitor may place any markers in any position she desires to aid her approach run. Also, a sighting marker such as a small cloth may be placed on top of the crossbar as a target.
6. The competitor must use a one-foot takeoff.

COMMON ERRORS

Most faults made by the high jumper occur at her takeoff point. The coach should station herself at various vantage points along the approach route to observe the jumper in action. Also, at times the coach should observe from a position in back of the jumper, from either side of the jumper, and from across the pit in front of the jumper to get a clear view of the girl's entire process of approach, takeoff, and clearance. From these vantage points the coach may be able to observe the following errors.

Too slow an approach does not give the jumper enough speed to convert horizontal velocity into vertical lift. Too fast an approach does not give her time to coordinate her action so that she can get a good plant against the ground.

When the jumper takes off too close to the bar, the angle of projection is too far beyond the bar, and the jumper will usually strike the bar on the way up. If the athlete takes off from a distance too far from the bar, she will come down on top of it.

Striking the bar with the thigh of the trailing leg in straddle jumping may indicate that the girl has started clearance too soon and needs to work harder on getting a much more solid lift from the ground. Failure to kick the lead leg upward before springing from the takeoff foot in straddle jumping will interfere with attaining height. It is important that the center of gravity be raised as high as possible at takeoff.

Too long an approach run is unnecessarily taxing and may interfere with timing. Too short an approach run does not provide sufficient velocity to get good upward lift.

In the back flop, failing to keep the hips forward causes the hips to knock off the crossbar. Allowing the feet to drop into the crossbar can be avoided in the back flop by making a concerted effort to lift them over the bar.

TEACHING SUGGESTIONS FOR THE BEGINNER

Jumping skills are first introduced to kindergarten children as they learn to move rhythmically in a variety of ways. Through participation in basic movement experiences, relays, and stunts, elementary school children learn the difference between a hop, a jump, and a leap. High jumping is usually introduced to upper elementary school children in physical education classes and in after-school play. Participation in junior high school physical education activities such as dance, stunts, trampoline, free exercise, rope skipping, tumbling, and relays affords many opportunities for jump training.

The various styles of jumping include the western roll, the straddle roll, the straddle roll with dive, and the back flop. Some styles involving the use of tumbling action over the bar have been experimented with. However, any style may be used with the beginner as long as it involves a firm one-foot takeoff and a fast lead leg with vigorous upward thrust.

Some instructors teach the scissors style of high jumping to elementary school children because it is easy to learn and a child can enjoy immediate success with it. If a safe landing pit is not available, the scissors style will have to be the only style used by the novice jumper. Since the flop style of jumping is a modified scissors style, there will be opportunity for carry-over learning at a later time when safe landing areas are available.

It is suggested that competitive straddle jumpers learn to use the western roll first and later change over to the straddle roll jumping style. Good fundamentals of jumping are employed in the western roll—a high upward kick and a good firm takeoff. The straddle jump is one of the most commonly used styles today, since jumpers can clear greater heights without lifting the total body mass as high as in the western roll. In the straddle roll the body lies flat over the bar with the jumper facing it, and the body's center of gravity need not be lifted as high as in the western roll to clear the bar at a given height. The dive has been added to this style, which further enhances the jumper's chance of clearing the bar. The back flop style of jumping has been gaining in popularity since the 1968 Olympics. Many coaches believe that the flop may be a more efficient style of jumping than is the straddle. The teacher will want to introduce various styles of clearing the bar and build on the developing competence of the individual jumpers.

High jumping fundamentals can be taught to the prospective jumpers in the gymnasium by using tumbling mats or similar floor padding for protection in landing. This is particularly beneficial when girls are prevented by inclement weather from going out to the field to use the jumping pit. The coach must provide sufficient padding to prevent injury to the jumpers. Sponge rubber and other synthetic materials are also satisfactory landing materials. Safe indoor landing pits are commercially available. Heavy cord or slender cane poles may be used as crossbars, and jump standards can be made quite easily out of beams set in weighted motor scooter tires. An elastic cord that is weighted on either end and prepared so that it slips easily off the uprights is probably the best substitute for a crossbar. A 2-foot length of ½-inch elastic tied to cords with bean bags attached to the ends is a substitute crossbar that is easy to carry around, stretches when a body part encounters it, and saves time because it does not have to be replaced on the uprights.

Jumping pits may be added to a regular outdoor playing field if such areas are not available. The entire area of one pit (20 by 20 feet is a convenient size) should be dug to a depth of not less than 18 inches and filled to overflowing with sawdust or fine wood shavings. Burlap bags filled with sawdust should outline the back and sides of the area to mark off the boundary and keep the filler from being dissipated. The landing area should be built up high enough so jumpers will be encouraged to jump to their greatest heights, knowing that the landing will not be an uncomfortable experience.

Pits may be constructed on top of the ground. The sawdust or wood shavings pit is 4 or more feet high. The sides of the pit are filled with grass sacks placed close enough together to contain the filler. Sometimes wooden sides are used to a height of 2 feet, with the sacks composing the rest of the border. However, the best pit is a portable one composed of foam rubber or air-filled material in a canvas container, which provides a very soft landing surface.

Teaching the western roll. Regardless of the girls' ages, the teacher must first discover girls who like to jump, have a natural leg spring for jumping, and are strong enough to jump or have the desire to develop the strength needed for jumping.

A good instruction plan to use in the beginning phases is to have the girls line up in two columns facing the front of the pit, with the jump bar set only a few inches off the ground. Then the girls are asked to hop over the bar. A hop consists of jumping into the air off the right foot and landing on the right foot, or taking off on the left foot and landing on the left foot. After repeated trials have been made to determine the best takeoff foot, those who hop better off the left foot are placed in the left column and those who hop better off the right are placed on the right side. The bar is raised a few inches at a time, and the girls continue to hop over it. The girls in the left column turn to the left after clearing the bar, and those in the right column turn to the right. With the bar set at a height of about 2½ feet, jumpers approach it from a line that is a definite distance away (a chalk or tape mark placed on the gymnasium floor or a line or stick used in outdoor situations), about five to seven strides from the bar. Now the jumpers are encouraged to kick the lead leg high in the air as they go over the bar. Any effort to use another style of jumping, such as diving or twisting, is discouraged at this time. A girl who attempts to do so must hop over a line on the ground or floor until the patterns of the western roll are reestablished.

The jumpers are encouraged to clear the bar by 6 to 12 inches if they can do so. At this point the height they attain is not especially important. This is the time that they should be praised, encouraged, and told to have fun and enjoy doing something that perhaps they thought they could not do at the beginning.

As experimentation reveals the interested and capable jumpers, instruction is carried a step further. The girls now run toward a slightly higher bar, kick the free leg up quickly, and hop over. As the body of each jumper goes over the bar, the arms reach down toward the takeoff foot, thus causing her to land on her two hands and the takeoff foot. At this point the jumpers understand they are executing a western roll. The jumpers now attempt to stride to the bar, kick the free leg up vigorously, and spring off the floor or ground with the takeoff leg raised as high as possible.

The length of the approach or run-up is determined by the use of the buddy system, whereby a friend helps check another's stride pattern. One girl stands with her back to the crossbar and faces outward at a 45-degree angle; then she runs as she would in approaching the jump bar. The other girl checks where her friend's seventh stride occurs and marks it. This process should be repeated a few times for verification of distance.

The location of an exact takeoff spot for beginning jumpers is best determined if the coach allows the girls to jump without mentioning the takeoff spot. At this stage the coach should place emphasis on just getting over the bar; the particulars of the takeoff procedure can be worked out at a later time. Nevertheless, she should inform the girls subsequently that the takeoff spot is usually about an arm's length from the bar. She should emphasize that the spring upward comes from a firmly placed foot that exerts a force against the ground, causing the body to rise vertically. Also, she can correct any inclination to lean into the bar by stressing that the head and chest are to be held erect, and that the eyes should focus on a point at which a higher bar will eventually be located.

The once popular western roll has all but disappeared from top-class competition; however, it is a good jump to teach beginners. Because there is near maximum lift at takeoff, it affords a relatively safe landing position, and the jumper is less likely to lean into the bar before maximum height is reached.

Teaching the straddle roll. The straddle roll is usually taught after the jumper has mastered the style of western roll high jumping (Fig. 11-1).

With the takeoff foot predetermined, the right-footed jumpers line up at an acute angle with their right side next to a line on the ground, and the left-footed jumpers place themselves at an acute angle with their left side next to the line. Girls walk to the line and step over it, transferring their weight from the right foot to the left. The left-footed jumpers transfer from left to right. With the takeoff foot next to the line the girl swings the free, or lead, leg up and over the line and springs off the takeoff leg, landing on the foot of the free leg. This action is repeated a number of times until the girl readily understands the transfer of weight from the takeoff foot to the foot of the lead leg. The above action is repeated with the jumper running easily on the approach, swinging the lead leg over the line, springing off the takeoff foot, and landing on the foot of the lead leg.

The jumper is then ready to try the straddle style of high jumping. She is first allowed to land on the back of her body to get the feel of landing in the pit. As the jumper takes off from the inside foot, kicking the lead leg up high, the trunk should be facing the same direction as the lead leg so the jumper will feel she is being pulled off the ground by the swing of the lead leg. This keeps her from leaning into the bar before maximum height has been reached. At this point in learning it is important that the bar be placed twice as high as the height of the jumper's knees. If the beginner fails to get lift and leans into the bar before she has left the ground, she should return to the western roll style of jumping for a few sessions.

The jumper will now use a three-step approach and jump to improve lead leg action, clearance of the bar, and landing using the straddle style. The bar is then raised to near what is considered her maximum jumping height, and the jumper works to attain a full swing of the lead leg at takeoff and to increase the power of the lift needed to get the body high into the air.

Teaching the back flop. For beginners wishing to learn the Fosbury flop, the takeoff foot is the foot farthest from the bar, so the left-footed beginning jumper will be approaching the bar from the right side. The jumpers will first resort to the old-fashioned scissors style of jumping, taking off with the outside or left foot and kicking the right leg up and over the bar, landing on the right foot. This is a natural action that need only be done a few times.

In executing the flop the girl will swing the right leg upward from a standing position as she springs from the left foot and land sitting in the foam pit, lifting both legs high as she falls on her back. This action is practiced without the use of a bar until the girl gets a substantial lift of the body and is bringing her legs up high as she sinks into the pit. Next, she takes a three-step approach (right-left-right-left) and then she takes off, and lands in the pit.

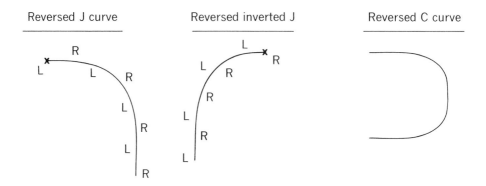

The jumper taking off with the left foot will approach a medium-height bar from the right side of the area. She will run with an easy stride in a straight line, starting on the right foot. On about the fourth step she will gradually curve left toward the center of the bar and continue to complete a reversed J curve until the predetermined takeoff spot is reached. She plants the left foot with a heel-ball-toe action and drives upward, extending the left leg and lifting the right knee, right arm, and body above the bar. The left foot begins a rotating action before takeoff that is carried through the hips and upper body as the jumper moves from a position parallel with the bar to one that is perpendicular and backward to the bar. The head and shoulders clear first, with the hips being lifted forward to clear. The knees are lifted over the bar followed by the ankles. The landing is taken on the upper back.

The eight-step approach for the jumper taking off with the left foot begins on the right foot. The jumper runs as if she is going toward a point in line with her start, and then she curves toward the takeoff point. To approach consistency with this style of jumping, there must be concentration on making the same curving action each time the bar is cleared. The jumper may be assisted in developing constancy by using a method of foot-printing. She could step lightly in lime, chalk dust, or water to see the path of her movement.

It will be observed that it is the fourth step that begins the curve to the left. There is gradual acceleration with the lengthening of the sixth and seventh strides to allow for a slight settling of the body and a lowering of the center of gravity. On takeoff the body is already starting to move upward, and the kick is coordinated with the upward swing of the arms and shoulders, primarily the arm closest to the bar. The back is turned to the bar as the body leaves the ground. The hips are lifted forward with the back arched to clear the bar. The knees are lifted, followed by the feet, with the arms reaching overhead to help accomplish clearance.

TRAINING PROGRAM

Proper conditioning of the body must be done in a continuous manner. The better the jumper's physical condition, the better she jumps. This is usually true of all track and field performers, but it seems to be especially true of high jumpers. Since active girls are interested in performing in several events, a wise coach will encourage the jumpers to take part in other events too. The use of special dance training exercises may prove valuable to jumpers. To develop proper strength and speed the jumper will need to follow the same training and conditioning schedule as sprinters do.

To win at high jumping, participation in a full strength-building and conditioning program is necessary. Weight training, running, jumping, and jump training are the essentials in such a program. Jump training designed to strengthen both legs is done by running up hills, running up stairs, hopping over barriers, and jumping or leaping from special vaulting boxes set at different heights (see Table 11-2 for standards of performance).

Conditioning during off-season. Weight-training exercises, such as using leg-press machines, performing one-half squats with added weight on the shoulders, and using iron boots in walking and running, can be individually designed for each girl. As progress is made, additional weights are added, and the number of repetitions is increased. It may be desirable to increase the weight and decrease the number of repetitions. The weight-training exercises may be performed two or three times a week.

Running is a good conditioner for jumpers. The jumpers could join the sprinters in their workouts once or twice a week to gain proper conditioning.

In such a program the jumper could run with exaggerated knee lift, stride with high knee lift 20 to 30 yards, run up stadium steps, run 100 yards emphasizing a bounce action and keeping on the toes. Work involving shorter runs at faster speeds is more desirable for jumpers.

Jumping, and lots of it, appears to be valuable for the jumper in the off-season period.

Table 11-2. Standards of performance for the high jump*

Age	Type of competition	Expected height †
10-11	School beginner	3 feet 6 inches
10-11	School experienced	4 feet
10-11	National record	4 feet 4¾ inches
12-13	School beginner	3 feet 10 inches
12-13	School experienced	4 feet 2 inches
12-13	National record	5 feet 1 inch
14-17	School beginner	4 feet 2 inches
14-17	School experienced	4 feet 6 inches
14-17	National record	5 feet 7 inches
Women	School beginner	4 feet 2 inches
Women	Experienced	5 feet
Women	National record	5 feet 10 inches
Women	World record	6 feet 4¾ inches

*From the wide range of heights shown in this table, the beginner can readily see how it is possible to improve greatly in the high jump.
†The height marks can serve as a guide for the beginner in anticipating degrees of success.

Developing proper technique as well as improving leg strength is a reason for actual jumping practice during this period. Repeated jumping practice in the off-season has great significance for back floppers in the development of consistent jumping style, particularly for those jumpers who appear to do well during the regular season with little jumping practice.

Participation in all workouts is to be preceded by a good warm-up, that is varied, progressively demanding, interesting, and of sufficient duration for the participant to feel that she is ready to perform her work-out assignment.

If training is varied and interesting, a girl will be motivated to achieve a higher level of conditioning. Through participation in a variety of training procedures, such as cross-country running, dancing activities, and performing fairly systematic circuit training activities, she should be able to maintain a fairly high level of conditioning.

When the regular track training season approaches, jumpers should give serious consideration to participating in jump training and to performing special exercises in addition to jogging and running wind sprints with the sprinters. Hurdle exercises, high leg kicks, and leg splits as well as abdominal and leg-stretching exercises are to be practiced regularly by the jumper to help her obtain flexibility, grace, and coordination. Skipping rope helps the jumper's timing and aids her in getting proper knee lift when jumping. Any imperfection of movement, such as toeing out at the takeoff, that might make jumping less effective should be corrected, and the use of good body mechanics should be emphasized at all times in all movements.

Practice sessions of no more than an hour's duration held 3 or 4 days a week seem to be adequate for many high school girls. During early training, emphasis is placed on the jumper's exhibiting proper form rather than achieving height. As the track season approaches and the jumper is well conditioned, attempts may be made to reach maximum height at certain times so that in competition the jumper will have developed the ability to withstand fatigue and stressful situations. However, jumping for height should not be done more than once a week. If girls using the back flop are jumping well in competition, they may jump infrequently in practice and concentrate on developing and maintaining leg strength, speed, and explosive power.

Weekly schedule for straddle jumpers

MONDAY
1. Warm up for 20 minutes.
2. Jump for form at low heights for 20 minutes.
3. Perform bouncing exercises for 10 minutes.
4. Run 50 yards six times, running on the toes for 10 minutes.
5. Warm down for 5 minutes.

TUESDAY
1. Warm up for 20 minutes.
2. Do light weight-training exercises for 30 minutes.
3. Perform flexibility exercises for 15 minutes.
4. Warm down for 5 minutes.

WEDNESDAY
1. Warm up for 20 minutes.
2. Jump for height for 30 minutes.
3. Run 40 meters six times in 10 minutes.
4. Warm down for 5 minutes.

THURSDAY
1. Warm up for 20 minutes.
2. Work on takeoff for 10 minutes.

    3. Jump within 2 or 3 inches of best height for 10 minutes.

    4. Run 30 meters eight times in 15 minutes.

    5. Warm down for 5 minutes.

FRIDAY   1. Warm up for 20 minutes.

    2. Work on clearing the bar for 20 minutes.

    3. Warm down for 5 minutes.

SATURDAY   Meet day.

SUNDAY   Do easy running.

Weekly schedule for back floppers

MONDAY   1. Warm up for 20 minutes.

    2. Work with sprinters for 30 minutes on 200 and 100 meters.

    3. Do jump training for 20 minutes.

    4. Warm down for 5 minutes.

TUESDAY   1. Warm up for 20 minutes.

    2. Do weight training for 40 minutes.

    3. Perform flexibility exercises for 15 minutes.

WEDNESDAY   1. Warm up for 20 minutes.

    2. Run 40 meters six times in 10 minutes.

    3. Do jump training for 30 minutes.

    4. Warm down for 5 minutes.

THURSDAY   Same as Tuesday.

FRIDAY   1. Warm up for 20 minutes.

    2. Do easy workout with sprinters.

    3. Work on second event.

    4. Warm down.

SATURDAY   Meet day.

SUNDAY   1. Do easy running.

    2. Do flexibility exercises.

PART FIVE

Throwing

CHAPTER 12

Putting the shot

HISTORY AND BACKGROUND

Throwing an object farther than one's playmates has always been a challenging game to young people. Ancient peoples enjoyed the challenge of throwing for distance and developed a skill for throwing a rounded stone of great weight. Modern man has standardized the weight and size of the shot and has given the sport written rules under which competition takes place in a restricted area. However, it is still a contest to determine how far the shot can be thrown while adhering to the rules.

Girls and women of the United States have not been as interested in the shot put event as have their counterparts in other countries. It is not that American girls are less strong than girls of other countries, but that in the past the shot put has not had the social acceptance of other events. However, young girls are now learning to perform the skills of shot-putting in schools throughout the country. Each year will find more and more girls learning the finer techniques of shot-putting at a championship level. Olympic results in the women's shot put are presented here to indicate the increase in distance that has taken place over a 28-year period.

1948	M. Ostermeyer, France	45 feet 1.5 inches
1952	Galina Zybina, U.S.S.R.	50 feet 1.5 inches
1956	Tamara Tychkevith, U.S.S.R.	54 feet 4 inches
1960	Tamara Press, U.S.S.R.	56 feet 9.75 inches
1964	Tamara Press, U.S.S.R.	59 feet 6.25 inches
1968	Margitta Gummell, East Germany	64 feet 4 inches
1972	Nadevh Chizhova, U.S.S.R.	67 feet 9.5 inches
1976	Ivanko Christova, Bulgaria	69 feet 5 inches

American women are far behind the 1976 distance mark; Earlene Brown's put of 54 feet 9 inches is the best mark made by an American. Marion Seidler, the 1976 top United States Olympic performer, puts the shot in the low 50-foot distance. Eastern European women dominate the international shot-put scene, with a 50-foot put being a poor effort. However, in America, this same throw would win most meets.

SPECIAL CONSIDERATIONS

A young girl who is physically strong (especially in the back, arm, and shoulder muscles) and who possesses good speed and coordination may very well choose the shot put as her competitive event. All other things being equal, the larger, stronger, heavier girl will have a greater opportunity to succeed in this event than the thinner, lighter, sprinter type with long lean muscles. Shot-putters spend a great deal of their practice hours building up strength in the upper torso, which in turn gives them greater explosive power at the release. Almost all top women shot-putters lift weights at least two or three times a week during most of the season.

The official weight of the iron or brass ball (called a shot) used in meets increases with the age of the competitor. The weight of the shot used by younger girls is 6 pounds; girls of high school age put the 8-pound shot; women put the 4 kilo shot (8 pounds 13 ounces). The rules governing the event state that the shot must be pushed rather than thrown with one hand only. The holding hand must be held in close proximity to the chin and cannot be dropped below this position during the act of putting the shot.

Furthermore, the shot must not at any time be brought behind the line of the shoulders in the rear. The top of the restraining toeboard is the foul line; if crossed, the put is disallowed—that is, a foul is recorded. A girl must leave the ring from the rear after the pushed shot has dropped for the put to be considered fair and measurable. (See Fig. 12-1 for ring dimensions.)

ELEMENTS OF PUTTING

Deep and utter concentration is essential while competing in this event because an athlete must use tremendous explosive power yet be careful to release the shot at the correct upward angle of about 42 degrees. The highly stylized method used in releasing the shot makes this concentration necessary. The proper performance involves rhythmic and continuous actions that build up the force behind the shot at the time of the release. A girl must have complete understanding of the movements to be made in the circle to have any degree of success. Emphasis should be placed on thrusting with the legs before putting the shot with the arms.

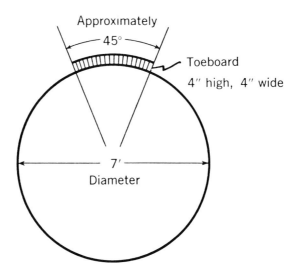

Fig. 12-1. Shot-put circle measurements. The inner edge of the stopboard must coincide with the inner edge of the circle. The stopboard should be made of wood and firmly fixed to the ground.

The method commonly used by most shot-putters of any stature is the so-called Parry O'Brien method, named after the great Olympic champion.

Holding the shot. As shown in Fig. 12-2, *A* and *B*, the shot is held by the thumb and first three fingers, which are spread behind it. The little finger curls below and helps the thumb support the weight. The shot rests along the base of the fingers rather than in the palm. Some women like to make use of the four-finger hold shown in Fig. 12-2, *C* and *D*, because of their small hands. When one is using this technique, the shot will rest more in

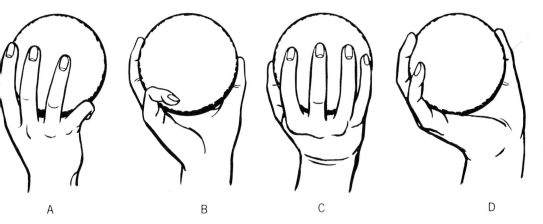

A	B	C	D

Fig. 12-2. Handholds used in shot-putting. Most girls use the three-finger method shown in **A** and **B**; However, girls with small hands may find it best to make use of the handholds shown in **C** and **D**. The shot will rest further down in the hand when a girl uses the four-finger method.

Fig. 12-3. This shot-putter is just starting to make her move across the ring from the rear facing position. She should be in a somewhat lower body position.

the palm of the hand. The elbow is held a little lower than the shoulder, with the shot resting below the rear of the jaw's curve.

Starting position in the circle. The starting position is at the back of the circle, and the performer faces to the back (Fig. 12-3). A girl (right-handed putter) should be in a relaxed position with her left arm held extended and almost above her head for balance. A "gathering" of the muscles should take place in preparation for action. As the movement begins, the feet are apart, with the right foot pointing to the rear and with a slight bend in the right leg. At this point the left foot is used for balance only and points slightly to the left. The body is bent low from the waist as the performer begins her action. The shoulders remain level, the body weight is placed over the right leg and the right hips, and the shoulders are held well back. The right elbow is held away from the body, and the right forearm is placed at about a 45-degree angle to the body. At this stage in the movement the left arm is at about shoulder height and bent slightly at the elbow. The putter must begin to feel a tremendous gathering of her body in preparation for the next phase in the action (Fig. 12-4).

A   B   C   D

E   F   G

Fig. 12-4. The shot put. **A,** This girl is in a relaxed upright balanced position. **B,** The body weight is centered over the right foot, and the left arm is extended for balance purposes. **C,** She is gathered in preparation for the glide across the ring. **D,** The left leg is thrust forward. **E,** The glide is almost completed. **F,** Note that the putting action is begun with both feet on the ground, and the right leg is extended prior to the completion of the putting action. **G,** The release has been accomplished at this point. Her feet are too close together and her arm appears to be extended upward rather than outward.

Glide or shift. The movement forward begins with the performer dropping her body very low, drawing her left leg under her, and then making a kick back (out, not up) with the left leg. The upper torso should be bent low over the bent right leg (Fig. 12-5). The object of this backward glide across the circle toward its center is to gain momentum and to place the body in the best position for thrusting the shot forward at release. The motion of moving backward—but across the circle to the forward part—with the right leg should be initiated by a strong kick of the left leg close to the ground and followed by a big drive of the right leg in gliding (not hopping) backward—but toward the front of the circle—in one gliding motion. The action should be smooth and continuous and should flow easily into the next part, the delivery or release. (See the foot pattern in Fig. 12-6.)

Release. At the release the right foot is planted in the center of the ring 35 degrees from its original starting point, with the left foot making about a 30-degree angle with the toeboard, resting very close to it, perhaps even against it. The bent right knee is ready to make a vigorous upward thrust (lifting action), since it will later be in a straight position as the shot is delivered. Thrust comes from the feet and legs.

The left leg is bent just before the release is made. The hips are swiftly rotated to the left, giving the body a half turnabout forward in the opposite direction. The shoulders are quickly rotated to the left, and there is a fast, forceful lifting action of the right shoulder.

Fig. 12-5. The hop across the ring has been completed. This shot-putter is almost ready to plant her front foot.

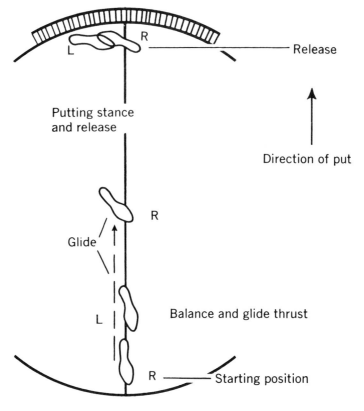

Fig. 12-6. Footwork pattern used by the shot-putter.

The head and eyes remain fixed until the turn is accomplished. Now, with the release effected, the eyes move upward. The head turns slightly to the left and is lifted upward in the general direction of the shot's flight (Fig. 12-7).

The right foot remains in a pushing position until the execution of the put is achieved. (The lift comes from the feet pushing against the ground and extension of the legs, which should occur as the actual release takes place.) As much momentum as possible should be developed; the shot should actually feel light as it is released. The release movement is upward and forward at about 45 degrees and is done as speedily as possible to maintain optimum force. Just after the release has been completed, the body weight is transferred almost entirely to the left foot. The action from the back of and across the ring must be continuous until the shot is released.

Follow-through and reverse. The wrist and fingers flex as the shot leaves the hand (Fig. 12-8, *C*). The right arm remains outstretched in a pronated position during the follow-through. It is essential to regain body balance after the proper follow-through has been accomplished, not only to avoid fouling but to get the greatest distance from the put. The final body action will indicate whether a correct thrust occurred and whether enough momentum was generated. The final action of any movement depends on several preceding actions. Thus an incorrect follow-through is a result of muscle action started before the

Fig. 12-7. This girl is getting ready to put the shot. Note her head and arm position. She will soon turn her head toward her left shoulder as she starts to release the shot.

actual follow-through took place. If any action is done incorrectly there will be a loss in the distance of the put.

The putter will reverse the position of her feet after the shot has been released so that her right foot is against the toeboard. She may find that she must hop once or twice (perhaps more) on her right foot to help her regain her balance after she releases the shot.

Discus spinning style. Some of the male and female shot-putters at the 1976 Olympics used a discus type spin in going across the shot-put circle. The final position and especially the release were the same as in the O'Brien method. This spinning form is described in Chapter 13. as it would be used by the "spinner" in shot-putting, it is the same method used in throwing the discus. It is believed that the spinning style will be used more and more by women performers in the future.

RULES

In all throwing events there are some rules that govern the competitors to ensure fair puts. Failure to comply with the following rules is a foul, and the attempt is not measured but counted as a trial.

Fig. 12-8. This series of drawings depicts the shot-putter after she has completed her hop and continues until she is ready to release the shot.

1. In all throwing events made from a circle, the competitor is permitted to touch the side of the toeboard (stopboard) with her foot. However, if she touches the top of it, it is a foul.
2. The competitor may not leave the circle until the shot touches the ground, and then she must leave from the rear half of the circle. She may not touch the ground outside the circle with any part of her body during the release or any part of the throw.
3. The shot must fall within the sector marked on the ground to be considered fair.
4. The shot must be put from the shoulder with one hand only. The putting hand must be in close proximity to the chin, and it must not be dropped below this position during the putting action. At no time may the shot be brought to the rear beyond the line of the shoulders.
5. All measurements must be made immediately after each throw. The measurement

must be taken from the nearest spot made by the fall of the shot on the ground to the inside of the toeboard, along a line to the center of the circle. Measurement is recorded to the nearest quarter inch, and the end of the tape showing the feet and inches is held by the official at the circle.

6. Three preliminary trials are allowed each competitor. There is one more finalist than the number of places to be scored, and each girl has three additional trials in the finals.

7. The circle and stopboard must meet specifications, as shown in Fig. 12-6.

COMMON ERRORS

Girls who wish to compete in shot-putting have to become almost machinelike in their actions during practice sessions. Failure to form a proper automatic pattern of execution is a grave error that affects the distance of the put and often creates fouling. The entire sequence of putting must be a mechanical action with a girl, so that she need not think about which foot goes where and when to turn but only about perfecting the execution of movement.

Certain technical points must be discussed with each girl as she develops an understanding of shot-putting. For example, each girl will have to work out her own patterns of movement under her coach's guidance, including the distance of glide, method of holding the shot, execution of the follow-through, use of the grunt for explosion of breath after release, and so forth.

Tension. Elimination of the tension that often occurs during the initial stance is important. The performer must be relaxed so that she will reach her peak efficiency. Again, the performer's ability to completely shut out all external stimuli during this initial phase of movement is essential. Tension is usually decreased as a performer gains experience.

Shot ahead of body. Any one of several technical errors happening to a girl during glide and delivery may account for her poor performance. In general, letting the shot get ahead of the body and having an incorrect angle to release create too flat a put angle or too steep an arc. These common technical errors result in puts of a short distance. There is also a tendency not to get low enough prior to making the glide, thus losing impetus.

Loss of balance. Finally, losing balance during the follow-through is usually caused by a failure to bring the right foot to the board immediately after the thrust is made. In other words, the reverse is not properly executed.

TEACHING SUGGESTIONS FOR A BEGINNER PROGRAM

The girl who has never seen a shot being put will think this event very difficult to perform. It does take time for a girl to master it. This event should follow in sequence the teaching of the more familiar throwing events, such as softball or basketball throws, which should have occurred previously in physical education classes. Although the actions used are not the same in putting the shot as in throwing other balls, a girl will have a feeling for hurling a round object into space for the greatest distance possible if shot-putting is presented after the other experiences.

Teacher experience. Because this event is simple but appears complicated in its actions, the teacher should certainly have some experience herself in putting the shot. She should be able to perform the actions correctly to fully understand the necessary kinesthetic movements involved. Without this experience she will not be able to fully appreciate the plight of the beginner in trying to learn such an unusual set of actions; indeed, she may not be able to teach the event correctly at all.

Demonstration. The class should have some opportunity to see a demonstration of shot-putting by a skilled performer. This person could be a member of the boy's track team or the staff, or it can be anyone available who can demonstrate the action. It may be necessary to have several demonstrations, as this event is considered difficult. The beginner will have to watch the correct action several times to have it firmly implanted in her mind. After the total action has been seen, the various parts of the putting action should be separated into segments and the movements for these component parts demonstrated. The class should try to perform each segment after seeing it demonstrated, from a stationary position at first, facing the desired direction of flight. As soon as possible the entire action should be executed.

Repetition. Each phase should be practiced until the girls are able to do it correctly in one smooth continuous action. It should be remembered that the beginner will probably do her throwing from a stationary position at first but should soon learn to perform all the action. Demonstrations from time to time will show the correct form to use. It may take a girl until her second or even third unit in track and field activities before she has enough ability to use the full turn, glide, and reverse effectively. It takes a while to learn the proper execution of these new skills; possibly two hundred or more practice puts will be necessary.

Progress charts. As mentioned in the discussion of the other events, the teacher should prepare charts indicating the progress the girls have made in learning to put. She should measure the throws at specified intervals and record the distances. When learning plateaus are reached and held for a while, the teacher should explain to the beginner that her progress may not be measurable at times. World records and records of other girls in similar age groups should be posted, including those performing in higher levels of competition. Thus the beginner can see what has been accomplished by women in this event. (See Table 12-1 for comparable standards.)

Table 12-1. Standards of performance for the shot put*

Age	Type of competition	Shot weight	Expected distance†
12-13	School beginner	6 pounds	23 feet
12-13	School experienced	6 pounds	32 feet
12-13	National record	6 pounds	40 feet 1¾ inches
14-17	School beginner	8 pounds	23 feet
14-17	School experienced	8 pounds	32 feet
14-17	National record	8 pounds	51 feet 5¼ inches
Women	College beginner	4 kilos	25 feet
Women	Experienced	4 kilos	35 feet
Women	National record	4 kilos	54 feet 9½ inches
Women	World record	4 kilos	69 feet 5 inches

*The shot put is one event in which the girl who practices diligently will improve noticeably.
†These distances can serve as guides for beginners in anticipating degrees of success.

Safety factors. Often the beginning putter will not be aware of the danger of being accidentally hit by a shot unless the instructor points this out to her. In the excitement of learning a new event, a young girl will think only of retrieving the shots and probably not remember that others are practicing with other shots. The girls must be trained to practice in a situation where one, two, or three shots are being used. They should follow certain rules to ensure their safety.

Squads. During the initial trials, the class should be divided into squads: each squad should be given a shot and assigned to separate practice areas. A leader should be appointed to take charge of each squad and to watch after the safety of the group. A throwing line or circle should be marked off in the grass or dirt, and all the girls but one should be instructed to remain behind the line at all times. A retriever should be the only one in the throwing area. However, she should be stationed well beyond the greatest distance that a girl could possibly put the shot. Therefore a second line some 40 feet away from the throwing circle could be marked off as the safety line for the retriever.

It is possible for girls to work in two groups, one member of each group facing the other, 40 or more feet apart. Only one girl at a time should put, and then she should return immediately to the end of her line. The members of each group should attempt putting, first a girl from one group, then one from the other group. Extreme care should be taken to keep the two throwing lines far enough apart to ensure that no injury results from anyone being hit with the shot.

Teaching progression. The following progressions and instructional suggestions might be considered for use with a class of beginners in shot-putting. When beginners are learning to put the shot, it is best to teach them to do it from a standing position (stationary) first. Often this is the only method many school girls will ever use, either from a lack of practice or from a feeling that this simple method of putting is enough for a member of the regular physical education class to learn. At any rate, the movement sequence should be taught with the put and release phase coming first, followed by the additional use of the Parry O'Brien method of gliding across the circle and ending up with the reverse.

Initially, the teacher should present the release phase of shot-putting. This can easily be practiced from a stationary position. The girl's feet are in the same position here as they would be after the glide is accomplished during the full action. The foot pattern drawing seen in Fig. 12-7 illustrates the proper foot placement to use. A girl should bend her right leg far enough to bring her body very low, and she should pivot over it. The push comes from the sequential actions made by the right foot, right leg, hip, turn of the hips, right side, right shoulder, right arm, right hand, and finally the fingers of the right hand.

A girl should practice the standing putting action without using the glide until she can successfully put the shot, using the correct body actions and doing the follow-through. She must learn to glide and put as soon as possible. She may or may not need to do the reverse action in this case. As a girl puts more effort into her thrusts, she will probably need to learn the reverse to stop herself from fouling.

It should be pointed out that a girl will have to practice in the ring repeatedly, possibly from fifty to eighty times during the initial training sessions, to learn the motions involved. She need not have the shot in her possession, but she should go through the actions with or without the shot until she feels comfortable doing them. She should, through her practice actions, strive for use of the correct form and proper angle of release.

As soon as a girl can shot-put using the stationary throw, she should be taught to glide across the ring; a girl who can glide properly will increase the distance of her puts considerably. At first the glide should be taught without using the shot. A good practice procedure is to have a girl assume her starting position and just glide backward repeatedly, using the vigorous left leg kick to add impetus to her glide. She should glide backward over a large area; that is, she should not be confined to the area of the ring. This is an exercise that should be repeated until the teacher thinks a girl has mastered the gliding (not hopping) and is able to use the tremendous left leg kick to help her move more rapidly.

Next in order is to present a combination of the glide and the release together. The beginner may have a tendency to stop between the glide and the start of her putting motion. The coach must not allow the girl to get into this bad habit. This stopping will tend to lessen the momentum gained in the glide. At this point a beginner may become discouraged because she cannot perform the actions adequately. She may feel that she is uncoordinated and complain that the actions feel jerky. She will probably have a tendency to "step into the bucket," that is, to turn or open up her hips far ahead in the direction of the line of flight with her left foot placed far to the left. This places her in a very bad position to get any power in her release. All she has left to push with is her forearm. The lifting action must be initiated from the extension of the legs.

The members of a team should practice together at the beginning of their training season, getting in as many puts as possible during the practice sessions. They should help each other and retrieve for each other, thus saving time. Circles drawn in the dirt and covered with chalk are good enough for use as practice rings.

A teacher should constantly remind the girls to release the shot high and aim for an angle of about 43 degrees. She should also point out that it can be released too high or too low, which will prevent the girl from attaining the distance normally expected.

Conclusion. The following points are reemphasized for the teacher in her presentation of the shot put in her track and field unit.

1. Teacher experience is essential.
2. Demonstrations of the event must be held so that the students may establish a visual concept of the correct techniques.
3. Repeated practices of the parts of the actions involved are necessary.
4. Beginners will probably use only the stationary putting position.
5. Progress charts should be kept to motivate the novice.
6. Safety factors must be stressed to prevent injuries.
7. The glide across the circle must be practiced many, many times to perfect it.

TRAINING SUGGESTIONS

During the early season, finger and hand strengthening exercises must be done so that girls will have enough hand strength to put the shot. Strength-building exercises are essential for the proper development of the back, arm, and shoulder muscles and are especially important during the early season practice sessions. Weight training must be participated in at least twice a week.

The pattern of improvement in shot-putting follows a staircase progression. There is a levelling off in performance as a peak is reached; this remains constant for a time; then improvement is seen until the next plateau is reached. Girls should be aware of this learning pattern so that they will not be disappointed when they do not show improvement after each practice session.

The following suggestions for a weekly training schedule are made for the midseason period. These are only suggestive in nature and are easily adaptable for most performers.

Midseason weekly schedule

MONDAY
1. Jog one lap.
2. Run three to four wind sprints of 50-meter distances.
3. Sprint 15 meters at top speed. Repeat.
4. Do stretching exercises.
5. Do puts from a standing position.
6. Do ten to twenty puts at all-out effort.
7. Perform strength exercises: three sets of ten fingertip push-ups.
8. Left light weights: five to ten sets of five repetitions, with speed action.

TUESDAY
1. Jog one lap.
2. Do three sets of five fingertip push-ups.
3. Perform stretching and loosening up exercises.
4. Do ten puts from a standing position.
5. Do ten to fifteen puts using the full circle at an all-out effort.
6. Take four to five starts from the blocks.

WEDNESDAY
1. Jog one lap.
2. Run wind sprints of 50 meters twelve to sixteen times, consuming a total distance of about two laps.
3. Do stretching exercises.
4. Practice on the moves involved in performing another field event.
5. Practice ten to fifteen puts from a standing position.
6. Perform ten to twenty puts at all-out effort.
7. Perform three sets of five fingertip push-ups.
8. Lift light weights: five to ten sets of eight repetitions, with speed action.

THURSDAY
1. Jog one lap.
2. Run wind sprints of 50 meters for two laps.
3. Perform stretching exercises and do selected calisthenic exercises.
4. Put ten times from a standing position.
5. Do five to seven puts at all-out effort.
6. Do three sets of five fingertip push-ups.
7. Jog one lap.

FRIDAY
1. Jog one lap.
2. Do not pick up the shot at all.
3. Get plenty of rest and sleep in preparation for the meet on Saturday.

SATURDAY
Meet day.

CHAPTER 13

Throwing the discus

HISTORY AND BACKGROUND

It is known that the discus was thrown by the Greeks in the ancient Olympic Games. In 1928, when women were permitted to participate in the modern Olympic track and field events for the first time, the discus throw was among the five events included. This beautifully coordinated feat, which combines grace and skill, was won in 1928 by a Polish girl with a throw of 129 feet 11⅞ inches. The only Olympic gold medal for discus throwing won by women of the United States is that won by Lillian Copeland in 1932 with a throw of 133 feet 2 inches. A world record of 230 feet 4 inches was established in Sweden in 1975 by Russia's Faina Melnik. At the 1976 Olympics Evelin Schlock of East Germany won the discus event with a throw of 226 feet 4½ inches.

The advantages of throwing the discus are numerous: it provides a good workout while it is being performed; success comes readily through practicing correct form; achievement is easily measured as distance increases; two people can enjoy competing against each other; and it does not require as much space or equipment as do some games. This international event, one of the oldest sports, could become an Olympic event for the girl whose temperament allows her to work consistently and carefully to master the performance techniques. Throwing the discus requires the performer to exhibit coordination, strength, and endurance. It also helps the performer develop character traits such as patience, perseverance, and self-dependence.

The object in throwing the discus is to develop an angular force so that momentum and body strength can be applied to the discus at the right moment as it is being released. The discus is one missile that in a sense does not get where it is going by being thrown there. It lands as a result of centrifugal force. What the golf swing does to the end of the club head to send the golf ball speeding down the fairway is the type of centrifugal action needed by the body and arm through the hand to put the discus into flight. (See Table 13-1 for standards of performance.)

SPECIAL CONSIDERATIONS

Discus throwing requires an extremely high level of skill and coordination. It is not necessarily reserved for the heavy or overweight girl. The girl of average build and strength and of average to tall height who is well coordinated, who has the temperament to concentrate on minute details, and who is able to work hard, can be successful in

Table 13-1. Standards of performance for the discus throw*

Age	Type of competition	Expected distance†
14-18	School beginner	75 feet
14-18	School experienced	100 feet
14-18	National record	155 feet
Women	Experienced	125 feet
Women	National record	179 feet 6 inches
Women	World record	230 feet 4 inches

*As may be seen by the various distances thrown by girls in the different age groups, the discus is another event in which the girl may improve greatly over her beginning efforts.
†The distances can serve as a guide for the beginner in anticipating degrees of success.

throwing the discus. Discus throwing is an event that requires a high degree of skill and training. It is one in which the highly skilled girl can achieve success.

The attitude of the performer has great influence on the ultimate achievement. The serious-minded girl who delights in competing against herself, who has a high capacity for concentration, and who enjoys self-discipline should find success and enjoyment in the discus throw. In this instance, attitude is much more important than body build. Kriemhild Hausman of West Germany, a former leading discus thrower in Europe and fourth-place winner at the 1960 Olympics in Rome (176 feet 11 inches) was a tall slender girl of average build. Edmund Piatkowski, the Polish 1961 world record holder for the men, possessed great strength and speed, but he was small for a male discus thrower. He stood 5 feet 11½ inches tall and only weighed 181 pounds.

It is true that the large active girl with long arms should have an advantage over the petite girl because strength and speed are factors to consider in predicting success. However, perhaps more important than brawn are concentration and the ability to develop the needed twisting (torque) force by practicing thousands of spins to perfect the proper techniques. Nevertheless, there is no discounting the value of strength, and the good discus thrower must develop strength in all parts of her body, especially her back and legs.

A strong body is necessary because muscles produce the force or forces that give the discus the initial velocity to gain distance in a throw. The legs drive the body across the circle in an angular movement. The center of the body moves upward at the end of the turns, giving the discus a velocity that takes a forward and upward direction as it is released by the fingers. The stronger the arm and shoulder muscles, the more force is available on release. The back and abdominal muscles must be strong to produce a forward and upward movement of the body when the discus is released. Flexibility in the trunk and throwing arm enables the discus thrower to twist her trunk and arm through a wide range of motion, thus imparting a great deal of momentum behind the discus.

It is necessary to have extra strength and flexibility in the wrists and fingers because the cocked wrist action is the last application of force before the discus is released. The fingers provide the gyroscopic spin as the discus is rolled off the index finger in a clockwise direction.

The forces behind the discus must be aimed in the direction the discus is to take, and they must be applied in the proper sequence. The larger slower forces of the moving legs and trunk are produced first, and the faster finer forces of the arms, wrist, and fingers are activated last. The total effort of producing these forces should be made in a constant and sustained movement resulting in a smooth application of force. The torque developed is dependent on the momentum accumulated by the discus thrower.

ELEMENTS OF THROWING THE DISCUS

Gripping the discus. The discus should be held in the hand with the first joint of each of the fingers over its edge. The fingers are relaxed and spread so that the discus is in a comfortable position and is easy to hold. It spins off the index finger clockwise rotation as it is thrown.

A discus at rest is not easy to hold, and without the centrifugal force to press it against the last joints of the fingers, it will drop out of the hand. It is at first held palm down and parallel with the ground, or nearly so. The discus will fall out of the hand at the end of each preliminary swing unless the left hand is used to steady it, since there is no centrifugal force to keep it against the palm. When the discus thrower is in motion, the discus

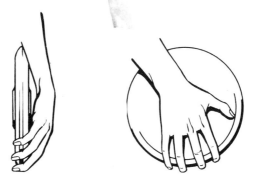

Fig. 13-1. Handhold style used by discus throwers, showing the widespread handhold style. Notice how the last joints of the fingers are placed over the edge of the discus.

Fig. 13-2. Discus throw. **A,** This girl is in a relaxed position before she begins her moves around the circle. **B,** She moves her left foot up to a parallel position with the right foot at the rear of the circle and swings her right arm far to the rear. **C,** She lowers her body and is ready to make a pivot turn. Her arm has been more to the rear prior to the position shown here.

will remain in her right hand without the support of the left hand. It is like whirling a bucket of milk; no milk is lost as long as the bucket is moving.

Positioning the feet. At the beginning the thrower stands with both feet at the back of the circle so that her back is toward the intended direction of the flight of the discus. The feet are comfortably apart, and the knees are kept loose, relaxed, and bent just enough for comfort and relaxation (Fig. 13-2).

From this position one or two preliminary arm swings are taken, and then a more accelerated swing is made as the girl starts her windup. She unwinds as she smoothly and rhythmically rotates (actually runs) around the circle in a one and three-quarters turn. The discus is released as the left leg is planted slightly left of center in the front part of the

D E F

G H I J

Fig. 13-2, cont'd. D, Note how she has turned her left foot. **E,** Her leg action here is not disimilar to that of a sprinter. Notice the high knee (sprinting action) lift of the right leg. **F,** The one and three-fourths turn is now almost complete. **G,** The hips should lead the rest of the body action (not enough hip lead is shown here). Note the position of the left foot. **H,** The discus is moved from a position low and close to the body to that seen in **I. I,** The release of the discus is accomplished at shoulder level and at an extended arm position from the body. **J,** A good follow-through is seen here, but the reverse has not been achieved as yet.

circle. The right leg pushes upward from its position in the middle of the circle as the arm starts its forward throwing motion. At this point the moment of release is a part of the entire movement. The last spin across the circle is accelerated as the discus thrower prepares for release.

The beginning position of the thrower is repeated here to give a clearer analysis of the movement to be made. In the starting position the left foot is first placed about 6 inches laterally from the right, but when the girl's motion is about to begin, it is moved to the back of the circle and about 14 inches from the right foot. (Fig. 13-3 shows the correct step pattern.)

Twisting the body (torque). The turn is accomplished by twisting the body to the right (Fig. 13-4) then untwisting to the left, with the weight shifting toward the left foot but with the right foot remaining in contact with the ground as long as possible. The upper body must remain relaxed as the pivot is made on the ball of the left foot and the hop run is done around the left leg. First the body weight is balanced over the bent right leg; then the left foot is pivoted to the left, and the body weight is shifted over it as the hop turn begins. The left leg will naturally reach toward the front part of the circle, left of the center line, if the movement is rotary and the body is balanced over the right leg (Fig. 13-4, *B*). This open

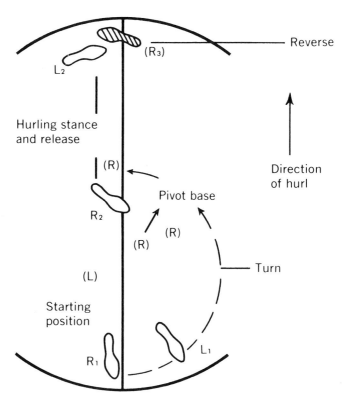

Fig. 13-3. Footwork pattern commonly used by discus throwers. The step pattern shown is the one and three-fourths turn and reverse style used by top discus throwers. Note that the position of L_2 at the time of the release is slightly to the left of center.

position allows the hips to lead the body movement in the throw. The actual throw is made at this time with the motion continuing through the last turn (Fig. 13-4, *C*). The throwing arm moves parallel with the ground as the drive of the legs causes the missile to be flung upward. The discus should be lifted upward gradually from the start of the throw and not just at the release. It is moved away from a position close to the hip as the performer

A
B
C
D

Fig. 13-4. A, Torque is accomplished by twisting the body to the right, then untwisting it to the left. **B,** Body position is balanced over the right leg just prior to release of the discus. **C,** The throw is attempted as the weight is shifted to the left foot. **D,** Discus is released with wrist in line with the intended flight.

completes the last hop. The discus is kept in the same horizontal plane throughout the turn and should be released as it is moved up nearly in line with the shoulder. The wrist is kept in line with the intended flight of the discus as the whiplike action of the wrist and fingers is applied (Fig. 13-4, *D*). The performer makes the final turn as rapidly as possible while still keeping her balance. She maintains a wide foot stance, with the knees bent as the discus is released. The discus revolves through the air in a clockwise direction.

Imparting the force. The right knee is extended forcefully as the hips lead the rest of the body in the turn. The chest is thrust out in advance of the trailing right arm, and the eyes are focused so that the head and shoulders remain on a level plane during the turning action. As the arm comes around, the weight is shifted to the left foot, and the wrist is uncocked as the last of the forces are exerted. The gyroscopic spin to the discus is imparted by the fingers. The index finger is the last to touch the discus when released.

Releasing the discus. As the discus is released with all the speed and power the thrower can generate, the thrower will have to reverse her foot position to stay in the ring. This is done after the discus has been released by placing the right foot parallel with the front edge of the circle, with the leg suspended in air as she whirls. After the performer has released the discus, she gradually dissipates the momentum she has generated.

RULES

The discus event has the following specific rules.
1. The discus may be made of wood bound with metal, composed of all metal, composed of heavier metal but hollow, or made of solid rubber.
2. The minimum weight of the discus is 2 pounds 3¼ ounces. The minimum diameter is 7 ³⁄₃₂ inches; the maximum is 7 ⁵⁄₃₂ inches.

The discus is not an expensive piece of equipment, and rubber discuses are especially economical to purchase.

The discus is thrown from a circle 8 feet 2½ inches in diameter. The circle is made of a band of iron, steel, or wood painted white and sunk in the ground. The ring is ¼ inch thick and 3 inches wide. The inside of the circle is ¾ inch lower than the outside ground. Practice circles can be chalked or painted on a concrete walk that is flush with the ground, or they may be chalked off with lime on a grassed playing field. At present the best discus circles are composed of cement sunk flush with the ground.

The discus must land within a 60-degree sector marked on the ground. The 2-inch radial lines form an angle of 60 degrees at the center of the circle (Fig. 13-5).

The rules further state that for a throw to be valid the competitor may not touch any part of the ground on or outside the circle until the discus has touched the ground or is marked, and she must leave the circle through the rear half after the throw is made.

COMMON ERRORS

In correcting errors the performer should let the major ones take precedence over the minor ones because there are many things that can go wrong in throwing the discus. It is important that performers not become discouraged with their early attempts. Many errors may be eliminated if in practice the feet are placed in the correct position in a marked circle (Fig. 13-3). Some of the errors to watch for follow.

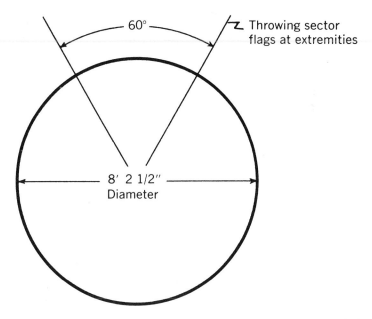

Fig. 13-5. Drawing of a discus ring. The ring should be placed on top of the circle so that the inside diameter of the circle is 8 feet 2½ inches. The throwing sector angle is 60 degrees according to NAGWS rules.

1. Too much tenseness, especially in the upper body
2. Allowing the shoulders or the head to drop too far forward during the turn
3. Hopping up rather than running around the circle; should be soft fast steps made from left to right (right-handed discus thrower) as the girl spins about the circle
4. Hurrying the turning action—sacrificing good form in an attempt to gain speed
5. Letting the discus drop too low during the turn
6. Letting the throwing arm get ahead of the body just before release
7. Throwing with a scooping action rather than releasing the discus in a near-horizontal position

TEACHING PROGRESSION FOR THE BEGINNER

Teaching girls how to throw the discus may present some difficulties to the instructor because it has to be taught by phases rather than by the whole-part-whole method. It is also a bit difficult to learn because it does not involve very many of the throwing motions previously learned.

The basketball throw with the flinging action made by the arm from the side of the body may be used as an indoor event for discus throwers. It provides a lead-up skill that can be used to teach throwing the discus.

The following sequences and procedures are suggested for use in teaching beginners how to throw the discus. The procedures suggested here are best introduced when a number of discuses are available. If each student does not have a discus available for her own use, the number in each group should be kept small so that everyone has an opportunity to throw the discus frequently.

1. The discus is carried at the right hip almost the same way a book or a purse is carried. The arms hand freely at the sides. The right arm is kept straight as the girl leans over and rolls the discus forward on the ground. As this is being done, the teacher will note and say aloud: "You are rolling the discus off the index finger."

2. From this same position of holding the discus near the hip, the extended arm is gently swung forward, and the discus is rolled off the fingers up into the air a few feet in front of and above the girl. The discus may also be rolled toward a target. These tosses and rolls are repeated a number of times.

3. The girl stands with her feet comfortably apart facing the throwing arc without a discus in her hand. Her knees are bent, causing her to assume a sort of a sitting position. The body is twisted to the right and the right foot is turned to the right, making a right angle with its former position. The shoulders are turned as far to the right as possible, and the weight of the body is almost entirely over the right foot. The left foot is placed slightly to the left of the center line so that the hips are free to move in leading the throwing action. Once the feel for this extreme twisted position is developed, the girl learns to twist and untwist into and out of this position in one continuous motion, causing her to feel that she can really unwind when she attempts to throw the discus. As the body is turned sharply to the left, at the simulated release, the right foot will trail as the weight is shifted over the left foot. The reverse completes the movement.

4. In the slight sitting position just described, the left arm is folded across the chest, and the right arm is allowed to dangle freely. The body is moved to the right in this extremely twisted position and then moved quickly to the left in the untwisted position as the right arm swings out and upward. This action is repeated again and again so that the athlete can get the feel of the extended arm being pulled rhythmically around as a result of the twisting force exerted by the trunk and leg muscles.

5. From the same position described previously, the discus is held at the hip and the turn is made sharply to the left, with the discus swung up and out a few feet forward. The idea is to sail the discus, keeping it nearly parallel with the ground. The arm is kept straight, palm down, and some slight pressure is applied against the discus with the right thumb if needed, so that the palm of the hand lies flat. If the hand is in a palm-up position at release, the discus will be scooped upward and go through the air in an upright rather than a horizontal (flat) position. Only short easy throws should be attempted, with emphasis placed on using a straight arm and keeping the discus flat in flight as the twisting-untwisting exercise is practiced.

6. Several circles 8 feet 2½ inches in diameter may be drawn with chalk on a concrete walk or with line on the field. The circles are divided into fourths and marked with an X or with an R and L to indicate the proper placement of the feet. There should be as many circles as there are discuses. The student stands at the back if the circle on the foot marks, facing away from the throwing areas with the body held erect but in the slightly bent (knees easy), crouched sitting position. The wind-unwind motion is then started, with the weight placed over the left foot as the girl pivots on the ball of the left foot; the right foot maintains contact with the ground. The right foot is then moved across the center line of the circle to the position marked for R_2. As the body continues to turn, the left foot lands in the forward left quarter of the circle where L_2 is marked (Fig. 13-4). This sequence is walked through until the performer knows exactly where each foot should be placed.

7. From the aforementioned starting position and without the use of the discus, the student smoothly and rhythmically winds and unwinds, but instead of stepping across she now springs or hop runs around the circle in a smooth continuous motion. The initial movement is made in an unhurried manner, and both feet are kept in contact with the ground as long as possible. The beginner needs to learn early to turn as far as she can to the left with the right foot still in contact with the ground. The athlete who can turn smoothly and land in a balanced position over the right foot is well on her way to becoming proficient in the execution of the hop turn.

8. The running turn is made across the circle. Ths discus is held near the hip and allowed to swing out easily 20 feet or so at the release. The presence of the discus may upset the smoothness of the execution of the hop-turn pattern, but the girl must concentrate on the execution of the drill movements to offset this problem.

9. The discus is held in the left palm at the very beginning of the action, as if it were a plate at a position near the right shoulder. The right hand then reaches across and grips the discus with the fingers spread apart and just over the edge; the grip must be relaxed. In this preliminary move the discus is brought back as far to the right as possible with an easy, smooth, comfortable swing. The arc of the swing at this time is nearly horizontal, and the discus is held palm down. The discus is now swung back to the position near the right shoulder, with the left hand touching it to keep it from dropping to the ground, and then it is swung back around to the right. The hop turn and throw are then executed. It is important to observe that the right arm (throwing arm) does not get ahead of the body during the hop turn. The right arm must be delayed so that the other body actions, such as those of the hips, trunk, and legs, precede it in completing their action or at least are not following the arm-throwing action.

10. No more than two preliminary swings should be made before each throw, and at this stage of training a controlled running turn ending in a strong throwing position should be worked for rather than distance of throw.

Coaching hints. Following are suggestions for the improvement of more skilled performers.

1. By moving the left foot forward a few inches ahead of the right foot in starting position, the thrower may be able to rotate the discus farther to the rear of the body and increase the distance through which momentum may be gained.

2. The delivery arm should be kept in an extended position from the start of the delivery because of the greater force and velocity that will be accumulated.

3. The discus should be held back as far as possible and at about hip height at the beginning of the throwing action so that proper pull and proper upward lift may be accomplished.

4. The initial motion of the turn should be an unhurried one, with the right foot staying in contact with the ground as long as possible.

5. The extension of the right leg at the release should be emphasized, and this drive should begin as soon as the right foot touches the ground at the completion of the hop turn. The vigorous upward lift of the discus (done with all possible speed) is accomplished as it passes the hip of the thrower. It is imperative that the throw be started with the right leg drive and ended with the left leg lifted to ensure a proper follow-through. Otherwise the discus will be thrown with the arm only, and the advantage of the

rotary movement will be lost. The amount of reverse needed to keep the thrower in the ring indicates the momentum attained by the discus at release. A vigorous reverse means that the discus accumulated a great deal of momentum.

TRAINING SUGGESTIONS

The serious athlete will need to follow a year-round training program. The more time that she can spend in conditioning activities and in actual throwing, the more proficient she will become.

The discus thrower will follow the same general conditioning program as do the other athletes. She should run with the sprinters, hurdle with the hurdlers, and put the shot. She should spend considerable time performing stretching and strengthening exercises. She should also do exercises that help increase trunk flexibility. The chinning bar and the parallel bars will be good equipment for her to use for exercise purposes. Much time should be spent in weight training. Emphasis should be placed on lifting reasonably light weights at great speed.

Participation in sports and dance activities will contribute to her general fitness. The discus thrower may find she needs to spend more time in perfecting the skills of her event than do the sprinters, jumpers, and hurdlers. A suggested workout schedule would include the following:

1. Jogging
2. Running wind sprints
3. Doing stretching exercises
4. Throwing from a standing position
5. Practicing the turn without throwing
6. Making complete throws
7. Experimenting with wind directions and their effect on the throw (Usually, if the wind is blowing toward the thrower and from the right—right-handed thrower— it will cause the discus to go farther.)
8. Performing strengthening exercises such as pull-ups, push-ups, sit-ups, leg lifts, vertical jumps, and so forth
9. Using weights at least twice a week to increase the strength of the shoulder, the chest, the back, and the legs
10. Running the 400 meters and 800 meters at a slow speed

Midseason weekly schedule

MONDAY
1. Jog 400 meters.
2. Do 15 minutes of stretching exercises.
3. Run wind sprints of 100 meters twice, jogging for rest between runs.
4. Take twelve to fifteen standing throws.
5. Do ten to fifteen push-ups; run relaxed for 8 to 10 minutes with the other girls.
6. Use weights at least once, and probably twice, a week.

TUESDAY
1. Repeat jogging and do stretching.
2. Run several 50-meter dashes.
3. Practice the turn without throwing.
4. Throw the basketball ten to fifteen times.
5. Make six to eight complete throws.
6. Run a relaxed 200 meters twice.

WEDNESDAY
1 Repeat jogging and do stretching.
2. Run four 70-meter wind sprints.
3. Take six to eight standing throws.
4. Rest. Make six to eight complete throws.
5. Run a relaxed 400 meters.

THURSDAY
1. Repeat jogging and do stretching.
2. Run four 70-meter wind sprints.
3. Practice putting the shot several times.
4. Practice the hop turn without throwing, fifteen to twenty times.
5. Run a relaxed 800 meters.

FRIDAY
No practice if there is a meet. If not, warm up by jogging and stretching.

SATURDAY
Participate in meet.

The weight training activities recommended for the early season program should be participated in twice a week during the regular season. They may be intensified by increasing either number of repetitions or the distances or weights used.

CHAPTER 14

Throwing the javelin

HISTORY AND BACKGROUND

The javelin has been thrown since ancient times. Primitive man was adept at using the spear in hunting and fighting. The Greeks had a spear-throwing event in the early Olympic Games.

Javelin throwing for women was introduced at the 1932 Olympics and was won by Babe Didrikson (Zaharias) of the United States with a throw of 143 feet 4 inches. A world record was set in Tokyo in 1964 when Elena Gorchakoua of Russia threw the javelin 204 feet 8½ inches. The American record is held currently by Kathy Schmidt, who has thrown a distance of 213 feet 5 inches. Ruth Fuchs of East Germany won the 1976 Olympic javelin throw with a toss of 219 feet 7 inches. Kathy Schmidt placed third in the 1976 Olympics with a throw of 209 feet 10 inches.

The javelin event is one of the most graceful events in track and field, and one that is thrilling and beautiful to watch; however, it is not widely participated in by American girls. This is most regrettable because success in throwing the javelin indicates achievement of a high level of skill. It is a physically demanding event to perform, it has great spectator appeal, and it brings rewarding satisfaction to the performer. The grace and beauty that the performers exhibit should have exceptional appeal for women. Pronounced flexibility is necessary for a successful performance, and women usually possess a high degree of flexibility. (See Table 14-1 for standards of performance.)

Javelin throwing may be introduced in high school or college programs or both as safely as throwing the discus or putting the shot. The rubber-tipped javelin increases safety and therefore the feasibility of its wide use. However, care must be taken at all times when practicing the javelin throw. The javelin should be thrown for form only in a physical education class. This will give variety to teaching throwing skills and allow girls a chance to discover an exciting field event. It will also provide opportunities for learning basic safety measures that must be observed in throwing the javelin. As girls become interested in throwing the javelin, they will want to join the track and field team and take part in the after-school athletic programs to perfect this skill.

SPECIAL CONSIDERATIONS

In informal meets the javelin must be thrown from behind a white line 10 feet long. The length of the approach runway is unlimited, but it can be no shorter than 30 meters. Its width is 4 meters and ends in a scratch-line arc (Fig. 14-1). The throw is made from

170

Table 14-1. Standards of performance for the javelin throw*

Age	Type of competition	Expected distance†
14-17	School beginner	65 feet
14-17	School experienced	90 feet
14-17	National record	175 feet
Women	College beginner	95 feet
Women	Experienced	125 feet
Women	National record	213 feet 5 inches
Women	World record	219 feet 7 inches

* As in other events where the proper technique is all-important, the beginner will be able to see rapid improvement in her javelin throw after much practice.
† These distances can serve as guides for the beginner in anticipating degrees of success.

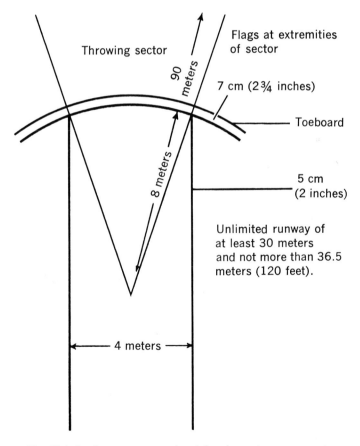

Fig. 14-1. Javelin runway approach and throwing sector measurements.

behind the scratch-line arc of a circle drawn with a radius of 8 meters. The scratch-line arc must be a white board composed of wood or metal 7 cm wide and sunk flush with the ground.

To be measurable a throw must fall within the inner edges of the lines marking the sector. The sector is formed by extending the radii through the extremities of the arc for a distance of 90 meters. The ends of the sector lines must be marked with flags.

The throw is measured from the nearest mark of the landing of the javelin to the inside of the center of the scratch line or to the center of the circle of which the arc is a part. The javelin must mark the ground with the point to be a measurable throw.

A good javelin has the largest possible lifting surface area, the highest possible stiffness, and a tilting movement that makes it land at the smallest possible angle that permits the javelin point to mark the ground. The javelin may be made of metal, plastic, or wood. Minimum weight and dimensions of a woman's javelin are 7 feet 2½ inches in length and 1 pound 5⅕ ounces in weight with a grip rope 5⅞ inches long.

Javelin throwing demands that the participant be in excellent physical condition. At the competitive level this event is for the exceptional athlete and the strong well-coordinated girl who will work hard and long and spend years conditioning and preparing herself to execute the correct throw. Most coaches think that such conditioning only comes from year-round training, 5 days a week, for a period of 4 years or more. The best single physical characteristic a successful performer can have is a good throwing arm. She must also be of a dedicated and determined character and have the will to succeed. Good arm speed coupled with explosive power and a strong flexible body to reinforce this power are essential for success in this throwing event. The girl who can successfully throw the javelin usually has good general athletic ability and will probably do very well in any physical activity, especially in a throwing event.

ELEMENTS OF THROWING

Handhold. The javelin is gripped firmly by one hand at its center. It must be held at the grip and thrown with an over-the-shoulder motion. The index finger is curled around the shaft of the javelin, with the middle finger folded over behind the special grip area

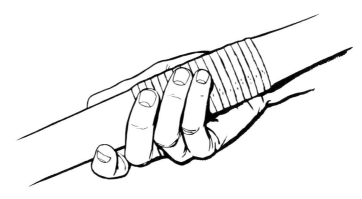

Fig. 14-2. Javelin handhold. When a girl uses this handhold, she places the javelin in the palm of her hand and along the inner portion of her forearm. The middle finger of her hand rests on the top part of the grip.

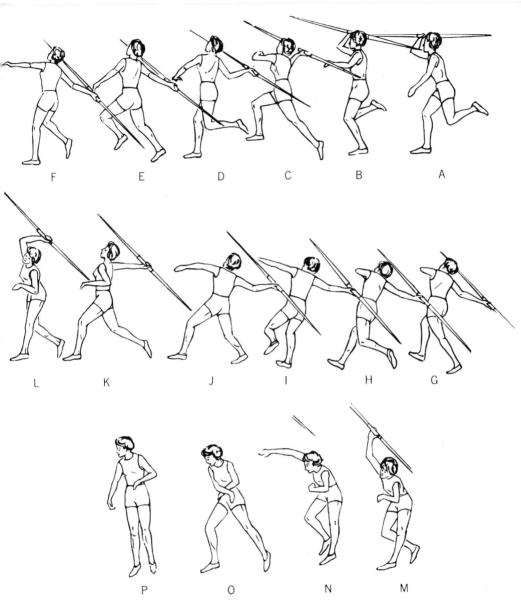

Fig. 14-3. The javelin throw. This girl is in a carrying position, **A,** with the javelin held parallel with the ground. Actually, the rear tip of the javelin was in an elevated position in the position previous to **A.** She has made most of her approach run and is getting ready to execute the crossover steps (**A** through **E**). Notice that her arm is extended well to the rear in **F** through **I.** A wide throwing stance is assumed in **K.** The elbow-leading position is seen in **L.** The release of the javelin and the subsequent follow-through is seen in **M** through **P.** Note that the tip of the javelin is pointed in the direction of flight. Also note action of left arm.

Fig. 14-4. Sequence of javelin throw. **A,** High carry. **B,** Long step. **C,** Crossover step. **D,** Last step. **E,** Release.

(Fig. 14-2). The javelin is held over the shoulder, and the point directed up during the approach run. It moves in rhythm with the body, and the throwing arm is held in a relaxed manner during the approach run (Figs. 14-3 and 14-4). Some coaches are advocating carrying the javelin very high during the approach to avoid up-and-down arm movements.

Approach. The approach can be as long or as short as the skill of the thrower demands; usually the girl will run about 15 meters or more. The speed of the run is determined by the ability of the thrower to transfer her speed to the throwing action. The use of a longer approach with the possibility of producing greater speed comes with improvement and mastery of the skill.

As the thrower reaches the last check mark (about 10 meters from the scratch line), the javelin is drawn back slowly and smoothly to transfer from the approach position to the stance used in preparing for execution of the throw.

Crossover step. Any type of foot movement used by a beginner (after the main run-up has been accomplished) during the last five strides is acceptable in preparation for the release. The steps used by a baseball outfielder just before he releases a throw to home plate may be used. The standard five-count or five-step crossover foot movements are best for good performers to use (Fig. 14-5). More steps may be decided on as skill improves. In the standard approach the performer's left foot strikes the check mark as the javelin is drawn back on the count of one, and the arm starts backward toward a fully extended

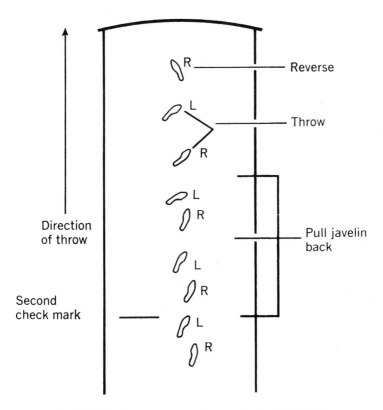

Fig. 14-5. Front crossover step pattern used by javelin throwers.

position to the rear; on the count of two, the right foot toes outward at an angle of about 45 degrees; on three, the left foot turns slightly as the step with the left foot is made; on four, the crossover with the right foot is made, and the right foot toes out far enough to line up the body in the throwing position; on five, the left foot moves forward with the stepping action and the javelin is thrown.

Release. The body is leaning backward as the right foot crosses over on the fourth count or stride; the pull of the javelin starts forward as this count is completed; the right elbow leads the hand as the count of five is completed, and the javelin is pulled through and over the shoulder as the arm is held high. The wrist snap gives the final impetus to the javelin (Fig. 14-6). The right shoulder is lifted vigorously just before release, and the follow-through is completed as the right foot steps forward in a reverse foot position to prevent fouling. The thrower begins her release some three or more strides before reaching the scratch line. This means that the five-count step procedure has been completed this far away from the scratch line. The same relative position of the arm and body are used regardless of the type of steps employed.

The point of the javelin must be kept in the direction of the desired flight during the crucial last five steps. If this is not done, the javelin will not go through the air in a straight line. Because of the aerodynamics of flight, the release is made at a fairly low angle of projection so that the javelin will travel the greatest distance. The thrower must be sure she throws so that her strong back muscles are utilized. Just as the throw is being completed, a whiplike action must take place for the greatest distance to be attained (Figs. 14-3 and 14-4). It will travel best in a crosswind and not as effectively in rear or backwind.

RULES

Following are rules of javelin competition.

1. The thrower must not turn her back to the throwing area after she has begun her approach run until the javelin is released.

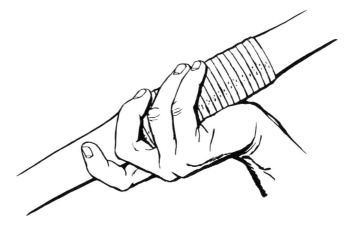

Fig. 14-6. Javelin handhold with cocked wrist position. The wrist is cocked to give additional thrust to the javelin when it is thrown.

2. The point of the javelin must break the ground first to count as a legal throw, and it must fall within the sector lines to be called a fair throw.
3. The competitor may not touch any part of her body or javelin on or over the runway lines or scratch line arc before the throw has been made, and she may not touch over the scratch line before the contact spot of the javelin on the ground has been marked.

COMMON ERRORS

For the beginner to learn the technique of throwing the javelin correctly the teacher should be on the lookout for errors. If the teacher corrects the following mistakes in performance, she will greatly help the novice to master this event.

1. An insecure hold on the javelin grip at release
2. An incomplete drawing back of the arm
3. A jerky, poorly coordinated run
4. Poor alignment of the front point of the javelin with the direction of flight
5. Too much tenseness in any part of the body
6. Throwing at too high an angle

TEACHING SUGGESTIONS FOR BEGINNER PROGRAMS

The beginner should have a chance to become familiar with the javelin before detailed instructions are given on how to throw it. Safety precautions should be stressed, and the beginner should be allowed many short throws to become accustomed to throwing the javelin. The teacher could mention some of the history of the javelin, including the fact that it was originally used as a weapon for killing game and as an instrument of war.

The number of students in a group should be kept small, and it is preferred that they work in couples. Careful attention should be given to the maintenance of safety at all times. Rubber-tipped javelins are very good for beginners to use, and canes, garden stakes, or laths from the lumber yard that are 7 feet in length and ¼ inch in diameter make excellent teaching implements. Perhaps as a lead-up skill the students could learn the softball throw for distance. Some teachers start beginners off by having them throw a tennis ball, using correct javelin leg and arm action.

Progression. Instruction begins with a discussion of the proper grip or handhold to use. The javelin should be held so that it lies diagonally across the hand in proper alignment for throwing, and the first or second finger can be placed around the shaft next to the cord. Care should be exercised to see that the grip is not held too tightly.

Standing throws are taught next. In the standing position the arm is drawn far back, and the body is turned at a right angle to the direction of the throw. The javelin shaft is pointed up at an angle. The arm is brought through gently and as high as possible over the head as the left foot is lifted slightly, then set down heel first and pointing straight ahead; the right foot is placed at an angle of 45 to 60 degrees to the scratch line. The right hip is turned to the front, and the thrower faces straight ahead in the direction of the throw. From the extended arm position to the rear a pull forward is made with the elbow leading the rest of the arm. Care is taken to move the arm so that the throw is made as close to the head as possible. The head and chest are held high. The throw is then executed with the javelin

Fig. 14-7. These drawings show the sequence of motion in a javelin throw. The wide stance and pulling action of the throwing arm begins the throw. The elbow is beginning to bend. In the release the right arm is almost fully extended.

being thrown with a whiplike action. The body weight is shifted from the right foot to the left foot as the throw is completed. The thrower could actually take a step with the left foot at this point to help her experience the weight of the body. Throwing from a standing position is repeated a number of times.

The high pull-through of the elbow can be further emphasized if a partner assists the thrower by pulling down on the extreme end of the javelin and then gradually letting it go so that the thrower may release it.

The carry is taught next. In the carry the arm is bent at the elbow as the javelin is carried over the shoulder, with the point of the javelin held slightly up. Several slow runs should be practiced, giving attention to keeping the javelin in proper alignment. Perhaps it would be best at first for the student to walk with the javelin in proper position and then throw it, before running and throwing it. Next the student learns to run with the javelin and shifts it from the carrying position to the throwing position. A number of running steps are taken, and without a break in the rhythm of the run the javelin is brought back by the extended arm to the throwing position and then returned to the carrying position. The student should repeat this drill by running the length of the field as often as necessary to ensure a smooth performance. When assuming the throwing position the right arm is brought straight back, and the javelin is held close and nearly parallel with the jaw. The left arm is bent in readiness to aid in body turn.

The next step is the carry and throw. A run of about 15 meters is made; the javelin is brought back, and attention is given to good alignment and arm extension as it is thrown forward. Once canes can be consistently thrown with good flight, the heavier javelin may be introduced.

The concept of the running approach, using either the baseball glide or the crossover step, and the throw are now introduced. In using the crossover step the student, standing with both feet together, begins the run by stepping forward at the left foot, counting as follows: 1—2—3—4—5—6—7—8—9—10—11—12; left—right—left—cross-step—left and throw (Fig. 14-5). The right leg is driven forward during the last cross-over step, and a pronounced backward lean of the body is made as the upward rotation of the right hip and the long pull-through of the arm with the javelin is begun. Next the left foot is planted on the ground, and the feet are spread in a wide stance as the throw is completed. The left arm aids in pulling the body around.

In the baseball glide the same general body action takes place, with the exception that the legs do not cross over one another during the last five strides.

After the run and throw of the javelin are taught by these simple progressions, it is up to the girls who hope to be good throwers to plan to spend a good deal of their time throwing. Like most field events, especially object-propelling events, the throwing of the javelin brings satisfaction and success only through adherence to systematic and constant practice. It will take a beginner hundreds of practice throws to perfect the skills for projecting the javelin.

The mastery of the cross-step is considered necessary in becoming a world or near world champion. The participant should practice drills especially designed for perfecting this skill. A good drill is one in which the athlete performs a number of cross-steps over a distance of 30 to 40 meters. However, less emphasis is being placed on the execution of the true or exaggerated crossover step. Perhaps more of a baseball glide step will be used in the future.

Regardless of the type of step or glide used, some teachers have their performers throw at a spot on the ground or into a bale of straw. The performer leans backward and throws with an easy motion at a particular spot, emphasizing the use of her back muscles.

Following are some hints for improving form:

1. From the beginning make a definite decision about the number of steps to use and then practice consistently, using the same count pattern each time.
2. Exercise the body into the best possible condition to become a good javelin thrower.
3. To avoid injury warm up thoroughly before a practice session or competitive situation.
4. Exaggerate the backward lean as the throwing action is commenced.
5. Start the pull of the javelin forward with the arm extended almost straight to the rear, and pull along the line of flight of the javelin.
6. Always point the javelin in the intended direction of flight.
7. Release the javelin at a fairly low angle of projection.
8. Wear regulation field shoes to help get a good grip on the ground.

TRAINING SUGGESTIONS

The javelin thrower needs to train hard and long to learn this event. The arm must be in perfect condition for the great effort made in throwing. The stress placed on the muscles and tendons demands that the body be in the best possible condition at all times. This high level of conditioning comes only through participation in systematic and continuous training programs.

Exercises that help develop the upper body, such as push-ups, pull-ups, horizontal and parallel bar exercises, mat exercises, and trunk extension exercises, will stretch and strengthen the muscles and tendons, making it possible to throw the javelin with a minimum of pulled or strained muscles. The hands and fingers should be strengthened to give a good final thrust to the javelin. Practicing handstand exercises, doing fingertip press-ups from the floor, and doing squeezing exercises on a spring grip or with a rubber ball will help the performer gain this strength.

Hurdle exercises will increase flexibility. Running over hurdles, using the right leg as the takeoff leg, is especially valuable in developing uniform stride for speeding down the javelin runway and for strengthening the drive of the right leg when executing the throwing motion.

Running sprints with the runners, jumping with the jumpers, and throwing the softball, basketball (in a javelin-type throwing action), and discus, as well as putting the shot will contribute to the overall strength and coordination needed for throwing the javelin. Special strengthening exercises with weights, inner-tube bands, or straps attached to the wall can be designed.

A typical practice session consists of a long warm-up period to be sure the body is sufficiently stretched and loose. This is followed by form throwing, in which various aspects are analyzed by the coach and the athlete. Then full-speed runs are made, with emphasis on the proper execution of the last five important steps prior to throwing the javelin. The javelin is thrown rather lightly at the end of each of these practice runs. The glide or cross-step drill is then practiced, and the workout is completed with practice in other events or participation in exercises designed to help build speed or strength.

Midseason weekly schedule

MONDAY
1. Jog one lap.
2. Do loosening-up, stretching, and twisting exercises.
3. Throw a ball several times, using the javelin throw form.
4. From a standing position throw the javelin easily ten to twenty times; this is called a jab into the ground.
5. Run through the throwing approach lanes for correct steps, using the cross-step. Throw five times at about half effort.
6. Take six to eight throws at about half effort, using the full running approach. Throw the last three with greater effort, trying for distance.
7. Run three sprints of 50 to 75 meters.
8. Take a shower.

TUESDAY
1. Jog one lap.
2. Run three wind sprints of 50 meters.
3. Do stretching, loosening-up, and twisting exercises.
4. Do jabbing practice fifteen to twenty times, using best form possible.
5. Participate in several cross-step drills.
6. Run through approach and take two to three throws, at two-thirds effort.

7. Throw twice at slightly more than two-thirds effort, then throw two to three times for distance at three-fourths effort.
8. Lift light weights; repeat set five times emphasizing speed.
9. Jog one lap.
10. Take a shower.

WEDNESDAY

1. Jog one lap.
2. Take two to three starts with the sprinters, running about 35 meters each time.
3. Do ten to twenty jabs into the ground from a standing position, throwing with greater velocity each time.
4. Take about five throws, using the proper approach run and cross-step and throwing at about half effort.
5. Throw three to four times at almost all-out effort.
6. Jog one lap.
7. Take a shower.

THURSDAY

1. Jog one lap.
2. Do several long jumps.
3. Participate in a weight training program, using light weights with emphasis on speed.
4. Throw a ball for distance; run over two or three hurdles; high jump or throw the javelin at about half effort or both.
5. Sprint 200 meters or run three wind sprints of 50 meters each.
6. Take a shower.

FRIDAY

1. Jog one lap.
2. Do stretching and loosening-up exercises.
3. Take a shower.

SATURDAY

Participate in meet.

PART SIX

Pentathlon

CHAPTER 15

Pentathlon

HISTORY AND BACKGROUND

The pentathlon, a contest in which each participant takes part in five different events, is gaining popularity in the United States and abroad. This event was permitted for the first time in the 1964 Olympic Games. The pentathlon includes the following and is run in the order listed: 100-meter hurdles, 4-kilo shot put, high jump, long jump, and 800-meter race. In 1977 the pentathlon was changed to include the 800-meter race instead of the 200 meters. The various points made by athletes prior to this time have included the 200 meters. After May, 1977, all international competition will include the 800-meter run and reflect the changed point system. The lesser known and less used triathlon consists of the 100-meter dash, high jump, and shot put.

Mary Peters of Great Britain was the 1972 Olympic penthathlon champion with 4,801 points. The holder of the United States championship is Jane Frederick. She was the leading United States contender and ranked as follows in the 1976 Olympics:

Long jump, eleventh, 19 feet 7¾ inches, 904 points
200-meter dash, sixth in her heat, 22.7 seconds, 873 points
100-meter hurdles, third in her heat, 13.54 seconds, 826 points
Shot put, sixth, 47 feet 8¾ inches, 870 points
High jump, fifth, 5 feet 9¼ inches, 993 points

Following are the final standings of all participants:

1. Siegrun Siegl, East Germany, 4,745 points
2. Christine Laser, East Germany, 4,745 points
3. Burglinde Poliak, East Germany, 4,740 points
4. Lludmila Popovskaya, U.S.S.R., 4,700 points
5. Nadejda Tkachenko, U.S.S.R., 4,669 points·
6. Diane Jones, Canada, 4,582 points
7. Jane Frederick, United States, 4,566 points
13. Gale Fitzgerald, United States, 4,263 points
17. Marilyn King, United States, 4,165 points

SPECIAL CONSIDERATIONS

It seems that a hurdler might be best equipped to succeed as a pentathlon performer, since three of the events demand speed as the essential component for success (100-meter hurdles, 800-meter race, and long jump). A hurdler would be far better prepared initially to perform most of these activities than would a field-event participant or a distance runner. With the change to the 800-meter race, instead of the shorter 200-meter sprint, the girl who has endurance might have an advantage now, provided she has the strength to lead in the shot put and jumps as well. Competitors must pace themselves in the 800 meters rather than running it as an all-out sprint, since failure to do well in this event can easily bring the point totals down. Also, it appears that a girl who possesses a very strong physique and has good sprinting speed would be more successful than a girl of slender build having average or less than average speed. For example, good arm, shoulder, and leg strength is necessary for success in shot-putting, and leg spring for success in high jumping. Besides regarding the hurdler as a potential pentathlon performer, the long jumper and sprinter should be considered.

Participation in the pentathlon may be the greatest single measure of determining a "great" athlete over a "good" athlete. The pentathlon is often considered the most demanding of all track and field events for women. One who excels in the pentathlon can easily be considered a true all-around athlete in every sense of the word, although she might not excel in any one of the individual events included in the pentathlon.

RULES

The rules for the pentathlon events differ slightly from those used in the same events in regular track meets. In the two running events a competitor is allowed two false starts; disqualification would occur on the third false start. A competitor must clear the starting height in the high jump before she is allowed to pass subsequent heights. Three trials are allowed in the shot put and long jump; three fouls disqualify a competitor in both events.

Scoring is based on a complicated table of points given for the various times and distances accomplished. The revised scoring table has changed to a point system whereby the high jump is now more heavily weighted. The point values for the other four events have been kept about the same for the various times or distances measured. Regardless of the weighted high jump scoring system, most coaches feel that a hurdler has the best chance of success in this event. Since the scoring procedure may change from time to time, it is not presented here.

TEACHING SUGGESTIONS FOR BEGINNERS

The young competitor in the pentathlon will have to learn to master the skills involved in each of the events. She should be trained to excel in the middle distances, hurdles, high jump, long jump and shot put, in that order. (She will undoubtedly be a member of a relay team as well if she becomes good in these events.) Competitive prospects start very early in their careers to gain speed and hurdle skill.

There are no particular teaching suggestions for pentathlon that are any different from the teaching of the specific events mentioned. Thus one should refer to those specific chapters that are pertinent to the five events. The triathlon is valuable for gaining experience in three of these activities, and it is easily conducted.

COACHING HINTS

Shot-putting is usually the pentathlon performer's least perfected skill. Most top international competitors do not put the shot more than 47 feet; in fact, they would consider a put of 47 feet a good effort. Therefore a girl could gain valuable points by being a good shot-putter, yet she must be good in the other events to score high.

An International Amateur Athletic Federation (IAAF) rule was changed to alter the distance of the hurdle race from 80 to 100 meters. The rule also changed the height of the hurdles from 30 to 33 inches. There are ten hurdles in the race, with the first hurdle being 13 meters from the start and with 8.1 meters between hurdles. Even with the additional 3 inches in hurdle height, it is believed that a hurdler will have the advantage over other specialists when competing in the pentathlon.

Pentathlon coaches commonly believe that it takes several years for a performer to become a top level pentathlon competitor and that her initial experience should be filled with as much track competition as possible. As her growth and strength increase, she should participate in a program of strength building but continue competing in several events. Perhaps she should alternate the events in which she participates while still maintaining her hurdle excellence.

It is not unusual for the Olympic pentathlon competitors to also represent their countries in some other track and field events. However, the pentathlon events during the Olympics are scheduled at the same time as other track and field events. This causes some difficulty for such competitors. Except for the Olympics, pentathlon meets are always scheduled at times other than during regular track meets to allow girls to compete in both types of meets.

TRAINING SUGGESTIONS

To succeed in this demanding event, the competitor must participate in a year-round program of conditioning and training. Because two of the events involve sprinting, she has to train as a sprinter and hurdler, participating in many sprinting activities. She must train hard for the 800 meters, running repeat 200- and 400-meter timed intervals to build stamina and speed. Her year-round conditioning program should include arm, shoulder, and leg strength exercises done with weights or against resistance. Also, it is recommended that these girls participate in indoor track meets to extend their competitive experiences during the year.

PART SEVEN

Management and planning aspects

CHAPTER 16

Conducting meets

Track and field meets can be made as exciting and interesting for spectators to watch as football, basketball, and baseball games or any other sporting event that draws large crowds. There are many opportunities in such meets to promote good human relationships and good sportsmanship. Since many educators agree that track and field participation has great social, intellectual, and physical advantages for those involved, it is important to encourage these aspects through well-organized and well-conducted track and field meets that are full of color, spectacle, and pageantry.

Successful track and field meets are the result of much hard work and involve careful planning and coordinating of many people. Giving attention to the comfort of the spectators helps to keep their continued interest and support.

KINDS OF MEETS

The kind of meet scheduled will depend on the number of competitors involved and the type of meet that will best serve these participants. Some examples are presented in the following sections.

Postal or telegraphic meets. A postal or telegraphic meet is one in which two or more schools compete against one another on their own separate tracks in events previously agreed on. The results are called in or telegraphed to each school to establish the winners. Although no travel is involved, competition occurs, even though it may be less interesting than knowing performers from other schools and competing personally against them. Competing against a record or a stopwatch is not nearly as challenging as competing against a live personality. Social and emotional development does not occur to the same degree, and it is usually less enjoyable for all. However, such a meet may be staged when travel is not feasible. Comparative results of both individual and composite team scores can be used to decide the winners.

Dual meets. A dual meet involves active competition between performers from two schools. Scheduling a dual meet between archrivals is a good promotional device to start off the season. Girls from the two schools could share the same dressing facilities to give them an opportunity to become better acquainted. This kind of meet can be conducted in a short period of time, and the competition may be of much interest to the spectators. Care must be exercised to see that the teams are not drastically mismatched for proper spectator interest and participants' enjoyment. This is also a good time to allow a larger number of entries per event, making it possible for third- and fourth-place competitors to find out what they can do in competition. Since it will not be necessary to conduct heats, the best times made by athletes should be submitted in advance to determine lane selections.

Double-header meets. A double-header meet involves participation of boys and girls. Performance in this kind of meet may be a rewarding experience for both groups; the girls are challenged by and learn from the superior performance of the boys, and boys develop an appreciation for the athletic ability of girls, as well as an understanding of the differences that exist between the sexes. Furthermore, boys are often pleased to perform before girls. The competition is conducted in the same way as in a dual meet; however, boys compete against boys, and girls compete against girls. A real advantage is the full utilization of meet officials, with men and women being used as officials.

Triangular meets. A triangular meet is one conducted among three schools. Often more interesting to watch than a dual meet, this type affords greater competition, increases the team effort, and may be more enjoyable for participants and spectators. Usually each team is allowed only two participants per event, depending on the number of lanes or the number of heats desired.

Double dual meets. In a double dual meet three schools participate in the same manner as in a triangular meet. However, the scoring is done between each of the two schools at one instance as in a dual meet. For example, if schools A, B, and C compete in such a meet, the competition would be as follows: A versus B; A versus C; B versus C. Such meets are common where one school has a particularly fine facility and each of the other schools would prefer using it to competing dually on their own sites. Judging and scoring have to be done accurately, as there are three places indicated for each dual scoring combination. This often necessitates recording as many as six places.

Indoor meets. An indoor meet is conducted in an indoor setting on a track, the circumference of which is usually smaller than the standard 400 meters—frequently 200 meters or less. However, such meets may be conducted in a standard-size gymnasium. Events such as the high jump, relays, indoor shot put, standing broad jump, and running long jump may be conducted with the use of mats and other safety equipment. Such a meet could be scheduled 3 to 4 weeks before the first outdoor meet as a promotional device to create interest in track and field by spectators and athletes. Indoor competition is increasing around the country as more indoor facilities are being provided. A demonstration indoor meet scheduled prior to the opening of the track season and composed of baton passing, sprint starting, high jumping, and perhaps a display of conditioning exercises may also help sell the track program to the students and the community.

Large meets. Large meets will involve the participation of many athletes. It may be a four-way meet or a county-wide, district, or state meet. It may also be an invitational, relay, composite-scoring, Olympic type, intrasquad, interclass, or intraclass meet. The proper conduct of these meets requires much advance and careful preparation, since large numbers create numerous details that must receive attention. It will be more difficult to provide dressing rooms, roped-off warm-up areas, additional equipment, and correct advance publicity. It will be necessary to have heats and trials, so drawing and seeding will be required. A large number of officials will be needed. Scoring will be more involved than in the smaller meets, and there is an increased chance that ties will occur. These meets may be time-consuming, and if there is a lag between events, spectator interest will also lag. However, if these large meets are carefully organized, they can be very interesting to the spectators and enjoyable for the contestants. A good method for ensuring a smoothly run meet is to stage a dry run by planning a less involved and smaller meet prior to the larger meet.

Relay meets. A relay meet is one in which competition is conducted primarily among three or more schools in relay races only. Field events may also be a part of this type of meet.

Composite-scoring meets. A composite-scoring meet is one involving the participation of performers from two or more schools; the contestants participate in various events, and the scoring is done by totalling the individual accomplishments of the members of each team in a particular event. For example, the total of the times of all performers on a team competing in a particular running event would represent the team's accomplishment in that event. The scoring will be determined as if all members of the team in an event were one person. In the field events a team's accomplishment would be the total distance or total height made by all participants from each team added together. Usually only three participants form a team's membership in an event. The number of places used in scoring in an event would be determined by the number of teams entering. The points awarded would depend on the number of teams and the number of places. In case the number of members of each team in an event cannot be the same, the team's score for each event could be determined by the average accomplishment of the contestants in that event from each school. In this type of meet each individual is recognized in relation to her performance for her team. Individual effort is recognized only as it contributes to the team's score; some might consider this a disadvantage, whereas others consider it an advantage.

Intrasquad, interclass, and intraclass meets. In addition to their value as screening devices, intrasquad, interclass, and intraclass meets serve as motivational procedures for keeping members of the squad and members of the class interested. They are also excellent for use in culminating the track and field unit of the physical education classes.

Olympic high school track meets. Olympic high school track meets are good promotional devices to use every 4 years in connection with the approaching Olympic Games. They help stimulate interest in the United States' representatives in the Olympics and may help to reveal promising performers in the high schools and colleges of the country. This kind of meet should embrace a large geographic area and include entries from fifty to seventy-five schools, with events for boys and girls. To avoid overlooking any excellent performances there should be a careful screening of all contestants. The results from all major meets conducted during the season should be carefully scrutinized by the screening committee (composed of men and women coaches); the best three boys and girls timed in any preliminary heat and the top five finishers in the finals of the track events should be considered. In the field events the best height or distance made by the top six boys and girls qualifying for any final competition should be given consideration. The sixteen outstanding athletes in each event should be selected, and accounts of the accomplishments of the ''top sixteen'' should be reported in the papers and on the radio. It may be expedient to run a qualifying meet several days before the Olympic finals to reduce the number of trials and heats that usually would be scheduled with a large group.

An "Olympic Fund High School Track Meet," with a decathlon event held on the days preceding it, has been sponsored by some schools. The events have included the 70-yard high hurdles, the 100-meter dash, the high jump, the discus throw, the 200-meter dash and the 120-yard low hurdles, the pole vault, the long jump, the shot put, and the 660-yard run. Those competing in the decathlon were not permitted to enter the open meet.

A decathlon (or septathlon) for girls could be held at the same time as the one held for boys and run in a similar fashion. Decathlon events for girls could include the 200-meter dash, 80-meter hurdles, long jump, shot put, high jump, 100-meter dash, standing broad jump, discus throw, softball throw, and 400-meter run. Septathlon events could consist of the 100-meter dash, 80-meter hurdles, long jump, shot put, high jump, standing broad jump, and 200-meter dash.

The opening ceremonies could be patterned after those used in an Olympiad. There could be a parade of the boy and girl participants, led by a color guard as they circled the track. While the athletes stand at attention facing the center of the track, short introductory speeches could be made by visiting dignitaries, and the meet could be officially opened by some outstanding track figure. This could be followed by a flag-raising ceremony and the release of white pigeons and the lighting of the Olympic flame by the two (boy and girl) winners of the decathlon held the previous day. They could run around the track together holding the symbolic torch. The meet could include all the pomp and splendor of an Olympiad, and the spectators would enjoy every minute of it.

ORGANIZING THE MEET

One of the steps to be accomplished in planning for a track and field meet is the appointment of working committees. Interested businessmen, former track stars, and women who are interested in girls' sports, including faculty members, could serve on the various meet committees. A ticket committee would have the responsibility for printing, distributing, and collecting admissions tickets. A program committee could prepare a program booklet (or even a single sheet) to be sold for a small sum. This booklet might contain interesting background information about the athletes and pictures of the various members of the track squad(s), and it should have the events listed in chronologic order with final qualifiers listed if this is a final meet. A list of past meet records and also state and national records in the various events could be included in the program booklet. The publicity committee should arrange for press, radio, and television coverage. This committee might be able to invite and entertain some outstanding sportswoman as a guest at the meet. A field committee could devise a method to use in selecting contestants, do the timing at the qualifying meets, and act as officials at the final meet. A special events committee could be responsible for conceiving ideas that would add color and sparkle to the meet. The Becky Boone Relays, held annually at Eastern Kentucky University, has used such ideas as pioneer bonnets for awards to the champion relay teams and a pioneer covered wagon as a first aid station (Fig. 16-1).

Time for conducting meets. Spring is the usual time for the staging of track meets. Twilight and evening meets are particularly popular. One of the best times for conducting a large meet is on a Saturday near the middle of May. If schools involved are in a closely

Fig. 16-1. A pioneer covered wagon used as a first aid station.

located geographic area, the meet may be scheduled on a school day. If travel of any distance is involved, Saturday meets are preferred. The length of the time of the meet is an important matter as far as spectator interest is concerned. The average spectator will enjoy a meet that can be completed in 90 minutes; this can be done if the meet is well organized. In such a well-planned meet, field events need to be started at least 30 minutes earlier than do the running events.

Number of meets. Because competition is necessary to help competitors develop or continue to improve their performances, a number of meets need to be scheduled. Six to eight meets is a reasonable number to schedule. In addition one big meet, such as an invitational meet, should be included in the schedule each year. A trip for the members of the track squad involving participation away from home can contribute to the development of proper social and psychological values for girls.

Promotion of the meet. Well-located bulletin boards containing timely articles, up-to-date special features, and action pictures colorfully displayed can help advertise and promote track and field meets. School and community newspaper articles can be used to call attention to the meet by citing unusual or spectacular events being planned and mentioning some of the outstanding performers who will be present.

School assemblies at which girls of the squad, dressed in their uniforms, are introduced helps create interest in track and field, especially in a forthcoming meet. Each girl might answer a few planned questions concerning the rules, scoring, or other items about her event and the competitors who will possibly perform at the various meets. The demonstration of certain actions and the mention of other skills to watch for in a meet calls attention to the meet in addition to increasing the understanding of the spectators. At such special assemblies, school spirit may be developed or increased by involving the cheer-leaders and the school band. Also, holding such an assembly in the stadium or at the site of the meet a few days before a track meet occurs is a good way to promote it.

Early in the season a nearby school may be invited to participate in a practice meet by sending three girls to compete in each event, each girl being allowed to enter only one event, and with a race being run every 6 to 8 minutes. No score would be kept in a practice meet. This adds much interest and helps prepare the athletes for the coming season. At such a meet wallet-sized cards made in school colors, with the coming season's track schedule and school track records printed on them, could be handed out to all spectators to help promote attendance at future meets.

The appearance of the coach before civic, service, and church groups for the purpose of creating booster organizations to publicize, support, and provide officials also helps promote track and field activities.

Conducting the meet

Official entry form. In a sense, the entry blank helps promote a track meet as much as it helps in conducting the meet. Letters containing general information about the meet should be sent to prospective competing schools at least 4 weeks before the date of a given meet so that teams may apply for acceptance if they desire to do so. (See information sheet on following page.) About 2 weeks before the meet, entry forms should be sent to each school, and from the number of entries received and accepted the schedule of events should be determined (Table 16-1). The time schedule and detailed instructions on the order of events, location of dressing rooms, practice areas, safety regulations, special requirements, and other pertinent information should be sent to each school so that there will be no misunderstanding about them. The entry form should also contain information indicating the deadline for submitting entries and an announcement as to when and where the scratch meeting is to be held. The entry forms should also contain a list of the events,

Table 16-1. Order of events and time schedule

Olympic sports day for high school girls	
Morning—Field events	Afternoon—Field events
10:00　Running long jump—trials 　　　　Shot put　　　　—trials 　　　　Softball throw　　—trials 　　　　Javelin　　　　　—trials 　　　　Discus　　　　　—trials	12:30　High jump—finals 　1:30　Long jump—finals 　1:30　Shot put　—finals 　2:00　Javelin　—finals 　2:00　Discus　—finals
Morning—Running events	Afternoon—Running events
10:00　　50-yard hurdles—trials 10:15　　50-yard hurdles—semifinals 10:30　　50-yard dash　—trials 11:00　　50-yard dash　—semifinals 11:15　　100-meter dash　—trials 11:30　　100-meter dash　—semifinals	2:00　　50-yard hurdles—finals 　2:10　　50-yard dash　—finals 　2:20　　100-meter dash　—finals 　2:30　　400-meter run　—heat 1 (in sections) 　2:35　　400-meter run　—heat 2 (based on 　　　　　　　　　　　　　　　time) 　2:40　　400-meter run　—heat 3 　2:45　　200-yard shuttle relay 　3:10　　400-meter pursuit relay

INFORMATION SHEET
EKU Women's Invitational
April 28, 1978
9:30 AM (Eastern Standard Time)

1. *Return entry blank* to Dr. Martha Mullins, Women's Physical Education Department, Eastern Kentucky University, Richmond, Kentucky, 40475, by April 24, 1978.
2. *Each college* may have two entries in each of the events. A girl may enter any four events.
3. Eastern Kentucky University can provide *locker room facilities* at Weaver Gymnasium.
4. *Food* may be obtained at the college cafeteria (near the track).
5. *Housing* information is enclosed.
6. *Campus parking* permits and a map will be sent to you at a later date.
7. *First aid care* and supplies are the responsibility of the individual teams. Emergency care confined to campus medical service will be available free of charge. Serious incidences must be handled by the local or nearby hospitals at team expense.
8. There will be a *scratch meeting* at 9:00 AM at the track.
9. *Participants* should not be on the track or infield unless performing.
10. *Coaches and spectators* are expected to remain in the stands or out of competition areas.
11. *AIAW Rules* will govern all events.
12. *Awards* will be presented to the first six place winners. Scoring will be 10-8-6-4-2-1.
13. *The track* is a grasstex surface. Performers should wear ¼-inch spikes.
14. *The height of the hurdles* will be 2 feet 6 inches.
15. *A tentative time schedule* of events is as follows:

Preliminaries

TRACK		FIELD	
10:00	100-meter hurdles	9:30	Shot put
10:15	400-meter dash	9:30	Long jump
10:30	100-meter dash	10:15	Discus
10:45	1500-meter run		
11:00	200-meter dash		

Finals

TRACK		FIELD	
11:15	100-meter hurdles	10:00	High jump
11:25	400-meter dash	11:00	Long jump
11:35	100-meter dash	11:00	Discus
11:45	800-meter run	11:30	Shot put
11:55	200-meter dash	11:30	Javelin
12:05	400-meter relay		
12:15	800-meter relay		
12:25	800-meter medley relay		

OFFICIAL ENTRY FORM

EKU Women's Invitational
April 28, 19___
9:30 AM (Eastern Standard Time)

Institution _____

NOTE: Each college may have two entries in each event. A girl may enter any *four* events. Please check, in the space provided, the events in which each participant will compete. The best previous performance of each participant should be indicated also.

Participant's name (please type)	100-meter dash	Best time	200-meter dash	Best time	400-meter dash	Best time	800-meter dash	Best time	1500 meters	Best time	100-meter hurdles (hurdle height is 2 feet 6 inches)	Best time	High jump	Best mark	Long jump	Best mark	Shot put	Best mark	Discus	Best mark	Javelin	Best mark
(Last) (First)																						
1.																						
2.																						
3.																						
4.																						
5.																						
6.																						
7.																						

SIGNATURE OF COACH _____

OFFICIAL RELAY ENTRY BLANK
(To be completed by teams entering the relays)

Please enter _____ in the following relays:
COLLEGE/UNIVERSITY

400-METER RELAY

Participant's name   *Best time*

1. _____

2. _____

3. _____

4. _____

Alternates

1. _____

2. _____

3. _____

4. _____

800-METER MEDLEY RELAY

Participant's name   *Best time*

1. _____

2. _____

3. _____

4. _____

Alternates

1. _____

2. _____

3. _____

4. _____

800-METER RELAY

Participant's name   *Best time*

1. _____

2. _____

3. _____

4. _____

Alternates

1. _____

2. _____

3. _____

4. _____

The 400-METER RELAY will be run in lanes all the way.

The fourth runner in the 800-METER MEDLEY RELAY and the third runner in the 800-METER RELAY may break for the inside lane as soon as the baton is received, according to NAGWS rules.

_____
SIGNATURE OF COACH

RETURN TO: Dr. Martha Mullins
Department of Physical
Education for Women
Eastern Kentucky
University
Richmond, Kentucky 40475
PHONE: (606) 622-5108

a blank space where each participant's name may be placed, indicating the competition she wishes to enter, and a place to list the participant's best time or distance. (See official entry form and relay entry blank on pp. 198-199.)

Drawing and seeding of the athletes. The coaches usually agree as to the number of participants to be entered in each event at a dual meet. This number is usually two or three participants from each school in each event. In a triangular or larger meet it is common for each team to be limited to the entry of two participants in each event. It will be necessary to conduct trial heats in all cases where the number of participants exceeds the number of lanes to determine the finalists. The clerk of the course has the responsibility of placing competitors in the various heats.

Table 16-2 shows a recommended pattern to follow when determining the heats that are used in qualifying runners for semifinal heats and finals. Heats are used when there are more runners in a race than there are lanes. Many meet directors do not wish to use heats in the longer races (400 meters and longer) because of the time it takes to complete such races. In this latter situation runners are put into flights rather than heats, and the places are determined by time rather than by who placed first, second, or third in a heat. When this method is used, the fastest girls are placed in one flight and the slowest in the last flight. To use this system accurately the times made previously by the girls must be turned in to the meet director.

When deciding which system to use, the determining factors are the experience of the competitors, the weather, the length of time it takes to conduct a meet, and the number of entries that have been received. Of course, the more qualifying heats that are run, the longer it takes to run off the meet. Also, if girls have been allowed to enter back-to-back races, many scratches will occur as the qualifying gets harder. All the girls and coaches should be aware of the number of heats, the number who will qualify, and whether the use of flights is planned before the competition begins.

Many meet directors wonder whether it is wise to have quarterfinals. They may wish to have fewer qualifying places and conduct only semifinals.

The number of heats required is determined by the number of lanes available and the number of runners and hurdlers entered in the meet. After all entries have been received and classified according to the reported times made in the events, the heats are formed. To have the best competitors in the finals, heat leaders (fastest girls) are seeded and distributed throughout the necessary heats. For example, if there are to be three preliminary heats, the three girls with the best times will be the heat leaders of each of the three heats. The next best times are also seeded so that the competition for each heat is comparable. In this example of three heats (involving eighteen girls) on a six-lane track, two girls would qualify for the finals in each heat, making a total of six finalists (Table 16-2). Semifinal heats may also be run if desirable. (See Appendix D for sample heat cards.)

When all heats have been formed, the games committee conducts the drawings to determine in which lanes to place the runners. In the semifinals and finals of the straightaway races the two girls with fastest times are placed in the two middle lanes, and the remaining competitors are placed to the right and left of them. This procedure enables the timers and finish judges to properly perform their duties of timing and selecting the

Table 16-2. Suggested pattern for determining heats*

Number of entries	Number of heats	Number to pick	Quarter-finals	Number to pick	Semifinals	Number in finals
For six lanes						
1 to 6	0	0	0	0	0	1 to 6
7 to 12	2	3	0	0	0	6
13 to 18	3	2	0	0	0	6
19 to 24	4	3	0	0	2	6
25 to 30	5	2	0	0	2 (of 5)	6
31 to 36	6	2	0	0	2 (of 6)	6
37 to 42	7	3	4 (5, 5, 5, 6)	3	2 (of 6)	6

For more entries, quarterfinals will be necessary.

For seven lanes						
1 to 7	0	0	0	0	0	1 to 7
8 to 14	2	3	0	0	0	6
15 to 21	3	4	0	0	2 (of 6)	6
22 to 28	4	3	0	0	2 (of 6)	6
29 to 35	5	2	0	0	2 (of 5)	6
36 to 42	6	2	0	0	2 (of 6)	6
43 to 49	7	2	0	0	2 (of 7)	6
50 to 56	8	3	4 (of 6)	3	2 (of 6)	6

For more entries, quarterfinals will follow the same pattern.

For eight lanes						
1 to 8	0	0	0	0	0	1 to 8
9 to 16	2	4	0	0	0	8
17 to 24	3	4	0	0	2 (of 6)	8
25 to 32	4	4	0	0	2 (of 8)	8
33 to 40	5	3	0	0	2 (7, 8)	8
41 to 48	6	2	0	0	2 (of 6)	8
49 to 56	7	2	0	0	2 (of 7)	8
57 to 64	8	2	0	0	2 (of 8)	8
65 to 72	9	3	4 (6, 7, 7, 7)	2	2 (of 8)	8

For more entries, quarterfinals will follow the same pattern.

For nine lanes						
1 to 9	0	0	0	0	0	1 to 9
10 to 18	2	4	0	0	0	8
19 to 27	3	3	0	0	0	8
28 to 36	4	2	0	0	0	8
37 to 45	5	3	0	0	2 (7, 8)	8
46 to 54	6	3	0	0	2 (9)	8
55 to 63	7	2	0	0	2 (of 7)	8
64 to 72	8	4	4 (of 8)	4	2 (of 8)	8

For more entries, quarterfinals will follow the same pattern.

*Parenthetical numbers indicate that the heats have an unequal number of runners. The figures indicate how many runners in the heats.

winners. It also enables the faster girls to keep track of the lane assignments of their competitors for the later races.

In races run around a curve the fastest girl is placed in lane number one, and the remaining competitors are placed according to the times they made in their qualifying heats. Usually they are placed so that the second fastest runner is in lane number two, and so on. At a dual meet where the best times made are not known, the visiting team members may be assigned to either the odd-numbered lanes or the even-numbered lanes as they desire, and the home team representatives take the opposite lanes. In field events the best competitors compete last. If no distances or heights are available, the order of performance or lane position is determined by drawing lots. Competitors may use Kelly pool balls for the drawing.

In the field events (discus, shot put, and javelin) at big meets each competitor has at least three trials, and the seven best competitors each have three additional throws. Each competitor should be credited with the best distance made in any of her trial throws. One more finalist than there are places to be awarded should be chosen. The girl with the best throw in the preliminaries should throw last. Sometimes it is advantageous to have the competitors take two trial throws in succession, and it may speed up the time spent running an event.

Equipment needed. The field should be arranged so that spectators are allowed to view all the events from one location; therefore the jumping pits and weight areas should be located in the center of the field and close to the edge, where the spectators will be seated. Sandbags, sawdust bags, dirt mounds, and foam rubber used in the high-jump pits can be placed on the playing field and removed after the season ends. Finish lines should be located in the center of the track close to the spectators. Everything possible should be done to help the spectators see the performers in their events. All finish areas should be kept free of nonparticipating athletes; faculty, helpers, the press, and the coaches should

Table 16-3. Chart for handicapping lanes for staggered starts (quarter-mile track)*

	2-turn stagger (440 and 880)	1-turn stagger (220)
30-inch lanes		
Lane 2 over 1 †	13 feet 7¼ inches	6 feet 9⅝ inches
Lanes 3 to 8 over next inside lane	15 feet 8½ inches	7 feet 10¼ inches
36-inch lanes		
Lane 2 over 1	16 feet 9 inches	8 feet 4 inches
Lanes 3 to 8 over next inside lane	18 feet 10¼ inches	9 feet 5⅛ inches
42-inch lanes		
Lanes 2 over 1	19 feet 10¾ inches	9 feet 11⅜ inches
Lanes 3 to 8 over next inside lane	21 feet 11⅞ inches	11 feet
48-inch lanes		
Lane 2 over 1	23 feet	11 feet 6 inches
Lanes 3 to 8 over next inside lane	25 feet	12 feet 6 inches

*This formula for staggered running must be followed when running races around a curve to make up for the length differential of the curved track.
†If Lane 1 is wider than the other lanes by 4 inches, the staggered schedule for Lanes 3 to 8 can be applied to Lane 2. This should eventually be phased out.

have a special place to sit so that the confusion that often results from their objection to decisions, as well as their instruction to their performers, is not apparent to the spectators.

The equipment necessary for conducting a track meet depends on the kind of meet planned and the scheduled events. The establishment of proper starting and finishing lines, the identification of baton exchange zones, and the proper marking of shot put, discus, javelin, and other throwing areas must be done according to the specifications in the rule book well in advance of the meet. (See Tables 16-3 and 16-4 for stagger markings and metric equivalents.)

It is obvious that the track and field area should be in the best possible condition on the day of the meet. Extra hurdles should be available in case of breakage. The proper number of starting blocks, a wheelbarrow to transport them, and hammers for students to properly set the blocks for each competitor should also be available. A steel ring for use in the discus throw and a toeboard made according to specifications for the shot put are also needed. Large sturdy signs placed at the various curved lines indicating the shot-putting distances help the fans to tell the approximate distance recorded on each put. Another method of marking the distance of each put is to use flag markers that are the colors of the participating schools. A white cloth flag located in the putting area at the national record distance could be used as an incentive to the athlete and a guide to the fans. There should be scales available to weigh each competitor's shot, and a steel tape, rake, tamp, shovel, broom, and benches for the contestants are also needed. The student helper should carry the shot back to the putting area after each throw rather than throwing it back, and the competitor should meet him halfway to receive it. A similar system is used with each

Table 16-4. Equivalents for the metric system*

Meters	Yards	Feet	Inches	Yards	Meters
1	1	–	3.37	50	45.72
5	5	1	1.48	100	91.44
10	10	2	9.70	110	100.58
50	54	2	0.50	200	182.88
80	87	1	5.60	220	201.17
100	109	1	1	300	274.32
200	218	2	2	440	402.34
400	437	1	4	880	804.67
1000	1093	1	10	1320	1207.01
1500	1640	1	3		

Feet	Meters	Feet	Meters
1	0.305	20	6.096
2	0.610	30	9.144
3	0.914	40	12.192
4	1.219	50	15.240
5	1.524	100	30.480
10	3.048	200	60.960

*More complete tables may be found in mathematics books, the AAU's *Track and Field Handbook*, or the NAGWS *Track and Field Guide*. For our present needs, however, the following is sufficient: 1 meter = 39.37 inches = 3.2808 feet = 1.0936 yard; 1 kilometer = 1000 meters = 0.621370 mile.

contestant in the discus contest. The student helper runs back toward the ring with the discus and does not attempt to hurl it back.

In the long jump a white board is used for the takeoff. Clay placed in front of this board will easily enable an official to determine a foul. Small red flags about 2 feet high, placed at each side of the takeoff board, will enable the jumpers to know where the board is located. A marker board in the pit will indicate the distance jumped. An adjustable red arrow mounted on a board can be used to show the leading distance attained by the top performer. A broom, rake, shovel, and steel tape are the equipment needed to conduct the long jump. All officials and helpers should be located on the side of the pit away from the spectators. A height marker large enough to be easily seen in the seating area of the stadium is needed to indicate to the fans the progress made by the high jumpers. Indicator cards to show fans the exact height attained by individual performers may also be used. Other equipment needed are extra crossbars, and a steel tape. Student helpers are often used to put the bar back into place after it has been knocked off by a competitor.

In addition to the necessary special equipment previously mentioned, the following general equipment is also needed:

Checklist
Event forms
Tables, chairs, benches
Clipboards
Pencils
Large blackboard
Large scoreboard to show current results
   and standings
Victory stand
Judges' stand
Officials' ribbons
Awards for winners
Wind gauge
Finish yarn or gauze
Field distance marking stakes
Steel tapes—300-foot, 50-foot, 8-foot
   lengths (suitable number for events)

Scorebook
Public address system
Area ropes and flags
Field event implements
Pit forks, rakes, and equipment
Hurdles
Starting blocks and mallets
Whistle
Starter's gun and blanks
Small blackboard for starter's gun smoke
   to be seen
Fluorescent sleeve
Batons
Stopwatches
Track and field rule book
First aid kit
Rest rooms, unlocked

A public address system is almost a necessity for properly conducting a meet. The meet director should check to be sure that one is available. The press, radio, and television personnel must be provided with the facilities they request and given copies of the schedule and background information on the various performers.

Selection of officials. Each official must be selected and assigned her duties well in advance of the meet. It is best to make these assignments before the season begins, and often an official can be placed in the same assignment from week to week and from year to year. A list of each official's duties should be mimeographed, and the rules pertaining to her event, along with a list of her duties, should be taped to the clipboard she uses at a meet for easy reference. Members of the male coaching staff, faculty members, girls from the officials' clubs, boys from track teams, and interested leaders in the community that have had track experience are good sources for securing officials. Incompetent officials should not be asked to perform these duties a second time. All officials must be properly identified by ribbons or tags. On the day of the meet, the meet director should have no definite assignment, so that she may coordinate the entire program and be available for any emergency. She should have two runners at her side at all times for emergency errands.

The following officials are suggested for meets in which three or more places are being scored. (Their duties are outlined in detail in Chapter 17.)

1 Meet director	1 Clerk of the course
1 Track referee	1 Marshall
1 Field referee	1 Scorer
1 Starter	1 Announcer
1 Assistant starter	1 Physician or nurse
7 Finish judges (including a chief)	1 Surveyor
7 Timers (including a chief)	1 Recorder of new records
6 Inspectors	1 Custodian of awards
Field judges (three per event, including a chief)	As many assistants as needed
1 Custodian of equipment	

Numerous helpers are needed to conduct a meet. These helpers should be contacted and a confirmation received from them early. Extra helpers are also needed for use in an emergency and should be contacted long before the date of a meet.

It is especially important to have a large scoreboard located on the field where everyone can read it and keep up with the progress of the meet. Events should be posted as they are completed, and a running score should be kept.

A good announcer is needed for many purposes, including notifying athletes that their event is ready to begin. The three-call method of notifying athletes, with a 5-minute interval between calls, is a good one to use. The announcer should also keep the audience well informed concerning school records, state and national records, and interesting information about local and visiting team members. The announcer should be someone who especially likes track, is accurate and thorough, and gives results immediately. The announcer can do a great deal to keep the audience interested and happy.

Good premeet planning includes a well-constructed system of checklist forms that contains all the details for administering a meet. These should contain a list of all the necessary information, people, equipment, and supplies needed, such as dressing room assignments, names, pertinent telephone numbers, various officials' assignments, names of alternate helpers for a late or absent official, and the names of the visiting coaches. It is important that one person be responsible for the checking out and in of the stopwatches, measuring tapes, markers, officials' badges, and so on.

A physician or nurse should be in attendance at a meet. A first aid station equipped with towels and blankets should be available but not conspicuously located near the spectators.

The events. The events that are to be scheduled will be determined by the age, training, and experience of the participants and the kind of meet desired. Table 16-5 is a suggested list of events that are usually included.

Order of events. The events should be arranged for expediency and the interest of the participants. (Except for the national AAU competitive meets, there is no established order of events.) It is common to begin the field events about 30 minutes before the running events, and it is best to have completed half the field events before participation in the

Table 16-5. Suggested track and field events

Event	Elementary	Middle school	Secondary	College and open
Running	50-yard dash	50-yard dash	50-yard dash	100 meters
	75-yard dash	100 meters	100 meters	200 meters
	100 meters	200 meters	200 meters	400 meters
	200 meters	400 meters	400 meters	800 meters
	400 meters	800 meters	800 meters	1500 meters
	800 meters	1500 meters	1500 meters	3000 meters
	1500 meters	1900 meters	3000 meters	5000 meters
	(1 mile cross-country)	(1½ miles cross-country)		10,000 meters
Relays	200-meter shuttle	200 meters	400 meters	400 meters
	200-meter pursuit	400-meter pursuit	800 meters	800 meters
	400-meter pursuit	800-meter pursuit	800-meter medley	800-meter medley
		800-meter medley	1600 meters	1600 meters
				3000 meters
Hurdles	50 yards	50 yards	50 yards	100 meters
		80 meters	80 meters	(2 feet 9 inches)
		100 meters	100 meters	
			(2 feet 9 inches)	200 meters
			200 meters	400 meters
Field	6-pound shot put	8-pound shot put	Shot put	Shot put (4 kilos)
	Basketball throw	Basketball throw	Softball throw	Discus
	Softball throw	Softball throw	Discus	Javelin
	Standing long jump	Standing long jump	Javelin	Long jump
	Running long jump	Running long jump	Running long jump	High jump
	High jump	High jump	High jump	

remainder is begun. This last procedure will enable some persons to officiate in the second as well as the first half of the events, thus facilitating the conduct of the meet (Table 16-1).

Participation in running events takes precedence over field events whenever a participant is scheduled in both simultaneously. In small meets the order of events need not follow a previously set pattern. However, the order should be made known to the coaches prior to the opening of the meet. It might be best to experiment with the order of events and make some changes for variety.

The hurdle races are usually held first because the hurdles can be placed on the track prior to the beginning of any other running events. They are removed immediately after the race is completed, thus avoiding interference with the other running events.

The sprint and the distance races should be so spaced that sufficient recovery time is afforded athletes who want to participate in more than one of each type. Relay races are usually conducted last, as this makes a fitting climax for the competitors, promotes good team effort, and comes as a thrilling experience for the spectators.

Scoring procedures. The methods of scoring that are used in a meet vary with the number of places to be counted as indicated in Table 17-2.

The finish judges' slips, head timer's reports, and field judges' reports are sent to the scorer's table immediately after a girl's participation in an event is completed, so that the information may be recorded on the master sheet. Individual and team scores are posted and should be made available to the coaches and the announcer. Up-to-the-minute reporting enables the announcer to reveal the winners soon after the event is completed, which increases the interest of the spectators.

Ribbons are excellent awards to give to all place winners. They are inexpensive, but often they mean a great deal to the girl who earns one. She will probably display it proudly on her bulletin board or mirror or in her scrapbook. The date, name of the meet, the event, and the order of finish should be included on the ribbon. Plaques or trophies may be awarded to the winning team. It is of utmost importance that winners be acknowledged as soon as possible after an event is completed. The announcer should announce the names of the winners to the spectators as they are presented their awards.

Follow-up procedures. Prompt follow-up letters containing expressions of appreciation are sent to officials and coaches to create good will and ensure future cooperation and participation. The coach of the host school usually sends these letters.

Care must be exercised to report the results of the meet correctly, and the final results of the meet are sent to the coaches of the visiting teams. The conduct of the meet should be evaluated, and suggestions for future improvements should be noted. Student helpers may be recognized in school assemblies and through the school paper for their part in the operation of the meet. The members of the track squad should discuss the conduct and performances of their participants, noting strengths and weaknesses. A squad may be recognized for good conduct and superior performance before the student body during a school assembly.

SUMMARY

A track and field meet should be a festive and fast-moving spectacle. The following suggestions are presented to help increase interest, ensure smooth conduct, and add color and pageantry to the meet.

1. Invite the guest school to participate against your team at least 4 weeks in advance of the date of the meet, and send entry blanks 2 weeks in advance of the date.
2. Secure key officials well in advance of the meet date. It takes many people to conduct a successful meet (sixty to one hundred people for a large track meet). If a few key officials are properly trained, other persons such as faculty members, members of the boys' track team, and other students may fill in and help effectively.
3. Prepare an interesting display of the trophies and prizes to be awarded, along with pictures of the track squad members, in a downtown store window.
4. Plan some special entertainment for the spectators that will add color and create interest in the track meet. If these special attractions are enjoyed by the spectators, they will have a good time at the meet and want to come to the next one.
5. Make special arrangements to have refreshments available for purchase by the spectators during the meet.
6. Have some prominent citizen act as honorary referee at the meet.
7. Boy and Girl Scout groups may be used effectively as color guards, ribbon girls, ushers, and/or student helpers.
8. Arrange for a public address system ahead of time, and check to ascertain whether it is still available the day before the meet.
9. Assume that at least one official will not show up and be prepared to substitute a

responsible person for the absent one. This usually means that a few extra people must be available for this purpose.

10. Arrange to have the track areas marked off well ahead of time. Be sure all equipment is in good repair and neatly arranged until it is time for it to be used.

11. At least one day before the meet post the following on the school bulletin board: the list of entries, details of the meet, location of meet, order of events, time schedule, the time squad members are to be excused from class, the time the school transportation will leave if meet is away from home, where to dress, and so on.

12. Have a desk placed on the field for the announcer and recorder, and have two responsible students stationed near the desk to be available for running errands.

13. Make one person responsible for checking out and in stopwatches, tapes, and all equipment for officials.

14. Have the participating athletes parade around the track before the meet led by a color guard.

15. Begin a meet on time, and follow the prescribed time schedule as closely as possible. Permit little time lag between events.

16. Have the announcer focus the fans' attention on specific areas of the field at certain times. He should notify the spectators of times and distances of the present records and call attention to records that are being shattered or threatened. Announce the winners as soon as possible after an event is completed, and be sure the spectators can see the winners receive their awards. If the winners receive their awards from a stair-step platform, as do the Olympic winners, it will add color to the meet. A bugler blowing victory notes also adds a dramatic touch to the ceremony.

17. As soon as possible send reports of the official results of the meet to the officials of the school or schools that took part in the meet.

18. Send notes of appreciation to all those who assisted in conducting the meet, and properly recognize student officials for their help.

A detailed set of guidelines for coaches to use for the beginners during meet participation follows:

1. Be sure that all performers know in what events they are entered, when the events are scheduled, and to whom they report.

2. Inform the girls of the meaning of first, second, and third calls that are made by officials.

3. Have a definite warm-up procedure and schedule in mind, indicating place, duration, and time to warm up.

4. Be certain that the girls know how to set their blocks and are able to manipulate the actual setting to fit their needs.

5. Have the girls able to run their race well, stay in their own lane, and sprint a few yards beyond the finish line after participating in a running event.

6. Be confident as a coach that the girls know the rules governing their event, what to expect from the official in charge, and what to do if there is some discrepancy in the conduct of the event.

CHAPTER 17

Officiating

The success of conducting a track meet depends largely on the capabilities of the officials in charge of running the meet. Securing enough qualified officials is an ever-present organizational problem, but it is essential to have them if the operation of any meet is to be efficient.

The duties of each official are important; they must be able to accurately judge, measure, and record the results made in the trials and finals. In meets of the caliber of league finals, championships, or others in which records are to be tabulated, the officials should be certified with the AAU, the National Association of Girls' and Womens' Sports (NAGWS), or other sponsoring agencies. The AAU recognizes new records only if three certified officials are present. Because of the large number of officials needed and the small supply available in any given school or area, alternate procedures have to be developed for accurately judging performances at meets. Some suggestions are presented later in the chapter concerning what steps to take when only a limited number of officials are available.

LIST OF NECESSARY OFFICIALS

1 Meet director
1 Track referee
1 Clerk of the course
1 Field referee
1 Starter
7 Finish judges (including a chief)
7 Timers (including a chief)
6 Inspectors (including a chief)
Field judges (three per event, includ-
    ing a chief)
1 Custodian of equipment

1 Marshall
1 Scorer
1 Announcer
1 Physician or nurse
1 Surveyor
1 Recorder of new records
1 Custodian of awards
1 Press steward
Assistants as needed by clerk, scorer,
    timer, field judge, meet director,
    and track crew

DUTIES AND RESPONSIBILITIES

Officials must know exactly what their duties and responsibilities are. Detailed instructions for and responsibilities of each official are included in this list. The descriptions are adapted from the AAU and other current rule books.

Meet director. The meet director must be responsible for the following:

1. Obtain permission for the use of the field and procure the necessary officials.
2. Purchase the medals.
3. Send out entry blanks and a brochure of the order of events.

4. Rule on all late entries or substitutions.
5. Procure all equipment needed for conducting the meet.
6. See that weights and measures are available on the field for checking field equipment.
7. Obtain the completed results of the meet from the scorer.

Track referee. The track referee must do the following:

1. See that the competitors are listed for the proper heats and lanes prior to the start of the meet.
2. Run the events and oversee the general operation of the program.
3. Inspect the track to see that it is properly marked.
4. Confer with the chief finish judge, head timer, clerk, scorer, and starter to be sure that each has sufficient assistants and personnel to carry out her responsibilities.
5. Inform the head officials of the number of heats needed in the running events and the names and total number of competitors who have qualified for the semifinals and finals.
6. Make final decisions on any disputes that arise for which there are no set rules and decide on any technical questions for which there are no established answers.
7. Make sure that only authorized personnel are allowed on the field; exclude any person (competitor or official) for improper apparel; make immediate decisions in regard to any protest or objection made about the conduct of a competitor or official.
8. Inspect, approve, and sign the scorer's records after the meet.

Clerk of the course. Smoothness and ease of operations when placing competitors in their proper lanes at the appointed time of the race is the principal duty of the clerk of the course. To accomplish her assignments she must do the following:

1. Obtain from the track referee the name and number of all competitors and the events and heats in which they are scheduled to participate.
2. Check the start and finish line of each race to determine if the proper distances have been established.
3. Supervise the drawings for the lanes prior to each trial, if the event is to be run in lanes. Place each competitor in the proper lane, and for relays be sure that each lead-off runner has a baton.
4. Obtain from the track referee the list of names and competitors for the semifinals and finals of each race and place them in the proper lanes before the races commence.

Field referee. This official has the same relative duties concerning the field events as the track referee has for the running events. Specifically, she must do the following:

1. Be sure that there is an adequate number of judges and assistants present to conduct all field events.
2. Obtain the list of contestants for the field events from the meet director and determine the order of competition and the number of finalists needed. Turn over to the head field judge the list of competitors scheduled to participate in each event.
3. Make sure that the necessary equipment for conducting all field events is available

and that the equipment meets the official standards. Rule on requests that contestants be permitted to use personal equipment.

4. Inspect all throwing areas to determine if the sectors and scratch lines are clearly marked, and check the jumping pits, runways, and crossbars to ascertain if everything is in readiness for competition.

5. See that the events start on time.

6. Inspect, approve, and sign the scorer's records at the conclusion of the meet.

Starter. The starter has the responsibility or authority to do the following:

1. Control the competitors at the starting line and be sole judge of any questions arising at the starting marks (Fig. 17-1). She must also wear a red jacket or have a red sleeve on the arm holding the gun.

2. Start all races with a gun of not less than 32 calibers, using a powder that gives a distinct flash. She must hold the gun in such a manner (using a background when necessary) that the flash is easily seen by the judges and timers at the finish. She must also have at least two blanks in the gun prior to the start of each race.

3. Issue instructions to competitors concerning the conduct of the race and the starting rules. She must also determine that all girls are on the starting line and ready to run before she fires the gun. The starting commands she should use are "On your marks!" and "Set!" Then the gun is fired.

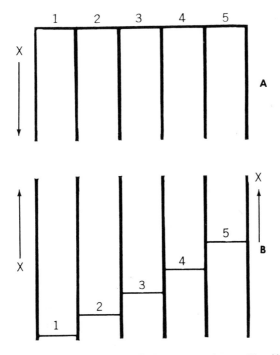

Fig. 17-1. Starter's *(X)* positions. **A,** From even starts. **B,** From staggered starts. (Key: X = position of starter.) The correct positions the starter should assume when running even and staggered starts are shown. The races from the staggered starting positions are run around a curve. The starter must be clearly visible to the judges and timers at the beginning of the races; however, it does not matter on which side of the track she stations herself.

4. Have the distance runners, who take a standing start, informed that the command will be "Set!" and then the gun will be fired.

5. Blow a whistle to receive the sign from the chief timer that judges and timers are ready.

6. Recall the runners in the case of a false start by firing the gun a second time. If any false start is made before the gun is fired, the starter must then call everyone off her mark and later reassemble them. One false start will disqualify the runner from the race.

7. Fire the gun after the set position when all competitors are motionless. This is to avoid giving an undue advantage to any competitor.

8. Use arm signals to coincide with vocal commands. After hearing the signal from the head timer, the starter is to raise the gun. ("Gun is up!" is the remark made by the head timer.) The other arm should be pointing at the ground to indicate runners are at their marks. On "Set!" the arm without the gun is raised sharply upward to shoulder height, signaling the set position to the timers.

9. During the races of more than one lap, fire a warning shot as the lead runners cross the starting line with one lap to go, indicating that the leaders have started the last lap of the race. This is referred to as the "gun lap."

Chief finish judge. The chief finish judge must do the following:

1. Assign the finish judges their places, pass out the judges' slips, and issue proper instructions about how they should be marked (if judges' slips are being used). (See Chapter 16 and Appendix D.)

2. See that the finish tape is ready and that there are two knowledgeable people available to hold it.

3. Observe the finish of each race and be prepared to make a decision in case of a tie vote by the judges concerning the finish placement of the runners. If there is a photographic device used in filming the finishes, the chief judge must review the pictures to make a final decision. If there is a disagreement among the judges after the photographic examination, relative to the finish position of the runners, the final decision is made by the track referee.

4. Collect all the completed finish slips and place them in their correct order, with the first-place winner on top. Slips should then be sent directly to the scorer.

5. Obtain the place results verbally from the judges and record them on the event card when the individual slips are not being used.

Finish judges. The finish judge's duties are as follows:

1. Pick the winners on the basis that at the moment any part of a contestant's torso reaches the nearest edge of the finish line she has crossed it.

2. Observe first the relative positions of the runners as they approach the finish line from 40 to 50 yards away. As the runners draw near the finish line (within 15 to 20 yards), the finish judge should turn her eyes to the finish line to observe the lanes and the positions to which each judge is assigned to pick the winning finishers.

3. Fill out her judge's slip and give it immediately to the chief finish judge without conferring with the other judges. If slips are not used, the judge should give the number of the contestant and the place she picked her to the chief finish judge on

request. If numbers are not being used, the judge should verbally give the name of the place she has picked to the chief finish judge.

Chief timer. The duties of the chief timer are as follows:

1. See that each timer receives an adequate supply of time slips, that there are approved watches for the timers to use, and that the watches are synchronized and wound. The watches should be previously checked to determine if they are in good working condition. (See Appendix D for samples of timers' slips.)
2. Acquaint herself with the previous records made in the particular event being run.
3. Assign timers for each place finisher, and advise the timers to give their undivided attention to the race being run and the timing of the race.
4. After the whistle of the starter signals the start of the race, the chief timer must listen to the report from the head finish judge that the judges are ready, check to see that her timers are ready, and signal back to the starter that all is ready for the start of the race.
5. Collect the timers' slips (if they are being used) and check the recorded time against the time shown on each watch. Place the slips in order with the first-place winner's time on top and send them to the scorer. If the slips are not being used, the chief timer should record the times made on the timer's card and check each time given with the time shown on the watch.
6. Give the order for the timers to reset their watches in preparation for the start of the next race.

Timers. The timers' duties are as follows:

1. Start watches with the flash of powder from the starter's gun.
2. Make sure their watches are wound after each race throughout the entire meet.
3. Stop the watch at the instant any part of the torso of a runner reaches the nearest edge of the finish line (Fig. 17-2).
4. Give the results of the time to the chief timer either by recording it on their slips or verbally. Present the watch for inspection of the time shown and reset the watch only when told to do so by the chief timer.

Inspectors. The inspectors are responsible for observing the competitors as they run and immediately reporting to the track referee any infractions of the rules that occur (Fig. 17-3). They should also observe the runners in the relays to determine if the correct baton passing procedures are being used, and in the 400- and 800-meter runs, to observe if lane infractions have been committed. They are not to make any decisions but only to report any infractions that occur.

Chief field judge of each event. The primary responsibility of the chief judge of each field event is the efficient operation of the competition procedures in that field event. She must do the following:

1. Supervise the drawing of lots if the order of competition has not already been determined.
2. See that equipment is available and that the pits and throwing areas are accurately marked and safely cleared. She must refer anyone who wishes to use her own throwing equipment in the competition to the field referee for a final decision.

Fig. 17-2. Finish of the pentathlon 200-meter race in the United States vs. Canada meet, August, 1972. The timers, judges, and recorder are seen here.

3. Instruct the field judges and assistants as to their duties—the methods of measuring, determination of fouls, and so on (Fig. 17-4).
4. Advise contestants as to the location of runways, sectors, and scratch lines. She must notify them of the order of competition, the number of contestants who will qualify for the finals, what are considered fouls, and so on.
5. Take measurements, read and record them, and call "foul" when a foul occurs.
6. Determine who will throw in the finals, and make this announcement to the competitors. Record the results of the final trials, determine how the contestants finish, sign the event sheets, and send the results to the scorer.
7. Collect all equipment and return it to the custodian.

Field judges. The judges of the various field events perform the following:
1. Measure distances after all preliminary throws are completed.
2. Measure long jump and shot put distances immediately after each trial (Fig. 17-5).
3. Collect equipment at the conclusion of the competition and return it to the custodian.

Fig. 17-3. Rounding the curve in the 220-yard sprint. The inspector in the background is checking the runners for any rule infractions as they round the curve. Notice the extreme concentration on the faces of the runners.

Fig. 17-4. High jump competition. This picture was taken during a meet in which this girl cleared 4 feet 2 inches in the high jump. She is in the 12- to 13-year age group. Notice the positions of the judge and his assistants.

Fig. 17-5. Long jumper in action. Note the officials at work and the spectators showing interest in the results.

4. In the high jump announce the starting height and the subsequent heights to which the bar will be raised at the end of each round. Raise it the necessary height as indicated by the head judge of the high jump.

Custodian of the equipment. The custodian of the equipment is responsible for all the equipment, implements, and items used in the track meet. She is to issue all necessary equipment, watches, clipboards, and so on to all judges, timers, and other officials, and see that such equipment is returned.

Marshall. The marshall acts in the capacity of a guard in preventing anyone not actually involved in the competition or officiating in the meet from entering the enclosure. She may have assistants aiding her and in this case should assign them to their various policing duties.

Scorer. The scorer must do the following things:

1. Record the order in which each competitor finished her event by using the record of the times made that was furnished to her by the timers and by using the results presented to her by the field judge. She will place the results on a master tally sheet.
2. Allot the proper number of points (if points are being scored) for the various winning places to the teams entered.
3. Notify the clerk of the course of the eligible competitors for the semifinals and finals.
4. Determine the lane placement of runners for semifinal and final races.
5. Have all the records checked, approved, and signed by the referee at the conclusion of the meet. Turn over all completed records to the meet director.

Announcer. The announcer is in charge of the public address system and is to inform the public of the progress of the meet, competitors' names, positions, and the results of each race, heat, and event. Furthermore, the announcer is to inform the athletes of the warning calls preparatory to each event and notify the finalists to report to their respective events.

Physician or nurse. Obviously, a physician or nurse should be on hand to administer to anyone who becomes ill or is injured.

Surveyor. The surveyor is to survey the track to determine the exact measurements of the distances marked off on it. This includes proper markings of the distances, throwing sectors, scratch marks, and other such areas specified for the conduct of the various events.

Recorder. The recorder is in charge of processing new records and completing application forms so they can be approved. It is her duty to see that these applications are properly filled out and signed by the proper referees and officials to ensure their acceptance.

Custodian of awards. The awards are in the sole care of the custodian of awards, who receives a list of the winners' names directly from the scorer. She then sees that all awards are properly given out in the prescribed manner.

Press steward. There can be more than one press steward. In any event, they should obtain (from the clerk of the course and scorer) the names of all contestants in each event, the names of the point winners, and the times recorded or distances made in each winning or record performance and keep the press thoroughly informed of the results of the meet.

RULES OF THE EVENTS

There are definite and clear-cut rules of competition under which a meet is conducted. Observance of them is essential to ensure that all are treated fairly and that conditions of competition will be the same for all events. The chapters dealing with specific events have included rules on conducting them.

From time to time rule changes are made for conducting various events, and the officials must be aware of these changes. The rules are kept up-to-date and are easily referred to in the NAGWS *Track and Field Guide,* which is published every 2 years, and in the AAU's *Track and Field Handbook,* a yearly publication. Both publications are easily obtainable and include the new and current rules as well as specifics for track measurements, equipment specifications, and so on.

Rules of track events. In all track competition run in lanes, the choice of lanes is drawn for in each heat. After the semifinalists or finalists are selected, the lanes are assigned with the two runners with the fastest times placed in the center two lanes, the next two fastest times placed on either side of the center lanes, and so on to the slower runners, who are placed in the outside lanes. In semifinals of races run on a curved track up to a distance of 400 meters, lane assignment will be decided by draw. In all races of 800 meters and longer, lane assignment will be determined by draw.

A false start at the starting line will result in the offending competitor being disqualified from that race. Each girl must be motionless after the set position has been assumed.

All competitors must run the entire distance of the race if they wish to be considered as competing in the race, and they must start with their hands behind the starting line and conclude with their torsos going over the finish line. Each girl must remain in her respective lane from the start to the finish in straightaway races. In races involving one or more turns she may not cross in front of another runner until she is at least 2 meters ahead. Any willful jostling or other interference with the progress of another competitor will disqualify a girl from that race.

No one may assist a runner in any way (such as coaching or pacing her), nor may a runner leave the track during the race and then return. In races run the entire distance in lanes, the competitor must stay within her lane for the entire distance.

Ties in running events. At times two runners may be judged as having tied for the same place. In this case, they are given the same time and the same place; the points in this case for both places are added together and divided equally, and their respective teams receive the same number of points.

In another instance, the judges may have properly identified two different places, but the timers have credited both contestants with the same time. In this event the judgment on the places stands, but identical times are recorded.

In the event of a tie, when awards are being given to the place winners, the usual procedure is for the judge to flip a coin to determine which girl will receive the medal for the higher ranking place.

Rules of field events. All measurement must be made with a steel tape. In field events other than the high jump each competitor will receive three trials. It is common practice to qualify one more finalist than there are places to be awarded. Each finalist will then receive three more trials, and her best mark will be selected from all her trials. In measuring the various field events, care should be taken to accurately and correctly use the tape in the manner described by the rules of track and field as presented in the appropriate chapters.

Each time a trial is attempted and a foul occurs, judges at the field events should be careful to mark it on the result sheets. This will eliminate the possibility of competitors taking illegal turns after fouling during that turn.

In the high jump event a competitor has the right to commence jumping at or above the starting height. She may pass her jumping attempt at any height, and it will not be counted as a trial. Even if she has failed once or twice at a specific height, she still may pass that height and attempt a higher mark. However, three successive failures disqualify the contestant from further jumping.

Ties in the high jump. If two or more competitors tie at the same height in the high jump, each will be credited with the cleared height, but the places will be determined by the fewest number of misses (failures) at that height and at preceding heights as far down as is necessary to break the tie. If the tie still remains, the next step is to give the higher place to the competitor with the fewest attempts or trials, whether successful or not throughout the competition. If the tie still exists, the bar may be raised or lowered to the heights announced before the competition began, and each girl in the tie may make one attempt to clear each height until the tie is broken.

If the tie still exists for any place other than first after all methods to attempt to break the tie have been exhausted, the tying competitors are awarded the same places, and the team points are shared. Very seldom do girls experience this close a tie in the high jump. The common practice is to have the tie broken by determining the fewest misses, and if this fails, to share the place and the points (Table 17-1).

Scoring ties. If a tie exists between two or more competitors, the points possible for the tying place plus the next one lower (and the next one lower if three are tying) will be added together and divided equally among the tying competitors. For example, in a two-way tie for third place in a meet in which four places are being given, the two points for third place are added together, with the one point for fourth place equalling three points. The two girls are each given one and a half points to add to each team's total. If there is a tie for last place, one point must be divided fractionally among the girls tying for last place.

Scoring. Official scoring for a meet is shown in Table 17-2.

Medals. As explained previously, it is customary to flip a coin when there is a tie for a place for which a medal is given. Although the record would show a tie occurred for that place, the awarding of the medal would have to be decided by chance.

Table 17-1. Resolving ties in the high jump*

	3 feet 10 inches	3 feet 11 inches	4 feet 0 inches	4 feet 1 inch	4 feet 2 inches	4 feet 3 inches	4 feet 4 inches	Total failures†	Total trials§	Position
A	– – –	x ✔	✔	x ✔	– – –	xx ✔	xxx	4	8	2
B	✔	✔	✔	x – – –	x ✔	xx ✔	xxx	4	9	3
C	✔	✔	x – – –	✔	xx ✔	xx ✔	xxx	5	—	4
D	✔	– – –	– – –	xx ✔	xx ✔	x ✔	xxx	—‡	—	1

A, B, C, and D all cleared the first height of 3 feet 10 inches, and they all failed at the last height of 4 feet 4 inches. Since D cleared 4 feet 3 inches on her second trial and the others on their third trials, D is the first-place winner. It is also seen that A and B each had four failures, whereas C had five. This makes C the fourth-place winner. A tie still exists between A and B, and it is seen that A took eight trials and B took nine; since A took the fewer trials, A becomes the second-place winner and B the third-place winner.

*This is an illustration of the method to use in resolving ties in the high jump: ✔ = cleared; x = failure; – – – = passed.
†Up to tying height.
‡Since D won with fewest misses at the preceding height, no total failures at last tying height are listed.
§At tying height.

Table 17-2. Scoring system used in computing team points and relay points

Number of places to be counted	First place	Second place	Third place	Fourth place	Fifth place	Sixth place
2	5	3	—	—	—	—
3	5	3	1	—	—	—
4	5	3	2	1	—	—
5	5	4	3	2	1	—
6	10	8	6	4	2	1

JUDGING

The finish judges are to make their decisions on the place winners they have picked without any discussion with other judges. If a dispute should occur, the chief finish judge will take the majority opinion, or if there is a tie decision, she will decide the issue.

Track events take precedence over the field events. That is, in the event that a girl is called to compete in a race and she is competing in a field event at that time, she must report to the judge of that field event and inform her that she is leaving to compete in the race. She will be allowed to take her entitled trials later except in the case of the high jump, where her absence will be recorded as a pass if the bar has been raised to a new height. The bar is never to be lowered for an absent competitor.

Fouls. Field event judges must be aware of the fouls that will probably occur in their particular event. When a foul is made, the judge should indicate it by saying ''Foul.'' In some meets the judges will also wave a red flag, indicating to the spectators that a foul has occurred and a white flag, indicating a fair throw or jump has been made. The latest rule books should be consulted regularly by the judges to be sure that they know the proper procedures to use in conducting an event.

OFFICIATING TECHNIQUES

Good officials will quickly and efficiently go about the business of running off their events. A timer will use the index finger of her strong hand in pressing the watch stem firmly. She should grasp the watch with the middle finger and the thumb. She should take up all slack in the stem before the gun goes off and prior to stopping it at the finish of a race. She must watch for the smoke from the starter's gun and use a quick firm action to start the watch. She should use the same action in stopping the watch.

Judges and timers at the finish line should station themselves so that the finish line is visible to them. Judges' stands that have steps are extremely useful, as they afford an unobstructed view of the finish (Fig. 17-2). All timers and judges should be cautioned to be aware of the runners on the inside lane closest to them. There have been sad instances of competitors finishing first and being completely missed by the judges and timers because they were running in the inside lane. Sometimes being below the vision line or at too close a range when judges are at track level causes a runner to be overlooked.

General procedures of officials. All officials should be sure of the date, time, and place when accepting an officiating assignment. The meet director should be notified well in advance if an official cannot keep her assignment. All officials should arrive at the track at least 30 minutes before the meet is to start. On arriving they should report to the meet director and to their respective head referees.

The clerk of the course should station herself in a section of the field easily seen and located by the athletes. At very large meets with several heats or flights in the races, she should have an assistant clerk who will help in directing the athletes to their respective lanes and heats before each race. This is an extremely helpful procedure to follow in dealing with young and inexperienced athletes. A particularly helpful technique is to have the lines of heats ready for the starter but stationed several meters away from the starting line. Each heat would then move up into position when called by the starter.

It is the responsibility of the meet director to provide equipment for proper officiating at each event. Clipboards, pencils, entry cards, tapes, foul flags, markers, and watches are to be in readiness for the head judge of each event at the officials' check-in table. The chief timer will obtain all watches, issue them to the individual timers, collect them after the meet, and return them as a unit to the table. Experienced officials will often bring their own kits with suitable items for conducting their specific events. For example, a long jump head judge might bring her own foul flag, brush for the runway, Plasticine for marking the area just past the takeoff board, tape, marker, and a straight-edge board to extend the take-off board for measurements.

Each head official should carry her own copy of the rule book under which a particular meet is being conducted. It is most helpful to have a copy of the summarized rules for each event taped to the clipboard for that event. This affords a quick reference source for answering questions that could arise in conducting an event, as well as an aid for new officials who might feel insecure.

Apparel. If there is an association or organization that supplies the officials for conducting a given meet, these officials probably will wear a special uniform while on duty. If not, the uniform of an official should be in keeping with the recommendations of the NAGWS or the requests of the meet director. This could include an appropriate skirt of dark blue or black, white blouse, rubber-soled shoes, and white or navy blue blazer. Starters must wear a red jacket or wear the red sleeve on the arm that holds the gun aloft.

If the officials are members of an officials' group, the proper identification insignia should be worn during the time of all meets. If no insignia is used, it is best for the meet director to have officials' ribbons issued for them to wear for identification purposes.

IMPROVISING FOR OFFICIALS

Rare is the women's track meet that has enough qualified officials on hand to run the meet. Therefore, steps must be taken to secure enough people to help with the judging and timing. The problem is compounded, since all officials' manuals state that at no time should an official serve in a dual capacity. The reasoning behind this rule is that if an official is doing all that she can do in carrying out her responsibilities, she will not have any time to devote to officiating any other activity during the meet.

However, experience and common sense will tell the meet director that she has several avenues open to her that are of great help in solving this problem. One avenue is to conduct the meet with fewer officials than are required and another is to double up on the assignments, even though she is cautioned against it. Timers are often asked to judge the finishes of races as well as keep time. It is not necessary to have a separate job distinction in the track referee, field referee, and meet director. The director may well assume these decision-making duties, thereby eliminating two other positions to be filled.

The assumption made by the rule books in listing the needed officials is that most meets are "full scale" and records are being sought. However, this is not true in the case of most school and playground meets for girls. At AAU meets, sanctions are required, and the requirements for any acceptance of records are quite clearly defined in the handbook and must be adhered to. For school, playground, or club meets, however, it is possible to allow much more latitude in the numbers of officials selected to conduct the meets.

Surveyor. The surveyor of the meet is in most cases the regular grounds keeper, who is also in charge of marking the track and field areas. The track would have been surveyed for proper lengths during construction, and these papers are usually on file with the school athletic department. This is a position that would not need to be filled for each meet.

Announcer. The announcer could easily be a member of the boys' track team of the local high school who has had experience in public speaking. Or it could be the regular announcer for the boys' track meets. People who regularly assist at the boys' meets are usually willing to help in officiating at the girls' meets at the high school or college level. Either the scorer or the meet director can serve as announcer and easily carry out other responsibilities as well.

Scorer, press steward, and recorder. The scorer, press steward, and recorder are often one and the same person, thus eliminating two positions to be filled. It is rare at a school meet that there is any need for having a recorder. At a full-scale women's meet, where it is likely that records will be broken, the scorer or her assistant or both can usually take care of seeing that the proper application forms are completed and results given to the press.

Chief field event judges. Chief field event judges are essential to the smooth running of field events. They should be experienced judges of these events. Their assistants might well be students assigned to the job of learning how to officiate a particular event. Boys from the school track team make excellent helpers in the events in which they are regular participants. There usually will not be enough people available to permit one person to be assigned as chief field event judge, so one of the event judges may also serve in this capacity.

At least three experienced timers and three finish judges must be secured. Some of these people can be faculty personnel from the host school or visiting schools. The head timer and head judge may be one of the timers and judges. The other timers and judges may very well be boys—again, selected from the track team. Also, girls who have had some previous training in timing and judging in the physical education track class may serve in the small meets as the assistant timers and judges.

Starter. The starter could be the coach of the boys' team. He has usually had years of experience in starting his own performers in practice and may very well be an official starter in his own right. In a very small meet the starter can also serve as the clerk of the course.

Clerk of the course. With the advent of structured leagues and conferences for conducting girls' athletics within schools and colleges, it is usually mandatory that one or more key officials be assigned to a meet by the officials' section of the league or conference. The one such assigned official is usually the starter, who is the only paid official at a track meet. However, it might well be that the league structure allows all officials for track meets to be secured by the hostess institution as a part of its responsibility. This usually is the case, and the school faces the problem of supplying enough officials to properly conduct a meet.

The clerk of the course should be experienced in working with girls and be able to fulfill the duties of the clerk of the course in an efficient manner. It is quite possible to train a mature high school student to become a good clerk of the course. The technique to use is to have a girl serve as an assistant several times, possibly at boys' meets. Then, after acquiring this experience, she could serve as clerk at a girls' meet.

Actually, most help should come from the boys who are on the boys' track team. If the boys' program has been in operation for a long time at a school, there should be a sufficient number of helpers for conducting meets. The inspectors could easily be selected from the hurdle crew, block boys, or field judges if they are not needed at the moment.

Assistants. All the assistants in the field events and the assistants to the track officials will probably be students. Some of the assistants that are needed are assistants to the clerk, to the head finish judge, to the meet director, and one to be located at the scoring table as a general messenger. Also, individuals are needed to serve on the hurdle and block crew as tape holders and assistants to the marshall. The tape could be tied to posts on both sides of the track, thus eliminating the need for two assistants. The tape would have to be very light.

It is even more difficult to obtain officials when meets are not conducted through the auspices of a school. Parents often have to be asked to serve as officials. However, a parent should not be the sole judge of the finish of a race in which his daughter may be running. This probably would not happen very often, but it could occur. Many parents will be glad to learn to officiate an event in which their daughters are not participating to be on the field and close to the scene of action. Some training must be conducted for the novice official; under no circumstances should novices be allowed to work alone until they have demonstrated knowledge of the event and shown that they can adequately officiate.

The procedure of duplicating assignments is very helpful when officials are scarce. Under these conditions the same official could conduct the shot, discus, and perhaps the javelin events. If the baseball throw is a part of a meet, the judge could conduct that event after she has completed officiating at another field event. Usually the high jump judge will not be assigned to officiate another event, since the high jump traditionally takes longer to run off than the other field events. However, as the entries are received from the various competitors and schools and the meet director has ascertained the number and caliber of the entries, she may plan duplications in assignments where it seems feasible.

TRAINING OF OFFICIALS

The training of a sufficient number of officials is probably the only procedure to use to help solve the ever-present shortage of qualified people to conduct a meet. The source of such officials is various school and nonschool personnel in a given community.

School groups. During the regular sessions of track teaching or coaching or both, a qualified teacher may easily train officials selected from the class to properly conduct various events. There are some girls who would much rather officiate in track and field than compete. Initially, each student official should go through the process of learning to execute all the skills in all the events, as do the students who are going to compete later on. This procedure is meant to ensure an understanding of the actions involved in the execution of the various events. Obviously, in cases of physical limitations, actual performance in the events might not be possible.

After being introduced en masse to all phases of track and field events, the entire group of girls in the class (performers as well as officials) should receive group instruction from the teacher in the techniques of conducting and judging each event. Explanations concerning governing rules, possible fouls, timing and judging procedures, and other procedures and infractions should be given. The novice officials should now receive practice in conducting the events during the practice sessions held for participants in those events. This would involve organizing the athletes for their trials as it would be done in a meet, measuring and marking the throws, judging and timing the races, and so on.

The teacher should plan at least one session specifically devoted to the training of the officials in timing and judging the track events. Beginners need more practice in this area than any other because of the judgment factor involved in the places to be picked and the coordination of stopwatch procedures with the starts and finishes. The use of two or three stopwatches, with one being held by the teacher to check the accuracy of the novices, is a good technique to adopt. Accuracy of timing should be checked after each practice sprint has been run.

It sometimes works well in a class situation to have the girls who are learning to officiate receive grades for officiating as well as for skill in performance of the events. If the track program is an after-school activity (such as Girls' Athletic Association or a varsity team) the officials should earn their letters or awards on the basis of their officiating, not necessarily on competing. This group is sometimes called Girl's Athletic Officials (GAO). Such girls often are a magnificent source of service to the school and other community athletic agencies.

It would be necessary for the teacher to schedule a separate session to instruct the scorer, announcer, recorder, and clerk about the performance of their duties. These girls should be very carefully selected and should have the ability to act decisively, since errors made here can be disastrous to the conduct of the meet and its conclusion. Classroom teachers interested in track and field may be invited to practice officiating skills during class and after-school activities. They are another source of trained officials.

Nonschool groups. Groups such as track clubs, parent groups, recreation personnel, school personnel, or AAU groups often conduct training sessions in the form of clinics and workshops. These sessions have proved to be successful. In all practice sessions the vital ingredient is the presence of the athletes. The trainees must have competitors to observe and judge so they can become proficient in officiating.

The teacher of these training sessions should give group instruction for conducting the various events somewhat as it is described here. She should give instructions in starting, demonstrate correct body positions, use proper voice commands, give correct signals, and use the gun for starting and recalling the track events. She should call attention to starting line fouls, proper use of the watch, judging the finish, determination of fouls in the race, and other details. The trainees should then practice the execution of their duties during simulated or abbreviated performances of the events. They should also learn the proper method of reporting the results to the head judge and timer. The teacher should assist and analyze the practice techniques used by the trainees during the officiating period, including the trainees' accuracy in the use of the watch and in picking places in close finishes.

The same procedure would be followed in the field events, including explanation of the event and the rules, demonstration of fair and foul trials, marking and measuring of distances, and the general conduct of the trials. The novice officials need to practice officiating techniques during the actual participation to gain the necessary experience for proper conduct of the events and adequate recognition of fouls.

A very good source of officials among the nonschool group is the parents who faithfully attend the workouts and meets. Since these parents usually spend many hours watching and waiting for their daughters, they might very well welcome the opportunity to serve as officials. Parents often love to time their daughters in practice and also enjoy being on hand to time them in competition. The prospective officials could practice during the team practice sessions, then offer their services to the meet director before the date of the meet. This method could be a big step forward in securing more qualified officials and could be easily instituted in most situations.

CHAPTER 18

Implementing track and field programs

Most colleges and universities have fairly adequate to excellent facilities for track and field. Many high schools have insufficient track and field areas because of the lack of space, funds, and enough personnel committed to track and field programs to work for the obtaining of such areas. Few elementary schools have the funds or the space for a quarter-mile track. The providing of adequate facilities and the regular maintenance and care of them is essential to any sports program. The presence of a track facility is a boon to the track program.

Just as the physical education program is somewhat limited by the space and equipment provided for its conduct, so the track and field program is limited to some degree in this respect. Good indoor and outdoor facilities that are safe, functional, and substantial should be provided by schools and communities for track and field use. If suitable facilities are not available, substitution areas will need to be found elsewhere.

Track and field activities can be conducted with a minimum of facilities and equipment. There are items that can be borrowed, constructed, improvised, and substituted. As long as the participants are actively involved in safe and interesting track and field activities and are challenged to improve themselves, the track and field program will not be severely handicapped because of lack of facilities (Fig. 18-1).

A good running track is certainly desirable but not an absolute necessity for conducting track and field activities. A playing field, a paved area, a little-used street, a park area, or a golf course can be utilized in place of a track. Lanes and distance lines can be painted on a nearby street, and arrangements can be made to stop traffic from going through this area during certain hours of the day. The longer distances, such as 400 and 800 meters, can be run by lapping back over the running area. No world records will be established on such a track, but girls could learn to perform track and field activities and experience the thrill of successful performance.

Golf courses and park areas are excellent places to train for participation in distance and cross-country running. Areas such as the county fairgrounds can be used as a location for staging meets. The horse-racing track can be marked off for conducting running events. The shot, discus, javelin, and other throwing event areas can be laid off in the center of the field, and the high jump and long jump pits can be constructed just off the edge of the horse-racing track but still near the grandstands.

226

Fig. 18-1. Competition in the high jump. This unique picture shows not only reasonably good high jump form but also how to hold a meet with less than perfect facilities. Notice the construction of the pit, the rural setting, and the great interest of the spectators. This meet was held in Kentucky.

The best plan for preparing the track area is to have a grounds keeper and a work crew attend to mowing, lining, and marking the areas and keeping the entire area in a safe usable condition. This chore may be the responsibility of the coach when there is not a maintenance crew available. The utilizing of school janitors, interested parents, members of booster clubs, and members of the track squad in the placing of equipment, caring for track, pits, and runways may be necessary for maintaining a safe and functional area.

FIELD

On a regularly prepared track and field area the sand-filled long-jump pits, foam landing high-jump facilities, and shot, discus, and javelin areas with well-marked throwing lanes contribute immeasurably to the interest, safety, enjoyment, and participation in, as well as spectator interest of, field events.

If such facilities are not available, there are some alternatives. Throwing areas may be chalked off or painted on grass or paved surfaces. Distance arcs or lines may be permanently painted on the street for the softball throw, rubber discus throw, and indoor shot put. The same lines and areas may also be chalked off on grassy areas. These areas could be any of the playground fields used for other sports.

A piece of chalk tied to a string measuring 3 feet 6 inches or 4 feet 1¼ inches is a good means of laying out shot and discus areas for practice. A sidewalk or other paved area facing a grassy surface can have 7-foot and 8-foot 2½-inch circles, respectively, circumscribed by centering the end of the string, stretching the radius with the chalk attached, and drawing the circle. Having eight or ten circles can provide areas for thirty-two or forty girls, working in squads of four, in which to practice moving across the circle to improve body position and performance in releasing the shot or discus.

High-jump areas may be constructed so that they are either temporary or permanent. For example, bales of straw secured from farmers may be laced or tied together to form the outline of the landing area, which may then be filled with wood shavings or sawdust and used as a temporary landing pit. A foam rubber factory may donate or sell very cheaply scraps of foam rubber that will make a desirable permanent landing area.

Long-jump pits may be dug out of the ground and filled with sand or sawdust. Sand is the more desirable to use, but sawdust can usually be secured merely for the cost of hauling it.

A long-jump takeoff board painted white, which meets standard specifications, can easily be built and sunk into the ground for the long jumpers. It is often convenient to have two separate jumping pits, although one area may suffice.

INDOOR FACILITIES

In some parts of the country the use of warehouses provides an indoor running area for the winter months when sleet and snow interfere with outside practice. Warehouses that have seasonal uses, such as tobacco warehouses, are empty around Christmas and may be available during January and February. Such an area is usually a rather large one and makes a very adaptable training area.

Portable landing pits may be located in a gymnasium. A trampoline with protective padding can make a safe landing area for high jumping.

The use of indoor discus and shot equipment allows these events to be practiced in the gymnasium when it is too cold and muddy to work outside. Nets can be hung as protective devices in which to throw, and vulnerable areas can be padded with mats.

IMPROVISING EQUIPMENT

Starting blocks. Starting blocks can be constructed in the workshop. However, if the running area is in a playing field, girls can dig holes for use as starting blocks. For practicing starts inside the gymnasium, a girl may scotch (support) another's feet with her own so that the sprinter gets the feel of pushing off blocks. A wooden block about 5 × 5 inches, with four huge spikes for driving it into the ground, makes a good starting block when practicing outdoors. It should be angled on its face so that the athlete can get foot leverage. The heads of the spikes should be cut off and driven up into drilled holes (Fig. 18-2).

Batons. Mailing tubes may be used in place of batons. It is a good practice to have a tube or baton for each girl to hold in her hand during participation in warm-up and practice sessions. This helps to familiarize the runner with this important piece of equipment. Broom or mop handles that have been cut into 12-inch lengths and taped on the ends to prevent splintering also make excellent batons. Plastic tubes used for separating golf clubs may be cut into 12-inch lengths and made to serve effectively as batons. These cost only a few cents each.

Starter's equipment. A starting gun can be borrowed, and a red sleeve can easily be

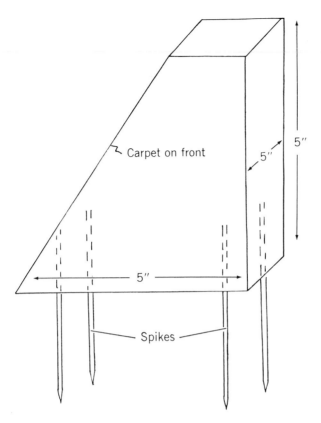

Fig. 18-2. Diagram of a sample handmade starting block. The heads should be cut off the spikes of this handmade starting block so they can be easily inserted into the drilled holes in the block. The parts of the spikes that extend beyond the block should be 3 inches in length.

sewn together for the starter. Clappers, consisting of two boards hinged together, may be used to start the runners in place of a gun.

Watches. It is very desirable to have a stopwatch, but any watch with a sweep-second hand will give a fairly reliable time of a running event for unofficial records. It must be understood that any records made will be unofficial under these circumstances.

Field markers. Sticks or tongue depressors are adequate for marking the distances made in the field events or for high-jump and long-jump stride patterns and takeoff indicators. The end of the stick should be cut to a point so that it will stick into the ground. The top end should have a number painted on it with India ink to identify the competitors, if used as distance markers.

It is very easy to have the school woodshop personnel (or any interested or qualified person) make very good field markers at low cost. These could be made from scraps of hardwood cut into pieces approximately 5 × 3 × 2½ inches. The head of a large spike should be cut off and the remaining spike driven up into the bottom of the wood marker into a drilled hole (Fig. 18-3). Both sides of the marker should be numbered with black paint or India ink, then shellacked to protect the numbers and the wood. The spike should be about 5 inches long, with about 2 inches of it inserted into the marker and 3 inches

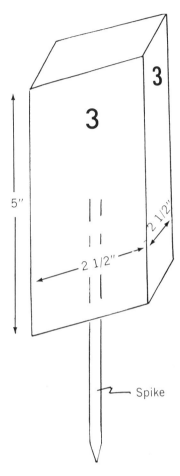

Fig. 18-3. Diagram of a sample handmade field event distance marker. The spike in this handmade marker should have the head cut away so that it can be easily inserted into the drilled hole in the wooden peg. The part of the spike that extends beyond the marker should be about 3 inches long to be strong enough to avoid being bent.

showing at the end to push into the ground. These markers can very easily be driven into the earth, even if there is no turf. A set of these markers will last for years, as they are very durable.

If a school uses metal archery quivers in its physical education instructional program, and these quivers happen to break at the top so that they are no longer usable, they may be used as flag markers in the javelin, shot, and discus events to indicate the throwing sector lines. A pennant can be secured to the top of the quiver and then stuck into the ground because it is pointed. Since these quivers are metal and have a small foot tab to press down into the ground, they make ideal marker stakes that last for years and are also easy to use.

Long-jump measure. Since metal (steel) tapes are quite expensive to purchase, they are usually scarce at most schools. However, the long jumpers like to have their jumps measured frequently to know how they are progressing. If a tape is not available, there is a simple method to use in making a permanent long-jump measuring board. Place a board along the running side of the pit, extending from the front edge of the takeoff board to the end of the pit. The board should be located on one side of the pit, not in it. On top of the board paint the feet and inches along its length, thus actually making a giant measuring tape. The board will then be shellacked for protection against the weather and securely fastened to the ground. Often there are wooden frames that help form the pit, and measurements could be painted on the top of this frame. It is not necessary to have every inch painted on, as the first few feet are not of importance, but the measurement could start with a minimum distance that anyone would be able to jump. If the same pit is used for the standing broad jump, then it would be necessary to start the measurements much closer to the takeoff board.

Crossbars. A cane pole will make a usable crossbar, but it will be necessary to secure an extra large supply of them since they are easily broken.

A functional practice crossbar, and one that could be used in competition, is a length of elastic weighted on each end by a bean bag. It saves time, since it stretches instead of being displaced, it can be used safely, and it can easily be carried to the jump area.

Other equipment. Iron balls of nearly the correct weight of the shot may be secured from building wrecking officials and substituted for the standard shot.

A ranger horn may be substituted for a public address system. Score sheets, entry blanks, judges' slips, and so on can be mimeographed or dittoed instead of being printed. Place ribbons can be made out of construction paper, or lengths of ribbon may be purchased and cut. All these items may be made available by having the school's art or print-shop students construct them as one of their projects.

Substituting events. Some events may be substituted for others if facilities and equipment do not allow the conduct of a full program. For instance, shuttle relays may be used in place of pursuit relays if an oval track is not available. The throwing of a softball and a basketball may be substituted for the shot put and discus throw, respectively. The standing long jump is a good event to schedule whether or not jumping pits are available, but it may also be used as a substitution for the long jump event.

A lack of facilities or a lack of equipment is not an excuse for failing to have a track and field program, since equipment can be borrowed, improvised, and constructed, and some events can even be eliminated to promote such a program. Events as well as equipment may be substituted to facilitate the scheduling of the track and field activities. Once the program is initiated and some success is realized, the addition to and improvement of facilities and equipment can be speedily accomplished.

Appendixes

APPENDIX A

Race walking

BACKGROUND

As track and field enlarges its horizon, girls and women often attempt to perfect skills in additional events to widen their competitive efforts. Race walking is one of the latest additions to the program and is suitable for almost all age groups. Walking in this setting, although somewhat comical in appearance, does have a following among many athletes.

Traditionally many male walkers have been former distance runners who turned to walking to extend their years of competition. Today, however, girls as young as 10 years of age are competing in the race walk for a distance of 1 mile (1500 meters). The AAU has approved distances of from 1 mile (1500 meters) through 6 miles (10,000 meters) for various age groups, with the women (14 years and older) being allowed to compete in distances of 3000 meters and longer. Competitive race walking is done on either a track or a road course.

Race walking is done primarily in California—it started in Southern California in 1972, an experimental year. The winning time for the mile walk at the district AAU meet that year was 7 minutes 59.4 seconds (women's division). The time in 1976 was 6 minutes 50.4 seconds, a record placed in jeopardy at each staging of the mile race walk. Young Susan Brodock of Rialto, California, is the world record holder at 1 mile, 1500 meters, and 5000 meters.

ELEMENTS OF RACE WALKING

Endurance is probably the greatest factor in helping develop a performer into a good walker. As in distance running, a slender individual is usually a more successful competitor than is a stocky one. Training is conducted in much the same manner as in distance running. The athlete will walk repeat distances at timed intervals, striving to build a paced race, with each segment of the race being walked in a specific time. They will "walk very rapidly" the last 200 meters (within the rules), just as the distance runners sprint; the sprint for a walker is walking as fast as possible but not running. Walkers will practice their "sprints" as well as other aspects of the race to build up their ability to have a "kick" left at the end of their races.

Teachers and coaches might find that the race walk is a good event in which to place girls who are having trouble winning or placing in other events. Because few people at present want to race walk, the field of competition is small; this event might prove to be

235

rewarding for certain girls, thus keeping up their enthusiasm for track and field competition.

RULES

The rules of race walking are simple. Unbroken contact with the ground must be maintained with one foot at all times. The advancing foot must contact the ground before the rear foot leaves the ground. During the period of each step in which a foot is on the ground, the leg must be straightened, and *not bent* at the knee, for at least one moment. In other words, the walker may not run, and this locking of the knee ensures that she will be walking, not running.

Judges, who are stationed all around the track, shall *caution* any competitor when *walking unfairly* (usually this means *not locking the knee on each step*); a second caution will disqualify the runner. However, immediate disqualification must occur if a competitor walks unfairly during the last 200 meters (200 yards) of a race.

Judges should use flags to indicate their cautions to the walkers. A white flag indicates a first caution and a red flag indicates disqualification. Walking may be done on either a track or on an open road.

APPENDIX B

General training programs

SUGGESTED CIRCUIT TRAINING PROGRAM

To encourage high school girls to participate in a circuit training program, the program must have great appeal for them. It must have variety, include activities that girls like, be difficult enough to challenge them, and provide progressive development of the skeletal muscles. Furthermore, it must include exercises that strengthen and develop the heart and lungs. Other fitness essentials must also be learned in such a program—agility, flexibility, balance, coordination, power, and dexterity.

The fact that a circuit training program allows for individual participation and at the same time permits the group to perform the work toward the attainment of group goals contributes to the popularity of circuit training with high school girls. The members of one squad may be pitted against those from another and seek to outdo each other in achieving the best times for negotiating the circuit. For example, the members of one physical education class of freshmen girls may attempt to outscore the girls of a sophomore class.

The popularity of circuit training is further increased because individual differences in connection with such things as exercise tolerance, levels of conditioning, and body builds are taken into account. It is interesting to note that some of the girls who turn in the best times are often not those who are the best in the class or even those who excel in performing particular activities. This naturally challenges the leaders to try harder and often motivates these girls, because of their new feeling of success, to try to do better every time they participate in the circuit training program.

The time involved in developing and maintaining a high level of conditioning is an important consideration to the modern girl. She is often interested in participating in many activities, and yet she may seriously want to become a good athlete. A training program that can be quickly established, demands little or no specialized equipment, can be conducted indoors or outdoors, and can be engaged in at any time helps solve this time problem of a busy girl. No attempt is being made here to suggest that circuit training should replace any of the better known and approved methods of training. Rather it is proposed that this method of training be utilized as a supplement to other types of training. It is believed that participation in circuit training should be done to bring the girls up to a certain level of conditioning so that serious training may then be commenced.

A suggested indoor program for girls is presented here. Since the only difference in the Black and Gold circuits is that more repetitions are required in the Gold, it was decided to present only an explanation of the Black circuit (Figs. B-1 through B-3).

General comments

1. The activities to be performed at the separate stations must be explained in detail to all participants (Fig. B-3).

2. The markers for the different stations should be easy to move, distinctly marked, and placed so as not to interfere with the performance of the activities at each station.

3. The arrangement of the stations should be such that participation in the activities is interesting and challenging.

4. The number of stations and the number of times that the circuit is run should be carefully determined. The age of the girls and the level of their conditioning are factors that must be considered.

A High School Circuit Training Program						
Item and Station No.	Black			Gold		
	1	2	3	1	2	3
1 Jumping jacks laps	10 1	15 1	20 1	25 1	30 1	35 1
2 Toe touch with high knee lifts	10	15	20	25	30	35
3 Jump rope	10 fwd. 5 bkd. 10 fwd.	15 5 15	20 10 20	25 10 25	30 10 30	35 10 35
4 Push-ups	5	8	10	10	10	10
5 Stair running and step test	1 10 1	2 15 2	2 20 2	2 25 2	3 30 3	3 35 3
6 Prone arch	5	8	10	10	10	10
7 Windmill laps (each side)	10 2	15 2	20 2	25 2	30 2	35 2
8 Sit-ups (each side)	5	8	10	10	10	10

Fig. B-1. Sample circuit training program.

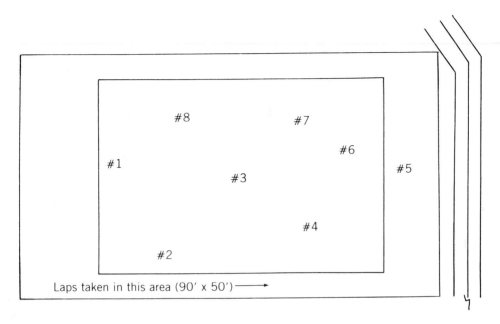

Fig. B-2. Location of eight circuit training stations in a gymnasium. (Scale: approximately 1 centimeter = 5 feet.)

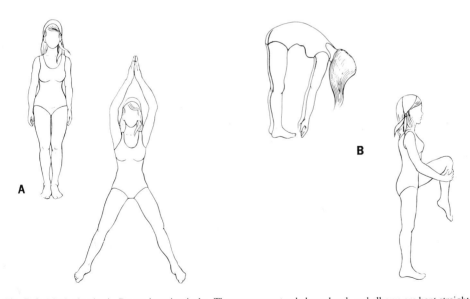

Fig. B-3. Black circuit. **A,** Do ten jumping jacks. The arms are extended overhead, and elbows are kept straight with the palms touching as the action takes place. When the legs are brought together, the arms are swung down to the side. One full lap of the track or gymnasium is run immediately after the jumping jacks are done. **B,** Do ten toe touches with a high knee lift between each one. The knees are kept straight while the palms of the hands are placed flat on the floor. The knee is then drawn up close to the chest, the hands grasping around the ankles. The knees are lifted alternately as indicated. *Continued.*

Fig. B-3, cont'd. C, Take ten forward skips of the rope. The feet may be kept together or touch the floor one at a time. Take five skips backward; take ten more skips forward.

D, Do five modified push-ups. The chest is allowed to touch the floor by permitting the elbows to bend. Then the arms are extended and the weight supported on the arms. The body must be kept in a straight line from the shoulders to the knees. The feet are raised from the floor, while the weight of the body rests on the knees and the hands during the lowered phase.

E, Run one time to the top of a five-stair bleacher; return to the bottom step. Perform ten step-ups, counting as one each time the right foot is placed on the top of the step. The step is done in a four-count rhythm: the right foot is first placed on the step, the left foot is then placed beside the right foot, the right foot steps down, and then the left foot steps down, thus completing one step-up. Run again to the top of the bleachers, touching the side of the wall before returning.

F, Do five prone arches. Lie in a prone position with the hands placed beneath the thighs. Lift the upper trunk from the floor and hold this position for a count of one. The body must be stretched; it is permissible to lift the feet from the floor.

Fig. B-3, cont'd. G, Do ten windmills to each side and then run two laps. Stand with the feet shoulder width apart and the arms extended sideward. Keeping the knees straight, stretch across to the opposite foot and place the hand on the floor outside the foot. Return to the beginning position between each of the windmills. Perform ten on each side, first to the left and then to the right.
H, Do five sit-ups to each side. Lie in a supine position with hands resting on top of the thighs. Then tighten the abdominal muscles and roll forward, curling the head and upper back as the ankle of the right leg is grasped. the knee is to be kept straight, and alternate ankles are grasped until five repetitions are accomplished on each side.

Specific information

1. A girl and her partner (both having similar general motor ability) are usually allowed to choose the station at which they wish to start their activities. A girl is not obligated to stay with her first partner if she can progress faster than her partner. The partner should serve as a motivator and as a check on each girl (if such is needed) to make sure she does not miss any repetitions.

2. The girls record the first beginning times and then check the times immediately after completing the activities at the last station. They are told that they are competing against themselves and are encouraged to surpass previous performances.

3. Daily, triweekly, or biweekly progress charts should be kept.

4. The consistent attainment of a certain score should prompt a girl to try to achieve the next level of excellence.

5. School colors are used to designate the stations at two circuits if more than one is used.

6. A completed course means that a girl has completed performing the activities in the circuit three times.

7. Eight stations were chosen for the suggested circuit, consisting of the following: (a) jumping jacks (and laps), (b) toe touch and high knee lift, (c) jump rope, (d) push-ups, (e) stair running and step test, (f) prone arch, (g) windmills and laps, and (h) sit-ups. (See Fig. B-3.)

Participation in this proposed circuit training program should cause the girls to improve progressively. They may gradually increase the intensity by first completing only one circuit. This can be accomplished as the warm-up phase of the physical education program. As performance is improved and girls are motivated to try to complete three circuits, circuit training will become an important device in conditioning girls for participation in track and field activities as well as in other sports activities.

In the suggested circuit program the following exercise benefits should be derived (Fig. B-3).

Jumping jacks and laps
   General conditioning
   Coordination
   Endurance
   Speed
Toe touch with high knee lift
   Hamstring stretching
   Trunk flexibility
Rope jumping
   Coordination
   Speed
   Endurance
   Leg power
   Rhythm and timing
Push-ups
   Shoulder girdle strengthening
   Muscular endurance
   Back strengthening

Stair running and step test
   Leg power
   Coordination
   Rhythm and timing
   Endurance
Prone arch
   Back strengthening
   Trunk flexibility
Windmills and laps
   Trunk flexibility
   Hamstring stretching
   Upper back stretching
   Endurance
Sit-ups
   Abdominal strengthening

SUGGESTED ISOMETRIC EXERCISES

An easy and interesting way to use isometric exercises is to implement a buddy system whereby a resisting force is created; explanations follow in the descriptions of specific exercises.

Anterior deltoid (arm) exercise. The performer stands with one foot in front of the other for balance, with the arms extended out from the shoulders in front of the body. The fingers are curled up to make a fist; the palm side is down. The budy resists by placing her hands at the wrist and pressing downward, not to the breaking point, but with sufficient pressure to cause the performer to exert maximum contractions for a count of 6 to 10 seconds. A few seconds are allowed between contractions for a rest cycle and then the exercise is repeated two more times.

Middle and posterior deltoid (shoulder and arm) exercise. The description here is the same as that given for the development of the anterior deltoid, except that the arms are extended sideward. The buddy offers resistance between the wrists and the elbows by pressing downward with sufficient pressure to bring about a maximum contraction.

Trapezius and pectoral muscles (neck and chest) exercise. The arms are stretched overhead obliquely at an angle of 45 degrees, with the palms facing outward. The buddy offers resistance at a point between the wrists and the elbows.

Rhomboid (back) exercise. The scapulas are adducted toward each other until they meet; the arms are extended straight down and back. The performer exerts a maximum effort to maintain the adduction of the scapulas as the buddy presses forward by placing her hands just above the wrists in an effort to push the arms forward.

SUGGESTED SEQUENTIAL PROGRESSION TRAINING

The teaching of new skills to girls should be based on those skills learned previously. Therefore it is suggested that the teacher consider the progression she selects in light of the experiences the students have had prior to enrolling in her class. A suggested progression follows.

Sprinting. In addition to the techniques of sprinting, girls must learn how (1) to run in a straight line, (2) to do starts, (3) to make use of the blocks, (4) to run through the finish, and (5) to run relays.

Standing long jump. The second step should be the standing long jump.

Long jumping. Long jumping should follow sprinting, as sprinting is an essential part of long jumping. The girl has already had experience jumping forward in learning to perform the standing long jump.

Longer races. After the sprint running techniques are mastered, the girls should be ready for information on how to run the longer distance races involving the use of a short stride and pacing. In preparation for running the longer distances the girls should condition themselves by jogging much longer distances than they have done previously so that such running will not be a shock to them.

Throws. The throws may be mastered at any time. Among the throws to be mastered are (1) the softball and baseball, (2) the soccer ball, (3) the basketball, (4) the shot put,* (5) the discus,* and (6) the javelin.*

High jump. The high jump should be taught to a girl after she has had experience in performing activities involving flight in the air, such as occurs in the long jump. She has only to adjust to going over a bar.

Hurdles. Since fear is so often present among the girls when attempting to jump over hurdles, they should have had previous experience in clearing an obstacle while travelling through space. Thus it is believed that hurdling should not be introduced until the girls have participated in the long jump and high jump.

WEIGHT TRAINING

The concept of using weights to improve performance in various track and field events is a well-accepted principle. For many years track coaches believed that lifting weights would make the athlete "muscle-bound." However, the most outstanding athletes in the past 10 to 15 years have taken part in weight training, especially those in throwing and field events. Although the results from studies are somewhat controversial, weight training has increased coordination, speed, or timing of some male and female performers and in most instances has increased strength. The optimum method of weight training has not been determined. Some successful male and female athletes use weight training as much as 4 out of 5 days of practice, but significant gains in strength have been attained by the use of weight training every other day and even every third day. Significant strength gains can be attained through the use of light weights and rapid movements without unduly increasing the muscle bulk. It is believed that girls and women would benefit from such experiences.

Tangible results from weight training cannot be obtained overnight; time and consistent work are required for significant results. Weight training should begin at least 8

---

*Do not teach the shot put, discus, and javelin throw to the novice at the same time because these skills are extremely difficult to master. The shot put should be taught about 2 years earlier, then one may teach the discus and the javelin throw in whichever order desired.

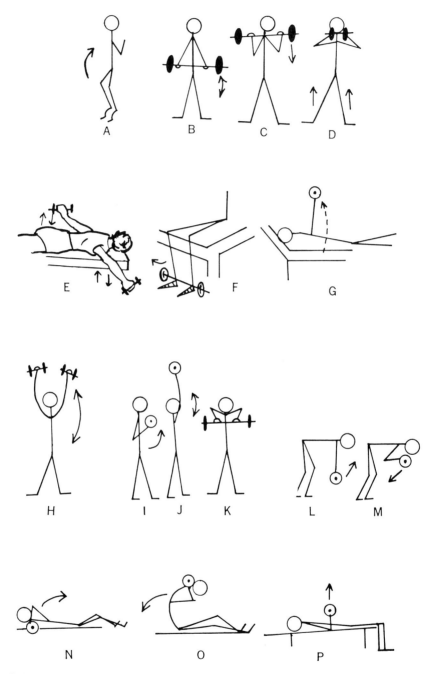

Fig. B-4. Some weight training exercises. **A,** Half squat; **B,** two-arm curl, first position; **C,** two-arm curl, second position; **D,** heel raise; **E,** prone horizontal flexion; **F,** extension with heavy boot; **G,** supine horizontal flexion; **H,** standing forward arm lift; **I,** military press, first position; **J,** military press, second position; **K,** standing rowing exercise; **L,** bending rowing exercise, first position; **M,** bending rowing exercise, second position; **N,** abdominal pull-up, first position; **O,** abdominal pull-up, second position; **P,** bench press.

months before the competitive season. The weight training sessions during the preseason should be more frequent than during the competitive season. The movements during the weight training sessions should be very similar to the movement of the event to be performed.

The degree to which the amount of weight to be lifted is increased depends on many factors, the foremost being the girl's strength and experience in weight training. Other factors include her need for increased strength, her progress rate, and the amount of time she devotes to this phase of training.

Suggested teaching plans for various age groups

GUIDELINES FOR DEVELOPING TRACK AND FIELD LESSONS

1. The length of the unit, available facilities, and the place of track and field activities in the total program must be determined.
2. Plans must be flexible to allow for class size, student's age (Tables C-1 to C-3), facilities, and inclement weather.
3. Teaching methodology may include the instructor's explanation, instructor or qualified student demonstration, class application, instructor and student evaluation, review, and further exploration of the ideas presented.
5. Attention needs to be given to safe conduct regarding all activities and to the learning of techniques for better performance.

PREPARATION OF INSTRUCTIONAL AIDS

The advanced preparation of teaching materials facilitates the teaching of track and field. There are many available prepared materials, and many others can be constructed by the teacher.

Footwork guides are templates of right and left feet for stencilling footprints in practice positions for the shot and discus circles.

Stenciled hints or "cues," reproduced on task cards, work sheets, or charts to remind participants of pertinent directions, are most helpful.

Audiovisual materials, such as films, slides, filmstrips, 8 mm loops, videotapes, sequence photographs, and magazine articles, can be obtained and filed for ready reference use. These can significantly aid the individualization of instruction.

Bulletin boards, for publicizing track events, calling attention to broken records, and posting other noteworthy events, are needed.

Charts that show training programs and records of training facilitate record keeping.

Written materials, for student and teacher/coach use, include mimeographed handouts of rules, strategy, history, and so on, free materials provided by equipment companies, AAHPER and AAU materials, textbooks, periodicals, and student handbooks.

Tests to determine potential sprinters, hurdlers, distance runners, high jumpers, long jumpers, and shot, discus, and javelin throwers need to be available to assist in the recruiting of future performers.

Suggested daily lesson plans for presenting track and field activities to fourth grade children follow.

DAILY LESSON PLAN

UNIT:	Four weeks in length
TIME:	Thirty minutes or more daily
PREPARATION:	It is assumed that the children have been adequately conditioned by taking part in physical education activities so that they will be ready to participate. They should be dressed in suitable clothes.
EVENTS:	Dashes
	Shuttle and pursuit relays
	Long jump
	Standing long jump
	High jump
	Softball throw
	Basketball throw
CLIMAX*:	There should be a school track meet conducted on the final day of the unit, preferably on Friday, in which all children participate in the three events they have previously selected.
NOTE:	Any item in this suggested program can easily be altered to suit any situation. It is merely a suggested progression in which the student moves from one event to the next in learning track and field activities.

First week

MONDAY:	Introduce sprinting, emphasizing good running form. Teach the crouch start without the use of blocks. Have the children run 20 meters for their longest distance. Allow either the crouch or standing start.
TUESDAY:	Continue sprinting practice. Stress form. Introduce the standing long jump.
WEDNESDAY:	Practice the sprints, having the children run two 20-meter distances, one preceding the other, followed by practice on the standing long jump.
THURSDAY:	Increase the sprinting distance to 40 meters. Introduce the use of the starting blocks. Introduce the softball throw, having children throw for form only, not for distance.
FRIDAY:	Have the children run 40 meters out of the blocks. Stress the proper finish to use. Practice throwing the softball and performing the standing long jump.

---

*There could be competition between members of classes, grades, or even other schools at this point. If it is not feasible to have a meet, the same type of competition could be arranged by having the children perform to determine their development of track and field skills. In this case, perhaps all should be required to perform in all the events.

Second week

MONDAY: Run 50 meters. Keep the tape available for measuring the distances made in the standing long jump so there will be an idea of the distances that they are jumping. See that markers are placed on the softball throwing area so they will have an estimate of the distances they they are throwing.

TUESDAY: Have them run 70 meters. Introduce the shuttle relay to the class. Have them practice the relay, running 20 meters for each shuttle distance. Have the students take several starts from the blocks.

WEDNESDAY: Introduce the pursuit relay and the passing of the baton. Have them practice passing the baton after running short distances of about 20 meters. Introduce the basketball throw.

THURSDAY: Have the relay teams run a 200-meter pursuit relay. Practice the basketball throw.

FRIDAY: Time the 40-meter dash in groups so it will be possible to get an estimate of all their times. Have them practice the basketball throw, softball throw, or standing long jump as they wait their turn to be timed or after they have finished their run.

Third week

MONDAY: Introduce the long jump. Practice the basketball throw for distance, using markers as the indicator of the distance.

TUESDAY: Practice the long jump. Have the children watch a demonstration of high jumping. Have them trot up to the bar, kick into the air, and then return to the approach spot to help them become accustomed to the bar.

WEDNESDAY: Practice the high jump. Practice the long jump.

THURSDAY: Practice the high jump. Have all relay teams run a 200-meter relay.

FRIDAY: Practice the high jump. Practice the long jump. Practice the pursuit relay.

Fourth week

MONDAY: Have the children run a 40-meter dash. Practice the high jump. Practice the long jump.

TUESDAY: Practice throwing the basketball for distance. Practice starts several times, then have them run 40 meters with all-out effort. Practice jumping for height in the high jump.

WEDNESDAY: Have the children decide which events they would like to participate in at Friday's meet. This day should be spent in perfecting their form of executing the various events. The relay teams should run twice, working on as smooth an exchange of the baton as possible.

THURSDAY: Go over the procedures to be used in the meet the next day to be sure that everyone understands exactly what is to be done and how the meet will be conducted. No practice should be scheduled.

FRIDAY: Hold a meet. This will serve as a climax to the track and field unit.

See Tables C-1 to C-3 for additional suggested events for various age levels.

Table C-1. Suggested events for college women*

Track	Field
70-meter dash	Long jump
100-meter dash	Standing long jump
200-meter dash	High jump
400-meter run	Shot put (4 kilograms)
800-meter run	Discus throw
1500-meter run	Javelin throw
100-meter hurdles	
200-meter hurdles	
400-meter relay	
800-meter relay (4 × 220)	
800-meter medley (200-100-100-400)	
3000-meter cross-country race†	

*Women 18 years and older are best suited to participate in these events. It is quite likely that the teacher of college women will find an extremely wide range of experience among her students. For this reason there is practically no limit to the events that college teachers can include in their track and field units.
†This event is run on a cross-country facility, not on a track.

Table C-2. Suggested events for senior high school girls*

Track	Field
40-meter dash	Long jump
70-meter dash	Standing long jump
100-meter dash	High jump
200-meter dash	Softball throw
400-meter run	Shot put (8 pounds)
800-meter run	Discus throw
1500-meter run	Javelin throw
400-meter relay	
800-meter relay (4 × 220)	
1600-meter relay	
800-meter medley	
50-yard hurdles	
70-yard hurdles	
3000- to 5000-meter cross-country race†	

*Time will not permit the average track and field teacher to include all these events. She should base her choice of activities on the previous experience of her students and the availability of facilities. There is less need for novelty events at the senior high school level than there is in the lower grades.
†This event is run on a cross-country facility, not on a track.

Table C-3. Suggested events for elementary school girls*

Track	Field
40-meter dash	Long jump
70-meter dash	Standing long jump
100-meter dash	High jump
200-meter dash	Softball throw
400-meter run	Basketball throw
50-yard hurdles (18 inches)	Shot put (6 pounds)
200-meter relay	
200-meter pursuit relay	
400-meter relay	

Novelties†
Soccer ball kick for distance
Standing hop, step, and jump
Sprint medley relays: 25, 50, 50, 75;
    50, 25, 25, 50; 100, 50, 50, 100 meters
Obstacle relay using the long jump pit
   or other innovations

*The enterprising teacher will be able to select activities from this list appropriate to the age and experience of her students. Obviously, the more training and experience a group of students has had, the more extensive the training that the group will receive in its unit of track and field.
†Novelty events may be used on special occasions, such as school field days and relay carnivals. In this case school records could be kept and compared with those of nearby schools. Coeducational teams from various rooms may also compete in some of these events.

"STICKS AND STONES" METHOD OF TEACHING HURDLING

The following teaching procedure should be used in hurdling when the "sticks and stones" method is employed.

1. Girls are divided into three groups according to their height or leg length.
2. The girls are assigned to three different lanes, and they run from a sprint start as fast as they can for about 50 meters. Each girl has a partner who observes her action. The girl marking her partner's foot positions notes the spot her lead foot strikes the ground between the eighth and ninth stride from the starting line and places a yardstick or lath there. This run is repeated by each girl until a consistent spot for placing the stick is determined. The girl then runs through 50 meters, and the checker notes in a similar manner the marks where three additional yardsticks are to be placed. However, these last markers are placed so that three strides may be taken between each one of them.
3. Each girl reruns the 50-meter distance three to five times, and the checker again notes carefully to see if the placing of the sticks is correct. She runs from the starting marks over the sticks through the ninth stride. Thereafter the checker counts her steps by saying "one, two, three" and places the next stick where it should be located. The checker begins to count again on the thirteenth stride, "one, two, three," and so on, until all the marks are placed and judged to be correct for the 50-meter hurdle run.

    The hurdle (eight strides to first hurdle) plan follows: 1, 2, 3, 4, 5, 6, 7, 8, stick; 9, 10, 11, 12, stick (step 1, 2, 3); 13, 14, 15, 16, stick (step 1, 2, 3); and 17, 18, 19, 20, stick (step 1, 2, 3).

4. A brick is placed face down under the edge of each stick as each girl runs down a lane at her own stride pattern. The brick is first placed on its side and then on end, making the barrier 8 inches high.

5. The height of the barrier is increased gradually and at the same time is gradually moved forward toward the ultimately prescribed hurdle distances of 39 feet 4½ inches to the first barrier, and 26 feet 3 inches between each successive barrier, as the girls gain confidence and ability.

6. The girls run each height of a given barrier five times. Until the height of two bricks is reached, the emphasis is strictly on running over the barriers in the same manner as in running the 50-meter dash. No change in running speed or cadence should occur as the barrier is being crossed. Girls are urged to run very fast, with a high knee lift.

7. The foregoing procedures are repeated until the height of 33 inches is gradually obtained and the correct distances used between the barriers have been reached.

Sample event result sheets

THE FIFTH NAGWS NATIONAL INTERCOLLEGIATE
TRACK AND FIELD CHAMPIONSHIPS

Sponsored by

The National Association for Girls' and Women's Sports
American Association for Health, Physical Education, and Recreation

and

Women's Athletic Department, Kansas State University
Manhattan, Kansas

May 11, 12, and 13, 19___

We are pleased that you are planning to participate in the Fifth NAGWS National Intercollegiate Track and Field Championships. Please read the following information carefully and note the deadline dates. Enclosed material includes:

1. Eligibility qualifications are revised for 19___ (Pink)
2. Map of area
3. Map of the university
4. University housing/meal reservation form (due April 10, 19___) (White)
5. Recommended off-campus housing (White)

May 1, 19___ is the due date for the return of:

6. Entry Fee (Blue)
7. Entry Form (Green)
8. Affidavit of Eligibility (Yellow)

If you have any questions that are not answered here, please contact the Meet Director.

TENTATIVE TIME SCHEDULE AND ORDER OF EVENTS

Friday, May 12, TRIALS

Event	Event no.	Time
Shot put	1	9:00 AM
Long jump	2	9:00 AM
200-meter hurdles	3	9:00 AM
400-meter dash	4	9:45 AM
100-meter dash	5	10:15 AM
1500-meter run	6	10:45 AM
100-meter hurdles (2 feet 9 inches)	7	11:15 AM
200-meter dash	8	11:45 AM
800-meter medley relay	9	12:15 PM

Friday, May 12, SEMI-FINALS

Event	Event no.	Time
High jump	10	2:00 PM
Discus throw	11	2:00 PM
Javelin throw	12	2:00 PM
200-meter hurdles	13	2:00 PM
400-meter dash	14	2:30 PM
100-meter dash	15	3:00 PM
100-meter hurdles	16	3:30 PM
200-meter dash	17	4:00 PM
800-meter run	18	4:30 PM
400-meter relay	19	5:00 PM

Saturday, May 13, FINALS

Event	Event no.	Time
Shot put	20	1:30 PM
Long jump	21	1:30 PM
High jump	22	1:30 PM
Discus	23	2:30 PM
Javelin	24	2:30 PM
200-meter hurdles	25	1:30 PM
400-meter dash	26	1:45 PM
100-meter dash	27	2:00 PM
1-mile run	28	2:15 PM
100-meter hurdles	29	2:30 PM
200-meter dash	30	2:45 PM
800-meter run	31	3:00 PM
400-meter relay	32	3:15 PM
800-meter medley relay	33	3:30 PM

SCRATCH MEETING: The *scratch meeting* will be held in Room 243 of the new Physical Education Building, Thursday, May 12 at 7:00 PM. Specific meet information will be distributed at this time and team packets may be obtained.

STANDARDS: *1976-1978 NAGWS Track and Field Guide* rules and standards will govern the meet.

ELIGIBILITY: The eligibility rules established by the Commission on Intercollegiate Athletics for Women (CIAW) will be used. A copy of these rules is included in this packet and should be read carefully. (Pink)

ELIGIBILITY AFFIDAVIT: Three forms, entitled Affidavit of Eligibility (yellow), are in this packet. TWO COPIES MUST BE RETURNED TO THE MEET DIRECTOR. PLEASE RETAIN ONE COPY FOR YOUR RECORDS. It is suggested that all possible participants be listed on the eligibility affidavit in order to facilitate last minute substitutions.

ENTRIES:	Entry forms are included in this packet (green) and must be postmarked no later than midnight, Monday, May 1, 19___. ENTRY FORMS MUST BE ACCOMPANIED BY ENTRY FEES AND ELIGIBILITY FORMS. Entries which are postmarked later than May 1 will not be accepted.
RECONFIRMATION OF ENTRIES:	In order to schedule the heats in the running events and flights in the throwing and jumping events, all entries must be RECONFIRMED by prepaid telephone call, telegram or letter no later than 4:00 PM Eastern Daylight Time, May 10, 19___.
ENTRY FEES:	The entry fee will be $2.00 per individual event and $4.00 per relay team. MAKE CHECKS PAYABLE TO NAGWS Track & Field Championship and send them to Nancy Lay, Meet Director. Non-AIAW Members will also be assessed $2.00 extra per performer.
LIMITATIONS:	Each participant may enter a maximum of four events. If four events are entered, the competitor may enter no more than three track events or three field events, provided that no more than two of these events are 400 meters are longer.
PUBLICITY:	If you have an outstanding performer on your team who will enter the meet, please send a photograph along with a statement of her accomplishment(s) at the same time you return your entry blanks.
CHAPERONE:	No participant will be permitted to attend a national championship without female supervision. A woman need not be from the same college as the participants she chaperones; however, she must agree to assume the following responsibilities: chaperones must be listed by name on the Summary Entry Form and, when other than the team coach, must be (1) registered at the meet, (2) in general attendance at the events, and (3) available when needed.
AWARDS:	NAGWS plaques will be awarded to the first three places in each event. Fourth, fifth, and sixth place contestants will receive certificates. The team scoring the highest number of points will also receive an award.
FACILITIES:	The meet will be held at Tom Black Track. The track is an all-weather tartan surface with nine lanes. Only ¼" spikes may be used. The high jump has a tartan approach apron and a foam rubber porta-pit landing. The shot and discus circles are concrete composition and meet Olympic specifications.
HEADQUARTERS:	The new Physical Education Classroom Building which is located just North of Tom Black Track will serve as Headquarters for the Meet. Reception attendants, just inside the main door, will answer your questions and provide general assistance.
HOUSING:	Insofar as rooms are available, participants will be housed in University dormitories close to Tom Black Track. Please see the campus housing/meal reservation form included in this packet. Reservations must be made no later than April 10, 19___. Due to a room shortage, coaches and chaperones must be housed off-campus. A recommended list of motels is included. Arrangements for this housing must be made directly with the motel. (White)
MEALS:	Those persons not in University housing may, at registration, purchase meal tickets for dining in University dining halls.

Meet:				At:		Date:				Scorer:	
Event	Time Dist.	First place	Sch.	Second place	Sch.	Third place	Sch.	Fourth place	Sch.	Fifth place	Sch.

Fig. D-1. Sample event result sheet for tabulating team scoring.

Meet:		At:			Date:				Scorer:			
Event	Sch.	Sch.	Sch.	Sch.	Sch.	Sch.	Sch.	Sch.	Sch.	Sch.	Sch.	Total
Totals												

Fig. D-2. Team score sheet.

Event_____   Date_____

Meet_____   Judge_____

Lane	Contestant	No.	School	Time	Order of finish	
1st			5th			
2nd			6th			
3rd						
4th						

_____ Finish judge

Timer _____

Scorer _____

Fig. D-3. Sample event card to be used for preliminary heats.

Event_____   **Date**_____

Meet_____   **Heat**_____

Lane	Name	No.	School	Place	Min.	Sec.	Tenths

_____   _____   _____
Timer   Judge   Scorer

Fig. D-4. Sample heat or finals event card. This card will fit on a card 5 × 8 inches.

Event_____   Date_____

Meet_____   Judge_____

Contestant	School	No.	ft.	in.	ft.	in.	ft.	in.	ft.	in.	ft.	in.	ft.	in.

1st _____ Dist. _____

2nd _____ Dist. _____

3rd _____ Dist. _____

4th _____ Dist. _____

5th _____ Dist. _____ Judge

6th _____ Dist. _____ Scorer

Fig. D-5. Sample field event card.

DATE _____ MEET _____

DIVISION/EVENT _____ FLIGHT _____ RECORDS:WORLD ___ AMERICAN ___ LOCAL ___

HEAD OFFICAL _____ OFFICAL _____ OFFICAL _____

ORDER	ATHLETE/CLUB	HEIGHT	PLACE
			MARK

1st _____ Ht._____ 4th_____ Ht._____   _____

2nd _____ Ht._____ 5th_____ Ht._____   _____ Judge

3rd _____ Ht._____ 6th_____ Ht._____   _____

Scorer

Fig. D-6. Sample high jump event card.

Meet:_____ Date:_____ Deadline:_____

Division:_____ From:_____
                                           (School)   (Coach)

100-m hurdles	400-m dash	Long jump
1._____	1._____	1._____
2._____	2._____	2._____
3._____	3._____	3._____

50-m dash	800-m run	High jump
1._____	1._____	1._____
2._____	2._____	2._____
3._____	3._____	3._____

75-m dash	400-m relay	Shot put
1._____	1._____	1._____
2._____	2._____	2._____
3._____	3._____	3._____
	4._____	

100-m dash	800-m medley (200 x 100 x 100 x 400)	Discus
1._____	1._____	1._____
2._____	2._____	2._____
3._____	3._____	3._____
	4._____	

220-m dash	Javelin	Mile run (1500-m)
1._____	1._____	1._____
2._____	2._____	2._____
3._____	3._____	3._____

Fig. D-7. Sample meet entry card.

9th 50-m dash	_____	_____	_____
8th 50-m dash	_____	_____	_____
7th 50-m dash	_____	_____	_____
9th 100-m dash	_____	_____	_____
8th 100-m dash	_____	_____	_____
7th 100-m dash	_____	_____	_____
9th 400-m dash	_____	_____	_____
8th 200-m dash	_____	_____	_____
7th 200-m dash	_____	_____	_____
9th High jump	_____	_____	_____
8th High jump	_____	_____	_____
7th High jump	_____	_____	_____
9th Long jump	_____	_____	_____
8th Long jump	_____	_____	_____
7th Long jump	_____	_____	_____
9th Shot put	_____	_____	_____
8th Shot put	_____	_____	_____
7th Shot put	_____	_____	_____
9th Softball throw	_____	_____	_____
8th Softball throw	_____	_____	_____
7th Softball throw	_____	_____	_____
9th Basketball throw	_____	_____	_____
8th Basketball throw	_____	_____	_____
7th Basketball throw	_____	_____	_____

Relay 400-m. (yes or no) 9th_____ 8th_____ 7th_____

Coach_____ School_____

Fig. D-8. Sample of group entry blank. This form is suitable for team entries for a junior high school meet.

The athlete whose signature appears below has been examined by me and found physically fit to participate in girls' and/or women's track and field events for the 19____ season.

_____
(Signature of M.D.)

Address:_____City:_____

Date:_____Athlete:_____
(Signature)

Address:_____City:_____

Birthdate:_____Affiliation:_____
(Month, day, year)

Return to:_____

Fig. D-9. Sample medical form. This sample form may be used by any group to ensure that the participating athletes have had a recent medical examination and are able to compete.

Finish Judge's Report
First Place

Event:_____

Heat:_____

Number:_____

School:_____

Signed:_____

Timer's Report
First Place

Event:_____

Heat:_____

Time:_____

Signed:_____

Sign card and return to head timer.

Fig. D-10. Samples of the finish judge's and timer's reports. If these slips are used, each timer and judge is to fill out one for each heat and one for each of the final races. The cards should be a different color for each place. The head timer and judge will collect the cards and make their final reports from them.

Meet: **Head timer:**

Event	1st Watches			2nd Watches			3rd Watches			4th Watches		

Fig. D-11. Sample of head timer's result sheet.

Initiating track and field programs

PRIMARY SCHOOL

Running, jumping, and throwing are the natural activities of primary school children and are fundamental for the growth and development of all children. Movement educators are concerned that children move their bodies with control through space as they learn to run and jump and manipulate themselves and other objects in a wide variety of ways. Whether children are performing rhythmic running, jumping a brook, doing a potato race, trying to jump and reach, or jumping "high waters" over a rope, they are participating in developmental activities that are very basic to the later accomplishment of track and field skills. These examples of primary children's movements, along with the many ways children are led to explore the environment and the capabilities of their bodies, suggest a foundation for the kinds of track and field experiences available in the developmental years. Furthermore, fitness activities provided by animal walks, such as the puppy dog run, the seal crawl, the crab walk, the lame dog, the turnover, the measuring worm, crab kicking, and the walrus walk, and combative stunts, such as scot tag, knee slap, torso touch, and step-on-toes, increase strength, quickness, flexibility, and to a certain degree, endurance. Agility runs, obstacle courses, rope jumping, and rope climbing stunts are other fun-filled activities that provide good opportunities for physical growth and neuromuscular skill development important to track and field learning.

These are the kinds of track and field experiences advocated for children of preschool and primary school ages. The main purpose of all physical activity for children in kindergarten through thrid grade is an opportunity for an abundance of running, jumping, and throwing for the sheer joy of moving, for good growth and development, and for learning how to control the moving body.

UPPER ELEMENTARY SCHOOL

Upper elementary school children, 9, 10, and 11 years old, are ready and eager for more specialized and challenging movement experiences. This is particularly true if the fundamental movement patterns that form the basis for all forms of movement have been presented to them during the years from age 2 to 8 in a learning climate structured toward exploratory and discovery experiences utilizing problem-solving techniques in performing a wide variety of movements. Upper elementary youngsters are ready to apply the fundamental movement patterns already learned to the refining of more complex movement skills.

Track and field skills appropriate for introduction to 9-, 10-, and 11-year-olds include the following:

Dashes
    30 yards—9
    40 yards—9
    50 yards—9, 10, 11
    75 yards—10, 11
    100 yards—11
Starts
    Standing start—9
    Sprint start—9, 10, 11
    Baton passing—10, 11
Relays
    Shuttle—9, 10
    Pursuit—10, 11

Jumps
    Standing long jump—9, 10, 11
    Running long jump—9, 10, 11
    High jump—10, 11
    Hop, step, and jump—11
Hurdling
    Soft hurdles—11
Distance running
    Striding to develop pace—10, 11
Throws
    Softball—9, 10, 11
    Volleyball—10, 11
    Basketball—11
    6-pound shot—11

MIDDLE SCHOOL

The track and field program for middle school youngsters, ages 12, 13, and 14, may range from the physical education class track and field activities to visiting organized competition in an area or all-city meet. It is of greater importance to provide for the participation of many children, who may find success in a variety of events, than for the creation of individual champions and meet winners. More opportunities for the encouragement of many participants will eventually result in more excellent performances at secondary levels.

The track and field events open to the middle school youngster comprise sprints, middle-distance, and short-distance runs, pursuit relays of different distances, hurdling at 30-inch heights, high jump and long jump, and throwing the 8-pound shot, softball, and basketball. The scheduling of an all-school track and field sports day composed of many relays and jumping and throwing activities, including novelty and fun events, will help generate much interest for middle school ages. All-comers meets are extremely popular with many performers during the late summer months and the cross-country season. Usually these meets have several different age groups involved, and the athletes simply show up in time for the meet and sign in on the field.

SECONDARY SCHOOL (HIGH SCHOOL)

The inclusion of a good instructional unit in track and field in the physical education program is of vital importance in helping to stimulate interest and in providing good experience for high school girls. The fast runners and good jumpers discovered here and in the intramural program, who are encouraged to compete in track and field events, will prove a good source of potential top level performers. The competition held in running, jumping, and throwing events between class squads, separate hourly classes, and separate grades should help the discovery of good track team members.

Early workouts should be fun and relatively easy for the participating girls. The essential equipment should be provided, although track is an activity that can be enjoyed with a minimum amount of equipment. All the girls should try out for all the events to learn about them, to find out where their strengths and weaknesses lie, and to discover in which events they enjoy participating the most.

The track squad will continue to show eagerness and enthusiasm if practice sessions are kept interesting by good organization and variation. Girls may be trained separately, or boys and girls may be trained simultaneously. If the latter plan is used, each will gain from the other by seeking social approval and acceptance. The girls learn a great deal about a given event by observing the performances of the boys; this will challenge them to extend themselves to learn and excel. The boys in turn work harder because they recognize an appreciative audience and want to perform well. They will also come to recognize that girl athletes have the ability to perform at high levels.

In the beginning the better competitors will be those with the better previous performance records; nevertheless, no one should be dropped from the squad. The coach will discover that some girls with no experience will be far better performers after some training than others with previous experience. Those who are willing to work hard in practice sessions may not win any races or receive great acclaim, but they usually improve their general health, strength, and coordination. Also, many of those who score no victories for a year or two may be the girls who find themselves becoming champions after 3 or 4 years of training.

For team members to perform to the best of their ability, there must be a careful and constant evaluation made of their performances. This evaluation may be accomplished by keeping records of performances in timed and measured practices as well as meet performances. Individual progress records should be kept by the coach and by each girl. One technique to follow is to have each girl keep a personal record book that would include personal data such as height, weight, medical records, and performance scores and for later use, a place to add ribbons, awards, news clippings, and photographs.

The scheduling of a dual meet with a nearby school will provide encouragement to those who have been training for track and field participation and will supply the impetus needed to really get a track program started. It is a good idea to follow up dual meets with a county-wide meet to have all the interested girls in the area involved in track competition. A number of dual meets coupled with some triangular meets and finally a large invitational meet scheduled at the close of the season will offer the competition needed by all participants and will increase their levels of performance.

Meet results

Table F-1. Results of a high school triangular meet*

Events	First	Second	Third
50-yard hurdles	8.2 seconds	8.5 seconds	9 seconds
100-yard dash	11.5 seconds	11.7 seconds	12 seconds
220-yard dash	27.2 seconds	27.5 seconds	27.9 seconds
440-yard run	66.5 seconds	67.5 seconds	70.2 seconds
Long jump	14 feet 7¼ inches	13 feet 5¾ inches	12 feet 11 inches
High jump	4 feet 10 inches	4 feet 5 inches	3 feet 10 inches
Standing long jump	7 feet 4½ inches	6 feet 7¼ inches	6 feet 6½ inches
Shot put	29 feet 11 inches	29 feet 2 inches	27 feet 6½ inches
Discus	96 feet 3 inches	80 feet 8 inches	76 feet 1½ inches

*These results are from a triangular meet held between three small high schools in the Midwest. It is apparent from the results that training in the long jump and the high jump was not as intensive as that given in track events. This is common when one person handles all coaching of events and a relatively short period of time is spent in training. Some events can take several seasons to master. A teacher often omits an event that she knows very little about, hoping that time will increase her knowledge of it.

Table F-2. Results of an invitational high school meet (eight schools)*

Events	Winning time and distance
50-yard dash	6.7 seconds
75-yard dash	9.8 seconds
100-yard dash	12.5 seconds
220-yard dash	29.5 seconds
440-yard run	68.2 seconds
50-yard hurdles	9.0 seconds
400-yard relay (shuttle)	47.4 seconds
Long jump	14 feet 7 inches
High jump	4 feet 6 inches
Standing long jump	7 feet 9 inches
Shot put	30 feet 9 inches
Softball throw	157 feet 1¾ inches

*Results are typical of those made by girls from small high schools where they receive training only in the school program. These girls are from a midwestern area in which physical education is not offered every day. It is possible, from looking at these results, to establish a standard of expectancy for girls of similar background and training.

Table F-3. Results of a California junior college track meet

Events	Time or distance
80-meter hurdles	15 seconds
440-yard run	64 seconds
50-yard dash	6.5 seconds
75-yard dash	10.6 seconds
100-yard dash	12 seconds
220-yard dash	28 seconds
440-yard relay	55.4 seconds
880-yard relay	2 minutes 12.2 seconds
Long jump	16 feet 6½ inches
High jump	4 feet 11 inches
Discus	100 feet
Shot put	30 feet 1 inch

Table F-4. Results of an Indiana NAGWS track and field meet (high school level)

Events	Winner	Results
100-yard dash	Lorene Spearman, Wawasee	10.7 seconds
220-yard dash	Lorene Spearman, Wawasee	23.9 seconds
440-yard dash	Pam Sedwick, Jeffersonville	57.1 seconds
880-yard run	Lorrie Swegman, New Palestine	2 minutes 18.9 seconds
1-mile run	Christy Wagner, Muncie North	5 minutes 12.3 seconds
80-yard hurdles	Rosemary Junk, Fort Wayne	10.7 seconds
Shot put	Gertrude Springfield, Indianapolis	42 feet 11 inches
Softball throw	Dru Cox, Plainfield	227 feet 3 inches
Long jump	Annette Dewenter, Lafayette	18 feet 5½ inches
High jump	Cindy Farrand, Castle	5 feet 7 inches
440-yard relay	Wawasee	49.2 seconds
880-yard relay	Fort Wayne, Northrop	1 minute 44.0 seconds
880-yard medley	Jeffersonville	1 minute 48.7 seconds

Table F-5. Results of a Kentucky NAGWS track and field meet (high school level)*

Events	First	Second	Third
50-yard hurdles†	7.1 seconds†	7.2 seconds	7.5 seconds
660-yard run	1 minute 53.3 seconds	1 minute 47.4 seconds	1 minute 50.1 seconds
50-yard dash	6.1 seconds	6.3 seconds	6.4 seconds
440-yard run	64.3 seconds	65.5 seconds	65.6 seconds
75-yard dash	9.1 seconds	9.1 seconds	9.1 seconds
100-yard dash	11.6 seconds	11.9 seconds	12.1 seconds
220-yard dash	27.4 seconds	27.9 seconds	28.3 seconds
440-yard relay	51.5 seconds	52.9 seconds	53.2 seconds
880-yard medley relay	1 minute 59.5 seconds	2 minutes 2.9 seconds	2 minutes 4.9 seconds
Shot put	33 feet 5¾ inches	32 feet 8½ inches	32 feet 2½ inches
Softball throw	208 feet ¼ inch	191 feet 5 inches	191 feet 1¼ inches
Standing long jump	8 feet 1 inch	7 feet 10⅝ inches	7 feet 9 inches
Long jump	16 feet 11 inches	16 feet 6¾ inches	15 feet 4 inches
Discus	103 feet 4 inches	100 feet 5½ inches	90 feet 1 inch
High jump	4 feet 7 inches	4 feet 6 inches	4 feet 5 inches

*This chart shows the results from a state-wide meet for high school girls in Kentucky. These girls had experience in track and field in their respective schools. Twenty-eight schools were represented. Individual and team points were kept. The winning school scored eighty-two points.
†The times reported are extremely fast for this event. It is unusual for high school girls to run this fast in a school meet.

Table F-6. Results of an AAU age-group meet

Events	9 years old and under	10 and 11 years old	12 and 13 years old
100-yard dash	13.0 seconds	11.8 seconds	11.3 seconds
220-yard dash	30.4 seconds	27.6 seconds	25.9 seconds
440-yard dash	68.1 seconds	64.7 seconds	59.7 seconds
880-yard run	2 minutes 30.4 seconds	2 minutes 27.7 seconds	2 minutes 21.1 seconds
1-mile run		5 minutes 30.1 seconds	5 minutes 10.1 seconds
50-yard hurdles			7.0 seconds
440-yard relay	58.8 seconds	54.0 seconds	50.1 seconds
880-yard medley relay		2 minutes 0.3 seconds	1 minute 54.0 seconds
1-mile relay			4 minutes 10.9 seconds
1-mile walk		9 minutes 59.7 seconds	8 minutes 38.4 seconds
High jump	4 feet 2½ inches		5 feet 2 inches
Long jump		15 feet 4¾ inches	17 feet 11 inches
Shot put			40 feet 3 inches
Discus			92 feet 4¼ inches
Javelin			114 feet 4 inches

Table F-7. Results of an AAU pentathlon 12- and 13-year-old age-group meet

Competitor	50-yard hurdles	Long jump	Shot put	High jump	200-meter dash	Total points
1. Lisa Kinsmaka	8.1 seconds	17 feet 2¾ inches	38 feet 9 inches	4 feet 10¼ inches	26.9 seconds	3,578
2. Lori Kaug	8.0 seconds	14 feet 2 inches	26 feet 6½ inches	4 feet 10¼ inches	28.8 seconds	2,968
3. Kerry Olmstead	8.7 seconds	13 feet 0 inch	30 feet ¾ inch	4 feet ½ inch	29.0 seconds	2,526

Table F-8. Results of district AAU championships, girls' division (14 to 17 years old)*

Events	Time or distance
100-yard dash	11.0 seconds
440-yard dash	57.6 seconds
880-yard run	2 minutes 13.5 seconds
1-mile run	5 minutes 12.7 seconds
80-yard hurdles	10.5 seconds
440-yard relay	48.9 seconds
1-mile relay	3 minutes 56.0 seconds
Long jump	17 feet 7 inches
High jump	5 feet 2¼ inches
Shot put (8 pounds)	45 feet 2¼ inches
Discus	139 feet 4 inches
Javelin	138 feet 6 inches

*This meet was sponsored by the Southern Pacific Association of the AAU in Southern California.

Table F-9. Results of AAU women's national championships*

Events	Time or distance	Competitor
100-meter dash	11.14 seconds (w)	Ashford
200-meter dash	22.62 seconds	Ashford
400-meter dash	51.55 seconds	Dabney
800-meter run	2 minutes 3.8 seconds	Latter
1500-meter run	4 minutes 8.2 seconds	Larrieu-Lutz
3000-meter run	9 minutes 0.2 second	Merrill
10,000-meter run	33 minutes 15.1 seconds	Neppel
100-meter hurdles	13.15 seconds (w)	Van Wolvelaere
400-meter hurdles	56.61 seconds	Ayers
440-yard relay	45.44 seconds	Tennessee State
880-yard medley relay	1 minute 39.3 seconds	Tennessee State
Mile relay	3 minutes 37.3 seconds	Atoms Track Club
2-mile relay	2 minutes 13.3 seconds	Los Angeles Track Club
5000-meter walk	24 minutes 10.1 seconds	Brodock
Shot put (4 kilos)	54 feet 1¼ inches	Seidler
Discus	193 feet 6 inches	Haist
Javelin	200 feet 7 inches	Schmidt
High jump	6 feet 1 inch	Huntley
Long jump	21 feet 9¼ inches (w)	Anderson

*These times and marks were made at the National Women's Track and Field Championships (AAU) in Los Angeles, California, in June, 1977.

Table F-10. Results of AAU district championship for women

Events	Time or distance
100-meter dash	11.5 seconds
400-meter dash	54.1 seconds
800-meter run	2 minutes 10.2 seconds
1-mile run	4 minutes 50.6 seconds
1-mile walk	7 minutes 59.4 seconds
100-meter hurdles	14.0 seconds
440-yard relay	47.5 seconds
1-mile relay	5 minutes 6.8 seconds
2-mile relay	10 minutes 47.8 seconds
Long jump	18 feet 11 inches
High jump	5 feet 9¼ inches
Shot put	49 feet 3¾ inches
Javelin	144 feet 11 inches

Table F-11. Results of 1976 Martin Luther King International Freedom Games (women's events)*

Events	Time or distance
440-yard relay	
1. Tigerbelle Track Club (Debra Oliver, Brenda Moorehead, Mary William, Chandra Cheeseborough)	45.5 seconds
2. Florida Track Club	45.6 seconds
3. Bahamas	47.6 seconds
4. Philadelphia Hawks	48.1 seconds
1500-meter run	
1. Cindy Bremser—Wisconsin TC	4 minutes 17.2 seconds
2. Brenda Webb—Ketering Striders	4 minutes 21.9 seconds
3. Gayle Olinek—Canada	4 minutes 25.9 seconds
4. Debbie Mitchell—Canada	4 minutes 27.6 seconds
5. Joan Benolt—Liberty AC	4 minutes 32.2 seconds
Shot put	
1. Vickie Smith—Florida State	42 feet 3¾ inches
2. Jackie Gordon—Florida TC	41 feet 10 inches
3. Kim Travers—Florida State	41 feet 9 inches
Discus	
1. Jackie Gordon—Florida TC	152 feet 1 inch
2. Kim Travers—Florida State	140 feet 10 inches
3. Vickie Smith—Florida State	112 feet 9 inches
High jump	
1. Karen Moller—Delaware SC	5 feet 10 inches
2. Paula Girven—unattached	5 feet 10 inches
3. Connie Dorsey—Terre Haute TC	5 feet 10 inches
4. Tie: Lyn Sheffield—Tennessee; Heidi Hertz—Florida TC	5 feet 4 inches
800-meter run	
1. Robin Campbell—Florida TC	2 minutes 5.2 seconds
2. Joan Wenzel—Canada	2 minutes 5.6 seconds
3. Kathy Hall—Suburban TC	2 minutes 6.5 seconds
4. Henrietta Nanols—New Orleans Super Dames	2 minutes 7.4 seconds
5. Francine Gendron—Canada	2 minutes 7.8 seconds
400-meter run	
1. Sheila Ingram—Coolidge H.S., Washington, D.C.	52.8 seconds
2. Deborah Armstrong—Florida TC	52.9 seconds
3. Debra Sapenter—Prairie View	53.3 seconds
4. Pam Jiles—New Orleans Super Dames	53.7 seconds
5. Sheila Choates—Tennessee State	53.9 seconds
100-meter dash	
1. Rose Allwood—Florida TC	11.3 seconds
2. Chandra Cheeseborough—Tigerbelle TC	11.3 seconds
3. Brenda Moorehead—Tigerbelle TC	11.5 seconds
4. Brenda Flinch—Jackson State	11.5 seconds
5. Pat Henderson—Chicago Murcherette	11.8 seconds
200-meter dash	
1. Chandra Cheeseborough—Tigerbelle TC	23.2 seconds
2. Deborah Armstrong—Florida TC	23.5 seconds
3. Brenda Moorehead—Tigerbelle TC	23.6 seconds
4. Rose Allwood—Florida TC	23.6 seconds
5. Pam Jiles—New Orleans Super Dames	23.9 seconds

*Greensboro Daily News, May 23, 1976.

Table F-12. Results of the 1976 Olympics

Events	Time, distance, or points
100-meter run	
Annegret Richter—West Germany	11.08 seconds
Renate Stecher—East Germany	11.13 seconds
Inge Helten—West Germany	11.17 seconds
Raelene Boyle—Australia	11.23 seconds
Evelyn Ashford—United States	11.24 seconds
Chandra Cheeseborough—United States	11.31 seconds
200-meter run	
Barbel Eckert—East Germany	22.37 seconds
Annegret Richter—West Germany	22.39 seconds
Renate Stecher—East Germany	22.47 seconds
Carla Bodendorf—East Germany	22.64 seconds
Inge Helten—West Germany	22.68 seconds
Tatyana Prorochenko—U.S.S.R.	23.03 seconds
400-meter run	
Irena Szewinska—Poland	42.29* seconds
Christine Brehmer—East Germany	50.51 seconds
Ellen Steidt—East Germany	50.55 seconds
Pirjo Haggman—Finland	50.56 seconds
Rosalyn Bryant—United States	50.56 seconds
Sheila Ingram—United States	50.90 seconds
400-meter relay	
East Germany	42.55 seconds
West Germany	42.59 seconds
U.S.S.R.	43.09 seconds
Canada	43.17 seconds
Australia	43.18 seconds
Jamaica	43.24 seconds
1600-meter relay	
East Germany	3 minutes 19.23* seconds
United States	3 minutes 22.81 seconds
U.S.S.R.	3 minutes 24.24 seconds
Australia	3 minutes 25.56 seconds
West Germany	3 minutes 25.71 seconds
Finland	3 minutes 25.87 seconds
Long jump	
Angela Voight—East Germany	22 feet 2½ inches
Kathy McMillan—United States	21 feet 10¼ inches
Lidiya Alfeyev—U.S.S.R.	21 feet 7¾ inches
Sigrun Siegl—East Germany	21 feet 7½ inches
Ildiko Szabo—Hungary	21 feet 6½ inches
Jarmila Nygrynova—Czechoslovakia	21 feet 5½ inches
High jump	
Rosemarie Ackermann—East Germany	6 feet 4 inches
Sara Simeoni—Italy	6 feet 3¼ inches
Yordanka Blagoyeva—Bulgaria	6 feet 3¼ inches
Maria Mracnova—Czechoslovakia	6 feet 2½ inches
Joni Huntley—United States	6 feet 2½ inches
Tatyana Shlyahto—U.S.S.R.	6 feet 1¾ inches

*Equals or betters the existing world record.

Continued.

Table F-12. Results of the 1976 Olympics—cont'd

Events	*Time, distance, or points*
Shot put	
Ivanka Khristova—Bulgaria	69 feet 5 inches
Ndayczhda Chizova—U.S.S.R.	68 feet 9¼ inches
Helena Fibingerova—Czechoslovakia	67 feet 9¾ inches
Marianne Adam—East Germany	67 feet 5 inches
Ilona Scholknecht—East Germany	67 feet 4¾ inches
Margitta Droese—East Germany	64 feet 11¼ inches
Discus	
Evelyn Schlaak—East Germany	226 feet 4 inches
Maria Vergova—Bulgaria	220 feet 9 inches
Gabriele Hinzman—East Germany	219 feet 3 inches
Faina Myelnik—U.S.S.R.	217 feet 10 inches
Sabine Engel—East Germany	216 feet 1 inch
Argentina Menis—Rumania	214 feet 6 inches
Javelin	
Ruth Fuchs—East Germany	216 feet 4 inches
Marion Becker—West Germany	212 feet 3 inches
Kate Schmidt—United States	209 feet 10 inches
Jacqueline Hein—East Germany	209 feet 5 inches
Sabine Sebrowski—East Germany	206 feet 11 inches
Svetlana Babich—U.S.S.R.	194 feet 11 inches
800-meter run	
Tatyana Kazankina—U.S.S.R.	1 minute 54.94 seconds*
Nikolina Chtereva—Bulgaria	1 minute 55.24 seconds
Elfi Zinn—East Germany	1 minute 55.60 seconds
Anita Weiss—East Germany	1 minute 55.74 seconds
Svetlana Styrkina—U.S.S.R.	1 minute 56.44 seconds
Svetla Zlateva—Bulgaria	1 minute 57.21 seconds
1500-meter run	
Tatyana Kazankina—U.S.S.R.	4 minutes 5.48 seconds
Gunhild Hoffmeister—East Germany	4 minutes 6.09 seconds
Ulrike Klapezynski—East Germany	4 minutes 6.09 seconds
Nikolina Schtereva—Bulgaria	4 minutes 6.57 seconds
Lyudmila Bragina—U.S.S.R.	4 minutes 7.57 seconds
Gabriell Dorio—Italy	4 minutes 7.27 seconds
100-meter hurdles	
Johanna Schaller—East Germany	12.77 seconds
Tatyana Anisimova—U.S.S.R.	12.78 seconds
Natalie Lebedeva—U.S.S.R.	12.80 seconds
Gudrun Berend—East Germany	12.82 seconds
Grazyna Rabsztyn—Poland	12.96 seconds
Esther Rot—Israel	13.4 seconds
Pentathlon	
Segrun Siegl—East Germany	4,745 points
Christine Laser—East Germany	4,745 points
Burglinde Pollak—East Germany	4,740 points
Liudmila Popovskaya—U.S.S.R.	4,700 points
Nadejda Tkachenko—U.S.S.R.	4,669 points
Diane Jones—Canada	4,582 points

*Equals or betters the existing world record.

Table F-13. American outdoor records for women

Events	Time, distance, or points
50-yard dash	5.7 seconds
100-yard dash	10.0 seconds
220-yard dash	22.6 seconds
440-yard dash	52.2 seconds
880-yard run	2 minutes 2.2 seconds
1-mile run	4 minutes 33.1 seconds
60-meter dash	7.3 seconds
100-meter dash	11.0 seconds
200-meter dash	22.6 seconds
400-meter dash	51.6 seconds
800-meter dash	2 minutes 0.8 second
1500-meter run	4 minutes 10.4 seconds
2-mile run	10 minutes 2.8 seconds
3000-meter run	8 minutes 52.8 seconds
3-mile run	16 minutes 32.8 seconds
5000-meter run	16 minutes 46.2 seconds
4-mile run	23 minutes 5.2 seconds
5-mile run	29 minutes 7.7 seconds
6-mile run	35 minutes 0.5 second
10,000-meter run	34 minutes 51 seconds
Marathon	2 hours 38 minutes 19 seconds
Long jump	21 feet 10¼ inches
High jump	6 feet ½ inch
Shot put	69 feet 7½ inches
Discus	187 feet 2 inches
Javelin	215 feet 6 inches
80-meter hurdles	10.5 seconds
100-meter hurdles	12.9 seconds
200-meter hurdles	26.1 seconds
400-meter hurdles	55.61 seconds
440-yard relay (4 × 110)	44.2 seconds
880-yard relay (4 × 220)	1 minute 37.3 seconds
880-yard medley relay (220-110-110-440)	1 minute 40.3 seconds
Mile relay (4 × 440)	3 minutes 33.9 seconds
3 × 880-yard relay	7 minutes 13.5 seconds
400-meter relay (4 × 100)	42.8 seconds
800-meter relay (4 × 200)	1 minute 35.5 seconds
1600-meter relay (4 × 400)	3 minutes 25.2 seconds
800-meter medley relay (200-100-100-400)	1 minute 41.7 seconds
2-mile relay (4 × 880)	8 minutes 53.6 seconds
Distance medley relay (440-880-1320-mile)	12 minutes 38.6 seconds
4-mile relay (4 × 1 mile)	20 minutes 40.8 seconds
Pentathlon	4,557 points
Race walk—1500-meter	6 minutes 50.4 seconds
1-mile	7 minutes 0.2 second
5000-meter	24 minutes 10.1 seconds

Table F-14. Results of 1977 AIAW championships

Events	Time, distance, or points
100 meters	
1. Ashford—UCLA	11.32 seconds
2. Lynch—Cal State Long Beach	11.37 seconds
3. Calmese—Kansas	11.75 seconds
4. Carter—Northeast Missouri	11.77 seconds
5. McRoy—Maryland	11.83 seconds
6. Day—Prairie View A&M	11.95 seconds
200 meters	
1. Ashford—UCLA	23.0 seconds
2. Lynch—Cal State Long Beach	23.1 seconds
3. Bowen—Arizona State	23.9 seconds
4. Nickson—Cal State Hayward	24.1 seconds
5. McRoy—Maryland	24.2 seconds
6. Calmese—Kansas	24.5 seconds
400 meters	
1. Bryant—Cal State Los Angeles	51.79 seconds
2. Forde—Long Island University	52.13 seconds
3. Weston—UCLA	53.07 seconds
4. Harvey—Stephen F. Austin	54.16 seconds
5. Mailey—Arizona State	54.20 seconds
6. Clagon—Morgan State	54.55 seconds
800 meters	
1. Brown—Cal State Northridge	2 minutes 2.88 seconds
2. Knudson—Colorado State	2 minutes 4.46 seconds
3. Latter—Michigan State	2 minutes 5.77 seconds
4. Vetter—Iowa State	2 minutes 5.78 seconds
5. Roberson—UCLA	2 minutes 7.49 seconds
6. McLaughlin—Otterbein	2 minutes 8.23 seconds
1500 meters	
1. Ennis—Montclair State	4 minutes 15.56 seconds
2. Vetter—Iowa State	4 minutes 15.77 seconds
3. Pearson—Texas El Paso	4 minutes 16.08 seconds
4. Brown—Cal State Northridge	4 minutes 18.03 seconds
5. Keyes—UCLA	4 minutes 21.02 seconds
6. Schilly—Iowa State	4 minutes 23.00 seconds
3000 meters	
1. Brown—Cal State Northridge	9 minutes 26.5 seconds
2. Lashley—Tennessee	9 minutes 27.4 seconds
3. Kinsey—Cal State Northridge	9 minutes 30.0 seconds
4. Spencer—Wisconsin	9 minutes 30.4 seconds
5. Bankes—Penn State	9 minutes 35.2 seconds
6. Quaiter—Seattle Pacific	9 minutes 45.6 seconds
5000 meters	
1. Webb—Tennessee	16 minutes 13.86 seconds
2. Kinsey—Cal State Northridge	16 minutes 17.50 seconds
3. Spencer—Wisconsin	16 minutes 23.30 seconds
4. Brown—Cal State Northridge	16 minutes 26.90 seconds
5. Lashley—Tennessee	16 minutes 38.70 seconds
6. Troffer—Cal State Northridge	17 minutes 06.80 seconds
100-meter hurdles	
1. Van Wolvelaere—USC	13.18 seconds
2. Oshikoya—UCLA	13.37 seconds
3. Esser—Iowa State	14.06 seconds

Table F-14. Results of 1977 AIAW championships—cont'd

Events	Time, distance, or points
100-meter hurdles—cont'd	
4. Baker—Nebraska	14.14 seconds
5. Ballew—Kentucky	14.23 seconds
6. Neal—La Salle	14.24 seconds
400-meter hurdles	
1. Esser—Iowa State	57.07 seconds
2. Ayers—Prairie View A&M	57.17 seconds
3. Levinski—Texas Women's University	58.67 seconds
4. Gainer—Prairie View A&M	59.66 seconds
5. Anderson—Cal State Northridge	60.26 seconds
6. Carlson—Central Missouri State	60.50 seconds
440-yard relay	
1. Prairie View A&M	45.95 seconds
2. Nevada Las Vegas	46.59 seconds
3. Cal State Los Angeles	46.79 seconds
4. Jackson State	46.82 seconds
5. Tennessee	47.04 seconds
6. USC	47.15 seconds
880-yard medley relay	
1. UCLA	1 minute 39.35 seconds
2. Cal State Los Angeles	1 minute 39.55 seconds
3. Nevada Las Vegas	1 minute 41.80 seconds
4. Morgan State	1 minute 43.65 seconds
5. Stephen F. Austin	1 minute 44.20 seconds
6. Prairie View A&M	No time
Mile relay	
1. Prairie View A&M	3 minutes 36.7 seconds
2. UCLA	3 minutes 40.1 seconds
3. Cal State Los Angeles	3 minutes 41.0 seconds
4. Iowa State	3 minutes 42.2 seconds
5. Michigan State	3 minutes 45.1 seconds
6. Cal State Northridge	3 minutes 47.0 seconds
2-mile relay	
1. UCLA	8 minutes 41.98 seconds
2. Iowa State	8 minutes 48.85 seconds
3. Oregon	8 minutes 50.76 seconds
4. Tennessee	8 minutes 51.34 seconds
5. Penn State	8 minutes 54.36 seconds
6. Cal State Northridge	8 minutes 54.78 seconds
Discus	
1. Haist—Tennessee	188 feet 5 inches
2. Griffin—Seattle Pacific	164 feet 5 inches
3. Marshall—Cal State Northridge	163 feet 4 inches
4. Pottle—Central Washington	158 feet 10 inches
5. Hansen—Seattle Pacific	155 feet 1 inch
6. Mecklenburg—Seattle Pacific	153 feet 3 inches
High jump	
1. Ritter—Texas Women's University	6 feet 1½ inches
2. Spencer—Seattle Pacific	5 feet 11 inches
3. Garrison—Washington	5 feet 9 inches
4. Remmling—UCLA	5 feet 9 inches
5. Girven—Maryland	5 feet 9 inches
6. Washington—Illinois	5 feet 7 inches

Continued.

Table F-14. Results of 1977 AIAW championships—cont'd

Events	Time, distance, or points
Javelin	
1. Smith—UCLA	197 feet 9 inches
2. Sulinski—Cal State Hayward	177 feet 5 inches
3. Gassen—Cal State Northridge	171 feet 5 inches
4. Wilkinson—Arizona State	168 feet 4 inches
5. Bennett—Seattle Pacific	161 feet 2 inches
6. Camarigg—Morehead State	156 feet 6 inches
Long jump	
1. Anderson—Cal State Northridge	21 feet 6 inches
2. Ray—Florida	20 feet 6¾ inches
3. Oshikoya—UCLA	20 feet 5¼ inches
4. Pettit—Prairie View A&M	20 feet 5 inches
5. Ferguson—Florida	19 feet 10¾ inches
6. Lee—Michigan State	19 feet 8¾ inches
Shot put	
1. Devine—Emoria Kansas State	51 feet 2½ inches
2. Patrick—Morehead State	49 feet 8¼ inches
3. Van Pelt—Washington	47 feet 10¼ inches
4. Haist—Tennessee	47 feet 10 inches
5. Griffin—Seattle Pacific	47 feet 6 inches
6. Dole—Cal State Long Beach	47 feet 3 inches
Pentathlon	
1. Collins—Arizona State	4092 points
2. Cornelius—Texas A&M	3990 points
3. Seippel—Eastern Kentucky	3950 points
4. Monteforte—Cal State Northridge	3815 points
5. Hertz—Florida	3771 points
6. Malloy—Colorado State	3761 points

Index